ENDS AND MEANS

ENDS AND MEANS

*An Inquiry into the Nature
of Ideals and into the Methods
Employed for Their Realization*

by

Aldous Huxley

GREENWOOD PRESS, PUBLISHERS
WESTPORT, CONNECTICUT

The Library of Congress cataloged this book as follows:

Huxley, Aldous Leonard, 1894–1963.
 Ends and means; an inquiry into the nature of ideals
and into the methods employed for their realization. New
York, Greenwood Press ₁1969, ᶜ1937₁

 386 p. 23 cm.

1. Social problems. ɪ. Title.

HN17.H84 1969   301   79–90533
SBN 8371-2252-X   MARC

Library of Congress   69 ₁3₁

Reprinted with the permission of Harper & Brothers,
Publishers

Reprinted in 1969 by Greenwood Press, Inc.,
51 Riverside Avenue, Westport, Conn. 06880

Library of Congress catalog card number 79-90533
ISBN 0-8371-2252-X

Printed in the United States of America

10 9 8 7 6 5 4 3 2

Contents

[v]

ENDS AND MEANS

I

Goals, Roads and Contemporary Starting Point

ABOUT the ideal goal of human effort there exists in our civilization and, for nearly thirty centuries, there has existed a very general agreement. From Isaiah to Karl Marx the prophets have spoken with one voice. In the Golden Age to which they look forward there will be liberty, peace, justice and brotherly love. "Nation shall no more lift sword against nation"; "the free development of each will lead to the free development of all"; "the world shall be full of the knowledge of the Lord, as the waters cover the sea."

With regard to the goal, I repeat, there is and for long has been a very general agreement. Not so with regard to the roads which lead to that goal. Here unanimity and certainty give place to utter confusion, to the clash of contradictory opinions, dogmatically held and acted upon with the violence of fanaticism.

There are some who believe—and it is a very popular belief at the present time—that the royal road to a better world is the road of economic reform. For some, the short cut to Utopia is military conquest and the hegemony of one particular nation; for others, it is armed revolution and the dictatorship of a particular class. All these think mainly in terms of social machinery and large-scale organization. There are others, however, who approach the problem from the opposite end, and believe that desirable social changes can be brought about most effectively by changing the individuals who compose society. Of the people who think in this way, some pin their faith to education, some to psycho-analysis, some to applied behaviourism. There are others, on the contrary, who believe that no desirable "change of heart" can be brought about without supernatural aid. There must be, they say, a return to religion. (Unhappily, they cannot agree on the religion to which the return should be made.)

At this point it becomes necessary to say something about that ideal individual into whom the changers of heart desire to transform themselves and others. Every age and class has had its ideal. The ruling classes in Greece idealized the magnanimous man, a sort of scholar-and-gentleman. Kshatriyas in early India and feudal nobles in mediaeval Europe held up the ideal of the chivalrous man. The *honnête homme* makes his appearance as the ideal of seventeenth-century gentlemen; the *philosophe*, as the ideal of their descendants in the eighteenth century. The nineteenth century idealized the respectable man. The twentieth has already witnessed the rise and fall of the liberal man and the emergence of the sheep-like social man and the god-like Leader. Meanwhile the poor and downtrodden have always dreamed nostalgically of a man ideally well-fed, free, happy, and unoppressed.

Among this bewildering multiplicity of ideals which shall we choose? The answer is that we shall choose none. For it is clear that each one of these contradictory ideals is the fruit of particular social circumstances. To some extent, of course, this is true of every thought and aspiration that has ever been formulated. Some thoughts and aspirations, however, are manifestly less dependent on particular social circumstances than others. And here a significant fact emerges: all the ideals of human behaviour formulated by those who have been most successful in freeing themselves from the prejudices of their time and place are singularly alike. Liberation from prevailing conventions of thought, feeling and behaviour is accomplished most effectively by the practice of disinterested virtues and through direct insight into the real nature of ultimate reality. (Such insight is a gift, inherent in the individual; but, though inherent, it cannot manifest itself completely except where certain conditions are fulfilled. The principal pre-condition of insight is, precisely, the practice of disinterested virtues.) To some extent critical intellect is also a liberating force. But the way in which intellect is used depends upon the will. Where the will is not disinterested, the intellect tends to be used (outside the non-human fields of technology, science or pure mathematics) merely as an instrument for the rationalization of passion and prejudice, the justification of self-interest. That is why so few even of the acutest philosophers have succeeded in liberating themselves completely from the narrow prison of their age and country. It is seldom indeed that they achieve as much freedom as the mystics and the founders of religion. The most nearly free men have always been those who combined virtue with insight.

Now, among these freest of human beings there has been, for the last eighty or ninety generations, substan-

[3]

tial agreement in regard to the ideal individual. The enslaved have held up for admiration now this model of a man, now that; but at all times and in all places, the free have spoken with only one voice.

It is difficult to find a single word that will adequately describe the ideal man of the free philosophers and the founders of religions. "Non-attached" is perhaps the best. The ideal man is the non-attached man. Non-attached to his bodily sensations and lusts. Non-attached to his craving for power and possessions. Non-attached to the objects of these various desires. Non-attached to his anger and hatred; non-attached to his exclusive loves. Non-attached to wealth, fame, social position. Non-attached even to science, art, speculation, philanthropy. Yes, non-attached even to these. For, like patriotism, in Nurse Cavell's phrase, "they are not enough." Non-attachment to self and to what are called "the things of this world" has always been associated in the teachings of the philosophers and the founders of religions with attachment to an ultimate reality greater and more significant than the self. Greater and more significant than even the best things that this world has to offer. Of the nature of this ultimate reality I shall speak in the last chapters of this book. All that I need do in this place is to point out that the ethic of non-attachment has always been correlated with cosmologies that affirm the existence of a spiritual reality underlying the phenomenal world and imparting to it whatever value or significance it possesses.

Non-attachment is negative only in name. The practice of non-attachment entails the practice of all the virtues. It entails the practice of charity, for example; for there are no more fatal impediments than anger (even "righteous indignation") and cold-blooded malice to the identification of the self with the immanent and transcendent more-than-self. It entails the practice of courage; for fear is a painful and obsessive identification of the self with its body. (Fear is negative sensuality, just as sloth is negative malice.) It entails the cultivation of intelligence; for insensitive stupidity is a main root of all the other vices. It entails the practice of generosity and disinterestedness; for avarice and the love of possessions constrain their victims to equate themselves with mere things. And so on. It is unnecessary any further to labour the point, sufficiently obvious to any one who chooses to think about the matter, that non-attachment imposes upon those who would practise it the adoption of an intensely positive attitude towards the world.

The ideal of non-attachment has been formulated and systematically preached again and again in the course of the last three thousand years. We find it (along with everything else!) in Hinduism. It is at the very heart of the teachings of the Buddha. For Chinese readers the doctrine is formulated by Lao Tsu. A little later, in Greece, the ideal of non-attachment is proclaimed, albeit with a certain, pharisaic priggishness, by the Stoics. The Gospel of Jesus is essentially a gospel of non-attachment to "the things of this world," and of attachment to God. Whatever may have been the aberrations of organized Christianity—and they range from extravagant asceticism to the most brutally cynical forms of *realpolitik*—

[5]

there has been no lack of Christian philosophers to re-affirm the ideal of non-attachment. Here is John Tauler, for example, telling us that "freedom is complete purity and detachment which seeketh the Eternal; an isolated, a withdrawn being, identical with God or entirely at-tached to God." Here is the author of "The Imitation," who bids us "pass through many cares as though without care; not after the manner of a sluggard, but by a cer-tain prerogative of a free mind, which does not cleave with inordinate affection to any creature." One could multiply such citations almost indefinitely. Meanwhile, moralists outside the Christian tradition have affirmed the need for non-attachment no less insistently than the Christians. What Spinoza, for example, calls "blessed-ness" is simply the state of non-attachment; his "human bondage," the condition of one who identifies himself with his desires, emotions and thought-processes, or with their objects in the external world.

The non-attached man is one who, in Buddhist phraseology, puts an end to pain; and he puts an end to pain, not only in himself, but also, by refraining from malicious and stupid activity, to such pain as he may inflict on others. He is the happy or "blessed" man as well as the good man.

A few moralists—of whom Nietzsche is the most cele-brated and the Marquis de Sade the most uncompromis-ingly consistent—have denied the value of non-attach-ment. But these men are manifestly victims of their temperament and their particular social surroundings. Unable to practise non-attachment, they are unable to preach it; themselves slaves they cannot understand the

[6]

advantages of freedom. They stand outside the great tradition of civilized Asiatic and European philosophy. In the sphere of ethical thought they are eccentrics. Similarly such victims of particular social circumstances as Machiavelli, Hegel and the contemporary philosophers of Fascism and dictatorial communism, are eccentrics in the sphere of political thought.

Such then, are the ideals, for society and for the individual which were originally formulated nearly three thousand years ago in Asia, and which those who have not broken with the tradition of civilization still accept. In relation to these ideals, what are the relevant contemporary facts? They may be summed up very briefly. Instead of advancing towards the ideal goal, most of the peoples of the world are rapidly moving away from it.

"Real progress," in the words of Dr. R. R. Marett, "is progress in charity, all other advances being secondary thereto." In the course of recorded history real progress has been made by fits and starts. Periods of advance in charity have alternated with periods of regression. The eighteenth century was an epoch of real progress. So was most of the nineteenth, in spite of the horrors of industrialism, or rather because of the energetic way in which its men of goodwill tried to put a stop to those horrors. The present age is still humanitarian in spots; but where major political issues are concerned it has witnessed a definite regression in charity.

Thus, eighteenth-century thinkers were unanimous in condemning the use of torture by the State. Not only is torture freely used by the rulers of twentieth-century Europe; there are also theorists who are prepared to justify every form of state-organized atrocity, from flogging and branding to the wholesale massacre of minorities and general war. Another painfully significant symptom is the equanimity with which the twentieth-century public responds to written accounts and even to photographs and moving pictures of slaughter and atrocity. By way of excuse it may be urged that, during the last twenty years, people have supped so full of horrors, that horrors no longer excite either their pity for the victims or their indignation against the perpetrators. But the fact of indifference remains; and because nobody bothers about horrors, yet more horrors are perpetrated.

Closely associated with the regression in charity is the decline in men's regard for truth. At no period of the world's history has organized lying been practised so shamelessly or, thanks to modern technology, so efficiently or on so vast a scale as by the political and economic dictators of the present century. Most of this organized lying takes the form of propaganda inculcating hatred and vanity, and preparing men's minds for war. The principle aim of the liars is the eradication of charitable feelings and behaviour in the sphere of international politics.

Another point; charity cannot progress towards universality unless the prevailing cosmology is either monotheistic or pantheistic—unless there is a general belief that all men are "the sons of God" or, in Indian phrase, that "thou art that," *tat tvam asi*. The last fifty years have witnessed a great retreat from monotheism towards idolatry. The worship of one God has been abandoned in favour of the worship of such local divinities as the nation, the class and even the deified individual.

Such is the world in which we find ourselves—a world which, judged by the only acceptable criterion of progress, is manifestly in regression. Technological advance is rapid. But without progress in charity, technological advance is useless. Indeed, it is worse than useless. Technological progress has merely provided us with more efficient means for going backwards.

How can the regression in charity through which we are living, and for which each one of us is in some measure responsible, be halted and reversed? How can existing society be transformed into the ideal society described by the prophets? How can the average sensual man and the exceptional (and more dangerous) ambitious man be transformed into those non-attached beings, who alone can create a society significantly better than our own? These are the questions which I shall try to answer in the present volume.

In the process of answering them, I shall be compelled to deal with a very great variety of subjects. Inevitably; for human activity is complex, human motivation exceedingly mixed. By many writers, this multifariousness of men's thoughts, opinions, purposes and actions is insufficiently recognized. Over-simplifying the problem, they prescribe an over-simplified solution. Because of this I have thought it necessary to preface the main arguments of the book with a discussion of the nature of explanation. What do we mean when we say that we have "explained" a complex situation? What do we mean when we talk of one event being the cause of another? Unless we know the answer to these questions, our speculations regarding the nature and cure of social disorders are likely to be incomplete and one-sided.

Our discussion of the nature of explanation brings us to the conclusion that causation in human affairs is multiple—in other words, that any given event has many causes. Hence it follows that there can be no single sovereign cure for the diseases of the body politic. The remedy for social disorder must be sought simultaneously in many different fields. Accordingly, in the succeeding chapters, I proceed to consider the most important of these fields of activity, beginning with the political and economic and proceeding to the fields of personal behaviour. In every case I suggest the kind of changes that must be made if men are to realize the ideal ends at which they all profess to be aiming. This involves us, incidentally, in a discussion of the relation of means to ends. Good ends, as I have frequently to point out, can be achieved only by the employment of appropriate means. The end cannot justify the means, for the simple and obvious reason that the means employed determine the nature of the ends produced.

These chapters, from the second to the twelfth, constitute a kind of practical cookery book of reform. They contain political recipes, economic recipes, educational recipes, recipes for the organization of industry, of local communities, of groups of devoted individuals. They also contain, by way of warning, descriptions of the way things ought not to be done—recipes for not realizing the ends one professes to desire, recipes for stultifying idealism, recipes for paving hell with good intentions.

This cookery book of reform culminates in the last section of the book, in which I discuss the relation existing between the theories and the practices of reformers on the one hand and the nature of the universe on the other. What sort of world is this, in which men aspire to good and yet so frequently achieve evil? What is the sense and point of the whole affair? What is man's place in it and how are his ideals, his systems of values, related to the universe at large? It is with such questions that I shall deal in the last three chapters. To the "practical man" they may seem irrelevant. But in fact they are not. It is in the light of our beliefs about the ultimate nature of reality that we formulate our conceptions of right and wrong; and it is in the light of our conceptions of right and wrong that we frame our conduct, not only in the relations of private life, but also in the sphere of politics and economics. So far from being irrelevant, our metaphysical beliefs are the finally determining factor in all our actions. That is why it has seemed to me necessary to round off my cookery book of practical recipes with a discussion of first principles. The last three chapters are the most significant and, even from the purely practical point of view, the most important in the book.

II

The Nature of Explanation

ABOUT the goal, I repeat, there has for long been agreement. We know what sort of society we should like to be members of and what sort of men and women we should like to be. But when it comes to deciding how to reach the goal, the babel of conflicting opinions breaks loose. *Quot homines, tot sententiae.* Where ultimate ends are concerned, the statement is false; in regard to means, it is nearly true. Everyone has his own patent medicine, guaranteed to cure all the ills of humanity; and so passionate, in many cases, is belief in the efficacy of the panacea that men are prepared, on its behalf, to kill and to be killed.

That men should cling so tenaciously to the dogmas they have invented or accepted, and that they should hate so passionately the people who have invented or accepted other dogmas, are facts that can be accounted for only too easily. Certainty is profoundly comforting, and hatred pays a high dividend in emotional excitement. It is less easy, however, to understand why such exclusive doctrines should ever arise, why the intellect, even when unblinded by passion, should be ready and even eager to regard them as true. It is worth while, in this context, to devote a few lines to the nature of explanation. In what does the process of explaining consist? And, in any given explanation, what is the quality which we find intellectually satisfying? These questions have been treated with great acuteness and an enormous wealth of learning by the late Emile Meyerson, from whose writings I have, in the ensuing paragraphs, freely borrowed.*

The human mind has an invincible tendency to reduce the diverse to the identical. That which is given us, immediately, by our senses, is multitudinous and diverse. Our intellect, which hungers and thirsts after explanation, attempts to reduce this diversity to identity. Any proposition stipulating the existence of an identity underlying diverse phenomena, or persisting through time and change, seems to us intrinsically plausible. We derive a deep satisfaction from any doctrine which reduces irrational multiplicity to rational and comprehensible unity. To this fundamental psychological fact is due the existence of science, of philosophy, of theology If we were not always trying to reduce diversity to identity, we should find it almost impossible to think at all. The world would be a mere chaos, an unconnected series of mutually irrelevant phenomena.

The effort to reduce diversity to identity can be, and generally is, carried too far. This is particularly true in regard to thinkers who are working in fields not subjected to the discipline of one of the well-organized natural sciences. Natural science recognizes the fact that there is a residue of irrational diversity which cannot be reduced to the identical and the rational. For example, it admits the existence of irreversible changes in time. When an irreversible change takes place, there is not an

* See *Du Cheminement de la Pensée* and *De l'Explication dans les Sciences* by Emile Meyerson.

underlying identity between the state before and the state after the change. Science is not only the effort to reduce diversity to identity; it is also, among other things, the study of the irrational brute fact of becoming. There are two tendencies in science; the tendency towards identification and generalization and the tendency towards the exploration of brute reality, accompanied by a recognition of the specificity of phenomena.

Where thought is not subject to the discipline of one of the organized sciences, the first tendency—that towards identification and generalization—is apt to be allowed too much scope. The result is an excessive simplification. In its impatience to understand, its hunger and thirst after explanation, the intellect tends to impose more rationality upon the given facts than those facts will bear, tends to discover in the brute diversity of phenomena more identity than really exists in them —or at any rate more identity than a man can make use of in the practical affairs of life. For a being that can take the god's-eye view of things, certain diversities display an underlying identity. By the animal, on the contrary, they must be accepted for what they seem to be, specifically dissimilar. Man is a double being and can take, now the god's-eye view of things, now the brute's-eye view. For example, he can affirm that chalk and cheese are both composed of electrons, both perhaps more or less illusory manifestations of the Absolute. Such reduction of the diverse to the identical may satisfy our hunger for explanation; but we have bodies as well as intellects, and these bodies have a hunger for Stilton and a distaste for chalk. In so far as we are hungry and thirsty animals, it is important for us to know that there is a difference between what is wholesome and what is poisonous. Their reduction to an identity may be all right in the study; but in the dining-room it is extremely unhelpful.

Over-simplification in regard to such phenomena as chalk and cheese, as H_2O and H_2SO_4, leads very rapidly to fatal results; it is rarely therefore that we make such over-simplifications. There are, however, other classes of phenomena in regard to which we can over-simplify with a certain measure of impunity. The penalty for such mistakes is not spectacular or immediate. In many cases, indeed, the makers of the mistake are not even aware that they are being punished; for the punishment takes the form not of a deprivation of a good which they already possess, but of the withholding of a good which they might have come to possess if they had not made the mistake. Consider, by way of example, that once very common over-simplification of the facts which consists in making God responsible for all imperfectly understood phenomena. Secondary causes are ignored and everything is referred back to the Creator. No more wholesale reduction of diversity to identity is possible; and yet its effect is not immediately perceptible. Those who make the mistake of thinking in terms of a first cause are fated never to become men of science. But as they do not know what science is, they are not aware that they are losing anything.

To refer phenomena back to a first cause has ceased to be fashionable, at any rate in the West. The identities to which we try to reduce the complicated diversities round us are of a different order. For example, when we discuss society or individual human beings, we no longer make our over-simplifications in terms of the will of God, but of such entities as economics, or sex, or the inferiority complex. Excessive simplifications! But here again the penalty for making them is not immediate or obvious. Our punishment consists in our inability to realize our ideals, to escape from the social and psychological slough in which we wallow. We shall never deal effectively with our human problems until we follow the example of natural scientists and temper our longing for rational simplification by the recognition in things and events of a certain residue of irrationality, diversity and specificity. We shall never succeed in changing our age of iron into an age of gold until we give up our ambitions to find a single cause for all our ills, and admit the existence of many causes acting simultaneously, of intricate correlations and reduplicated actions and reactions. There is, as we have seen, a great variety of fanatically entertained opinions regarding the best way of reaching the desired goal. We shall be well advised to consider them all. To exalt any single one of them into an orthodoxy is to commit the fault of oversimplification. In these pages I shall consider some of the means which must be employed, and employed simultaneously, if we are to realize the end which the prophets and the philosophers have proposed for humanity—a free and just society, fit for non-attached men and women to be members of and such, at the same time, as only non-attached men and women could organize.

III

Efficacy and Limitations of Large-scale Social Reform

AMONG people who hold what are called "advanced opinions" there is a wide-spread belief that the ends we all desire can best be achieved by manipulating the structure of society. They advocate, not a "change of heart" for individuals, but the carrying through of certain large-scale political and, above all, economic reforms.

Now, economic and political reform is a branch of what may be called preventive ethics. The aim of preventive ethics is to create social circumstances of such a nature that individuals will not be given opportunities for behaving in an undesirable, that is to say an excessively "attached," way.

Among the petitions most frequently repeated by Christians is the prayer that they may not be led into temptation. The political and economic reformer aims at answering that prayer. He believes that man's environment can be so well organized that the majority of temptations will never arise. In the perfect society, the individual will practise non-attachment, not because he will be deliberately and consciously non-attached, but because he will never be given the chance of attaching himself. There is, it is obvious, much truth in the reformer's contention. In England, for example, far fewer murders are committed now than were committed in the past. This reduction in the murder rate is due to a number of large-scale reforms—to legislation restricting the sale and forbidding the carrying of arms; to the development of an efficient legal system which provides prompt redress to the victims of outrage. Nor must we forget the change of manners (itself due to a great variety of causes) which has led to the disparagement of duelling and a new conception of personal honour. Similar examples might be cited indefinitely. Social reforms have unquestionably had the effects of reducing the number of temptations into which individuals may be led. (In a later paragraph, I shall consider the question of the new temptations which reforms may create.) When the absence of temptation has been prolonged for some time, an ethical habit is created; individuals come to think that the evil into which they are not led is something monstrous and hardly even thinkable. Generally, they take to themselves the credit that is really due to circumstances. Consider, for example, the question of cruelty. In England the legislation against cruelty to animals and, later, children and adults was carried through, against indifference and even active opposition, by a small minority of earnest reformers. Removal of the occasions of indulging in and gloating over cruelty resulted after a certain time in the formation of a habit of humanitarianism. Thanks to this habit, Englishmen now feel profoundly shocked by the idea of cruelty and imagine that they themselves would be quite incapable of performing or watching cruel acts. This last belief is probably unfounded. There are many people who believe themselves to be fundamentally humane and actually behave as humanitarians, but who, if changed circumstance offered occasions for being cruel (especially if the cruelty were represented as a means to some noble end) would succumb to the temptation with enthusiasm. Hence the enormous importance of preserving intact any long-established habit of decency and restraint. Hence the vital necessity of avoiding war, whether international or civil. For war, if it is fought on a large scale, destroys more than the lives of individual men and women; it shakes the whole fabric of custom, of law, of mutual confidence, of unthinking and habitual decency and humaneness, upon which all forms of tolerable social life are based. The English are, on the whole, a good-humoured and kindly people. This is due, not to any extra dose of original virtue in them, but to the fact that the last successful invasion of their island took place in 1066 and their last civil war (a most mild and gentleman-like affair) in 1688. It should be noted, moreover, that the kindliness of the English manifests itself only at home and in those parts of their Empire where there has been for some time no war or threat of war. The Indians do not find their rulers particularly kindly. And, in effect, the ethical standards of Englishmen undergo a profound change as they pass from the essentially peaceful atmosphere of their own country into that of their conquered and militarily occupied Indian Empire. Things which would be absolutely unthinkable at home are not only thinkable, but do-able and actually done in India. The Amritsar massacre, for example. Long immunity from war and civil violence can do more to promote the common decencies of life than any amount of ethical exhortation. War and violence are the prime causes of war and violence. A country where, as in Spain, there is a tradition of civil strife, is far more liable to civil strife than one in which there exists a long habit of peaceful co-operation.

We see, then, that large-scale manipulation of the social order can do much to preserve individuals from temptations which, before the reforms were made, were ever-present and almost irresistible. So far so good. But we must not forget that reforms may deliver men from one set of evils, only to lead them into evils of another kind. It often happens that reforms merely have the effect of transferring the undesirable tendencies of individuals from one channel to another channel. An old outlet for some particular wickedness is closed; but a new outlet is opened. The wickedness is not abolished; it is merely provided with a different set of opportunities for self-expression. It would be possible to write a most illuminating History of Sin, showing the extent to which the various tendencies to bad behaviour have been given opportunities in the different civilizations of the world, enumerating the defects of every culture's specific virtues, tracing the successive metamorphoses of evil under changing technological and political conditions. Consider, by way of example, the recent history of that main source of evil, the lust for power, the craving for personal success and dominance. In this context we may describe the passage from mediaeval to modern conditions as a passage from violence to cunning, from the conception of power in terms of military prowess and the divine right of aristocracy to its conception in terms of finance. In the earlier period the sword and the patent of nobility are at once the symbols and the instruments of domination. In the later period their place is taken by money. Recently the lust for power has come to express itself once again in ways that are almost mediaeval. In the fascist states there has been a return towards rule by the sword and by divine right. True, the right is that of self-appointed leaders rather than that of hereditary aristocrats; but it is still essentially divine. Mussolini is infallible; Hitler, appointed by God. In collectivized Russia a system of state capitalism has been established. Private ownership of the means of production has disappeared and it has become impossible for individuals to use money as a means for dominating their fellows. But this does not mean that the lust for power has been suppressed; rather it has been deflected from one channel to another channel. Under the new régime the symbol and the instrument of power is political position. Men seek, not wealth, but a strategic post in the hierarchy. How ruthlessly they would fight for these strategic posts was shown during the treason trials of 1936 and 1937. In Russia, and to a certain extent in the other dictatorial countries, the position is very similar to that which prevailed in the religious orders, where position was more important than money. Among the Communists, ambition has been more or less effectively divorced from avarice and the lust for power manifests itself in a form which is, so to say, chemically pure.

This is the cue for smiling indulgently and saying: "You can't change human nature." To which the anthropologist replies by pointing out that human nature has in fact been made to assume the most bewilderingly diverse, the most amazingly improbable forms. It is possible to arrange a society in such a way that even so fundamental a tendency as the lust for power cannot easily find expression. Among the Zuñi Indians, for example, individuals are not led into the kind of temptation which invites the men of our civilization to work for fame, wealth, social position or power. By us, success is always worshipped. But among the Zuñis it is such bad form to pursue personal distinction that very few people even think of trying to raise themselves above their fellows, while those who try are regarded as dangerous sorcerers and punished accordingly. There are no Hitlers, no Kreugers, no Napoleons and no Calvins. The lust for power is simply not given an opportunity for expressing itself. In the tranquil and well-balanced communities of the Zuñis and other Pueblo Indians all those outlets for personal ambition—the political, the financial, the military, the religious outlets with which our own history has made us so painfully familiar—are closed.

The pattern of Pueblo culture is one which a modern industrialized society could not possibly copy. Nor, even if it were possible, would it be desirable that we should choose these Indian societies as our model. For the Pueblo Indians' triumph over the lust for power has been secured at an excessive cost. Individuals do not scramble for wealth and position, as with us; but they purchase these advantages at a great price. They are weighed down under a great burden of religious tradition; they are attached to all that is old and terrified of all that is novel and unfamiliar; they spend an enormous amount of time and energy in the performance of magic rites and the repetition, by rote, of interminable formulas. Using the language of theology, we can say that the deadly sins to which *we* are peculiarly attached are pride, avarice and malice. *Their* special attachment is to sloth—above all to the mental sloth, or stupidity, against which the Buddhist moralists so insistently warn their disciples. The problem which confronts us is this: can we combine the merits of our culture with those of the Pueblo culture? Can we create a new pattern of living in which the defects of the two contrasted patterns, Pueblo Indian and Western-Industrial, shall be absent? Is it possible for us to acquire their admirable habits of non-attachment to wealth and personal success and at the same time to preserve our intellectual alertness, our interest in science, our capacity for making rapid technological progress and social change?

These are questions which it is impossible to answer with any degree of confidence. Only experience and deliberate experiment can tell us if our problem can be completely solved. All we certainly know is that, up to the present, scientific curiosity and a capacity for making rapid social changes have always been associated with frequent manifestations of the lust for power and the worship of success.* As a matter of historical fact, scientific progressiveness has never been divorced from aggressiveness. Does this mean that they can never be

* See in the last chapter the discussion of the relations existing between enforced sexual continence and social energy.

divorced? Not necessarily. Every culture is full of arbitrary and fortuitous associations of behaviour-patterns,
thought-patterns, feeling-patterns. These associations
may last for long periods and are regarded, while they
endure, as necessary, natural, right, inherent in the
scheme of things. But a time comes when, under the
pressure of changing circumstances, these long-standing
associations fall apart and give place to others, which in
due course come to seem no less natural, necessary and
right than the old. Let us consider a few examples. In
the richer classes of mediaeval and early modern European society there was a very close association between
thoughts and habits concerned with sex and thoughts
and habits concerned with property and social position.
The mediaeval nobleman married a fief, the early-mod-
ern bourgeois married a dowry. Kings married whole
countries and, by judiciously choosing their bed-fellows,
could build up an empire. And not only did the wife
represent property; she also *was* property. The ferocious
jealousies which it was traditionally right and proper to
feel, were due at least as much to an outraged property
sense as to a thwarted sexual passion. Hurt pride and
offended avarice combined with wounded love to produce the kind of jealousy that could be satisfied only
with the blood of the unfaithful spouse. Meanwhile the
faithful spouse was ornamented and bejewelled, occasionally no doubt out of genuine affection, but more
often and chiefly to gratify the husband's desire for self-
glorification. The sumptuously attired wife was a kind of
walking advertisement for her owner's wealth and social
position. The tendency towards what Veblen calls "con-

spicuous consumption" came to be associated in these cultures with the pattern of sexual behaviour. I have used the past tense in the preceding passage. But in fact this association of conspicuous consumption with matrimony—and also with fornication—is still characteristic of our societies. In the other cases, however, there has been a considerable measure of dissociation. Spouses do not regard one another as private property to quite the same extent as in the past; consequently it no longer seems natural and right to murder an unfaithful partner. The idea of a wholly gratuitous sexual union, unconnected with dowries and settlements, is now frequently entertained even among the rich. Conversely there is a quite general belief that even married people may be sexually attached to one another. This was not so in the time of the troubadours; for, in the words of a recent historian of chivalry, chivalrous love was "a gigantic system of bigamy." Love and marriage were completely dissociated.

There are many other associations of thought-patterns, feeling-patterns and action-patterns which have seemed in their time inevitable and natural, but which at other times or in other places have not existed at all. Thus, art has sometimes been associated with religion (as in Europe during the Middle Ages or among the ancient Mayas) ; sometimes, on the other hand, it has not been associated with religion (as among certain tribes of American Indians and among Europeans during the last three centuries). Similarly commerce, agriculture, sex, eating have sometimes been associated with religion, sometimes not. There are some societies where almost all activities are associated with negative emotions, where it is socially correct and morally praiseworthy to feel chronically suspicious, envious and malevolent. There are others in which it is no less right to feel positive emotions. And so on, almost indefinitely.

Now, it may be that progressiveness and aggressiveness are associated in the same sort of arbitrary and fortuitous way as are the various pairs of thought-habits and action-habits mentioned above. It may be, on the other hand, that this association has its roots in the depth of human psychology and that it will prove very difficult or even impossible to separate these two conjoined tendencies. This is a matter about which one cannot dogmatize. All that one can say with certainty is that the association need not be quite so complete as it is at present.

Let us sum up and draw our conclusions. First, then, we see that "unchanging human nature" is not unchanging, but can be, and very frequently has been, profoundly changed. Second, we see that many, perhaps most, of the observed associations of behaviour patterns in human societies can be dissociated and their elements re-associated in other ways. Third, we see that large-scale manipulations of the social structure can bring about certain "changes in human nature," but that these changes are rarely fundamental. They do not abolish evil; they merely deflect it into other channels. But if the ends we all desire are to be achieved, there must be more than a mere deflection of evil; there must be suppression at the source, in the individual will. Hence it follows that large-scale political and economic reform is not enough. The attack upon our ideal objective must be made, not only on this front, but also and at the same time on all the others. Before considering what will have to be done on these other fronts, I must describe in some detail the strategy and tactics of attack upon the front of large-scale reform.

IV

Social Reform and Violence

"THE more violence, the less revolution." This dictum of Barthelemy de Ligt's is one on which it is profitable to meditate.*

To be regarded as successful, a revolution must be the achievement of something new. But violence and the effects of violence—counter-violence, suspicion and resentment on the part of the victims and the creation, among the perpetrators, of a tendency to use more violence—are things only too familiar, too hopelessly unrevolutionary. A violent revolution cannot achieve anything except the inevitable results of violence, which are as old as the hills.

Or let us put the matter in another way. No revolution can be regarded as successful, if it does not lead to progress. Now, the only real progress, to quote Dr. Marett's words once more, is progress in charity. Is it possible to achieve progress in charity by means that are essentially uncharitable? If we dispassionately consider our personal experience and the records of history, we must conclude that it is not possible. But so strong is our desire to believe that there is a short cut to Utopia, so deeply prejudiced are we in favour of people of similar opinions to our own, that we are rarely able to command the necessary dispassion. We insist that ends which we believe to be good can justify means which we know

* See *Pour Vaincre Sans Violence* (English translation published by Routledge) and *La Paix Créatrice* by B. de Ligt.

quite certainly to be abominable; we go on believing, against all the evidence, that these bad means can achieve the good ends we desire. The extent to which even highly intelligent people can deceive themselves in this matter is well illustrated by the following words from Professor Lasky's little book on *Communism*. "It is patent," he writes, "that without the iron dictatorship of the Jacobins, the republic would have been destroyed." To any one who candidly considers the facts it seems even more patent that it was precisely because of the iron dictatorship of the Jacobins that the republic was destroyed. Iron dictatorship led to foreign war and reaction at home. War and reaction between them resulted in the creation of a military dictatorship. Military dictatorship resulted in yet more wars. These wars served to intensify nationalistic sentiment throughout the whole of Europe. Nationalism became crystallized in a number of new idolatrous religions dividing the world. (The Nazi creed, for example, is already implicit and even, to a great extent, fully explicit in the writings of Fichte.) To nationalism we owe military conscription at home and imperialism abroad. "Without the iron dictatorship of the Jacobins," says Professor Lasky, "the republic would have been destroyed." A fine sentiment! Unfortunately there are also the facts. The first significant fact is that the republic *was* destroyed and that the iron dictatorship of the Jacobins was the prime cause of its destruction. Nor was this the only piece of mischief for which the Jacobin dictatorship was responsible. It led to the futile waste and slaughter of the Napoleonic wars; to the imposition in perpetuity of military slavery,

[29]

or conscription, upon practically all the countries of Europe; and to the rise of those nationalistic idolatries which threaten the existence of our civilization. A fine record! And yet would-be revolutionaries persist in believing that, by methods essentially similar to those employed by the Jacobins, they will succeed in producing such totally dissimilar results as social justice and peace between nations.

Violence cannot lead to real progress unless, by way of compensation and reparation, it is followed by non-violence, by acts of justice and good will. In such cases, however, it is the compensatory behaviour that achieves the progress, not the violence which that behaviour was intended to compensate. For example, in so far as the Roman conquest of Gaul and the British conquest of India resulted in progress (and it is hard to say whether they did and quite impossible to guess whether an equal advance might not have been achieved without those conquests), that progress was entirely due to the compensatory behaviour of Roman and British administrators after the violence was over. Where compensatory good behaviour does not follow the original act of violence, as was the case in the countries conquered by the Turks, no real progress is achieved. (In cases where violence is pushed to its limits and the victims are totally exterminated, the slate is wiped clean and the perpetrators of violence are free to begin afresh on their own account. This was the way in which, rejecting Penn's humaner alternative, the English settlers in North America solved the Red Indian problem. Abominable in itself, this policy is practicable only in underpopulated countries.)

The longer violence has been used, the more difficult do the users find it to perform compensatory acts of non-violence. A tradition of violence is formed; men come to accept a scale of values according to which acts of violence are reckoned heroic and virtuous. When this happens, as it happened, for example, with the Vikings and the Tartars, as the dictators seem at present to be trying to make it happen with the Germans, Italians, and Russians, there is small prospect that the effects of violence will be made good by subsequent acts of justice and kindness.

From what has gone before it follows that no reform is likely to achieve the results intended unless it is not only well intentioned, but also opportune. To carry through a social reform which, in the given historical circumstances, will create so much opposition as to necessitate the use of violence is criminally rash. For the chances are that any reform which requires violence for its imposition will not only fail to produce the good results anticipated, but will actually make matters worse than they were before. Violence, as we have seen, can produce only the effects of violence; these effects can be undone only by compensatory non-violence after the event; where violence has been used for a long period, a habit of violence is formed and it becomes exceedingly difficult for the perpetrators of violence to reverse their policy. Moreover, the results of violence are far-reaching beyond the wildest dreams of the often well-intentioned people who resort to it. The "iron dictatorship" of the

Jacobins resulted, as we have seen, in military tyranny, twenty years of war, conscription in perpetuity for the whole of Europe, the rise of nationalistic idolatry. In own own time the long-drawn violence of Tsarist oppression and the acute, catastrophic violence of the World War produced the "iron dictatorship" of the Bolsheviks. The threat of world-wide revolutionary violence begot Fascism; Fascism produced re-armament; re-armament has entailed the progressive de-liberalization of the democratic countries. What the further results of Moscow's "iron dictatorship" will be, time alone will show. At the present moment (June 1937) the outlook is, to say the least of it, exceedingly gloomy.

If, then, we wish to make large-scale reforms which will not stultify themselves in the process of application, we must choose our measures in such a way that no violence or, at the worst, very little violence will be needed to enforce them. (It is worth noting in this context that reforms carried out under the stimulus of the fear of violence from foreign neighbours and with the aim of using violence more efficiently in future international wars are just as likely to be self-stultifying in the long run as reforms which cannot be enforced except by a domestic terror. The dictators have made many large-scale changes in the structure of the societies they govern without having had to resort to terrorism. The population gave consent to these changes because it had been persuaded by means of intensive propaganda that they were necessary to make the country safe against "foreign aggression." Some of these changes have been in the nature of desirable reforms; but in so far as they were calculated to make the country more efficient as a war-machine, they tended to provoke other countries to increase their military efficiency and so to make the coming of war more probable. But the nature of modern war is such that it is unlikely that any desirable reform will survive the catastrophe. Thus it will be seen that intrinsically desirable reforms, accepted without opposition, may yet be self-stultifying if the community is persuaded to accept them by means of propaganda that plays upon its fear of future violence on the part of others, or stresses the glory of future violence when successfully used by itself.) Returning to our main theme, which is the need for avoiding domestic violence during the application of reforms, we see that a reform may be intrinsically desirable, but so irrelevant to the existing historical circumstances as to be practically useless. This does not mean that we should make the enormous mistake committed by Hegel and gleefully repeated by every modern tyrant with crimes to justify and follies to rationalize—the mistake that consists in affirming that the real is the rational, that the historical is the same as the ideal. The real is not the rational; and whatever is, is not right. At any given moment of history, the real, as we know it, contains certain elements of the rational, laboriously incorporated into its structure by patient human effort; among the things that are, some are righter than others. This being so, plain common sense demands that, when we make reforms, we shall take care to preserve all such constituents of the existing order as are valuable. Nor is this all. Change as such is to most human beings more or less acutely distressing. Accord-

[33]

ingly, we shall do well to preserve even those elements of the existing order which are neither particularly harmful, nor particularly valuable, but merely neutral. Human conservatism is a fact in any given historical situation. Hence it is very important that social reformers should abstain from making unnecessary changes or changes of startling magnitude. Wherever possible, familiar institutions should be extended or developed so as to produce the results desired; principles already accepted should be taken over and applied to a wider field. In this way the amount and intensity of opposition to change and, along with it, the risk of having to use measures of violence would be reduced to a minimum.

V

The Planned Society

BEFORE the World War only Fabians talked about a planned society. During the War all the belligerent societies were planned, and (considering the rapidity with which the work was done) planned very effectively, for the purpose of carrying on the hostilities. Immediately after the War there was a reaction, natural enough in the circumstance, against planning. The depression produced a reaction against that reaction, and since 1929 the idea of planning has achieved an almost universal popularity. Meanwhile planning has been undertaken, systematically and on a large scale in the totalitarian states, piece-meal in the democratic countries. A flood of literature on social planning pours continuously from the presses. Every "advanced" thinker has his favourite scheme, and even quite ordinary people have caught the infection. Planning is now in fashion. Not without justification. Our world is in a bad way, and it looks as though it would be impossible to rescue it from its present plight, much less improve it, except by deliberate planning. Admittedly this is only an opinion; but there is every reason to suppose that it is well founded. Meanwhile, however, it is quite certain, because observably a fact, that in the process of trying to save our world or part of it from its present confusion, we run the risk of planning it into the likeness of hell and ultimately into complete destruction. There are cures which are worse than disease.

Some kind of deliberate planning is necessary. But which kind and how much? We cannot answer these questions, cannot pass judgment on any given scheme, except by constantly referring back to our ideal postulates. In considering any plan we must ask whether it will help to transform the society to which it is applied into a just, peaceable, morally and intellectually progressive community of non-attached and responsible men and women. If so, we can say that the plan is a good one. If not, we must pronounce it to be bad.

In the contemporary world there are two classes of bad plans—the plans invented and put into practice by men who do not accept our ideal postulates, and the plans invented and put into practice by the men who accept them, but imagine that the ends proposed by the prophets can be achieved by wicked or unsuitable means. Hell is paved with good intentions, and it is probable that plans made by well-meaning people of the second class may have results no less disastrous than plans made by the evil-intentioned people of the first class. Which only shows, yet once more, how right the Buddha was in classing unawareness and stupidity among the deadly sins. Let us consider a few examples of bad plans belonging to these two classes. In the first class we must place all Fascist and all specifically militaristic plans. Fascism, in the words of Mussolini, believes that "war alone brings up to its highest tension all human energy and puts the stamp of nobility upon the peoples who have the courage to meet it." Again, "a doctrine which is founded upon the harmful postulate of peace is hostile to Fascism." The Fascist, then, is one who believes that the bombardment of open towns with fire, poison and explosives (in other words, modern war) is intrinsically good. He is one who rejects the teaching of the prophets and believes that the best society is a national society living in a state of chronic hostility towards other national societies and preoccupied with ideas of rapine and slaughter. He is one who despises the non-attached individual and holds up for admiration the person who, in obedience to the boss who happens at the moment to have grabbed political power, systematically cultivates all the passions (pride, anger, envy, hatred) which the philosophers and the founders of religions have unanimously condemned as the most maleficent, the least worthy of human beings. All fascist planning has one ultimate aim: to make the national society more efficient as a war machine. Industry, commerce and finance are controlled for this purpose. The manufacture of substitutes is encouraged in order that the country may be self-sufficient in time of war. Tariffs and quotas are imposed, export bounties distributed, exchanges depreciated for the sake of gaining a momentary advantage or inflicting loss upon some rival. Foreign policy is conducted on avowedly Machiavellian principles; solemn engagements are entered into with the knowledge that they will be broken the moment it seems advantageous to do so; international law is invoked when it happens to be convenient, repudiated when it imposes the least restraint on the nation's imperialistic designs. Meanwhile the dictator's subjects are systematically educated to be good citizens of the Fascist state. Children are subjected to authoritarian discipline that they may grow up to be simultaneously obedient to superiors and brutal to those below them. On leaving the kindergarten, they begin that military training which culminates in the years of conscription and continues until the individual is too decrepit to be an efficient soldier. In school they are taught extravagant lies about the achievements of their ancestors, while the truth about other peoples is either distorted or completely suppressed. The press is controlled, so that adults may learn only what it suits the dictator that they should learn. Any one expressing unorthodox opinions is ruthlessly persecuted. Elaborate systems of police espionage are organized to investigate the private life and opinions of even the humblest individual. Delation is encouraged, tale-telling rewarded. Terrorism is legalized. Justice is administered in secret; the procedure is unfair, the penalties barbarously cruel. Brutality and torture are regularly employed.

Such is Fascist planning—the planning of those who reject the ideal postulates of Christian civilization and of the older Asiatic civilization which preceded it and from which it derived—the planning of men whose intentions are avowedly bad. Let us now consider examples of planning by political leaders who accept the ideal postulates, whose intentions are good. The first thing to notice is that none of these men accepts the ideal postulates whole-heartedly. All believe that desirable ends can be achieved by undesirable means. Aiming to reach goals diametrically opposed to those of Fascism, they yet persist in taking the same roads as are taken by the Duces and Fuehrers. They are pacifists, but pacifists who act on the theory that peace can be achieved by means of war;

they are reformers and revolutionaries, but reformers who imagine that unfair and arbitrary acts can produce social justice, revolutionaries who persuade themselves that the centralization of power and the enslavement of the masses can result in liberty for all. Revolutionary Russia has the largest army in the world; a secret police, that for ruthless efficiency rivals the German or the Italian; a rigid press censorship; a system of education that, since Stalin "reformed" it, is as authoritarian as Hitler's; an all-embracing system of military training that is applied to women and children as well as men; a dictator as slavishly adored as the man-gods of Rome and Berlin; a bureaucracy, solidly entrenched as the new ruling class and employing the powers of the state to preserve its privileges and protect its vested interests; an oligarchical party which dominates the entire country and within which there is no freedom even for faithful members. (Most ruling castes are democracies so far as their own members are concerned. Not so the Russian Communist Party, in which the Central Executive Committee acting through the Political Department, can override or altogether liquidate any district organization whatsoever.*) No opposition is permitted in Russia. But where opposition is made illegal, it automatically goes underground and becomes conspiracy. Hence the treason trials and purges of 1936 and 1937. Large-scale manipulations of the social structure are pushed through against the wishes of the people concerned and with the utmost ruthlessness. (Several million peasants were de-

* See "Planned Society," edited by Findlay Mackenzie, p. 837. (New York, 1937.)

liberately starved to death in 1933 by the Soviet planners.) Ruthlessness begets resentment; resentment must be kept down by force. As usual the chief result of violence is the necessity to use more violence. Such then is Soviet planning—well-intentioned, but making use of evil means that are producing results utterly unlike those which the original makers of the revolution intended to produce.

In the bourgeois democratic countries the need for using intrinsically good means to achieve desirable ends is more clearly realized than in Russia. But even in these countries enormous mistakes have been made in the past and still greater, still more dangerous mistakes are in process of being committed today. Most of these mistakes are due to the fact that, though professing belief in our ideal postulates, the rulers and people of these countries are, to some extent and quite incompatibly, also militarists and nationalists. The English and the French, it is true, are sated militarists whose chief desire is to live a quiet life, holding fast to what they seized in their unregenerate days of imperial highway-robbery. Confronted by rivals who want to do now what they were doing from the beginning of the eighteenth to the end of the nineteenth century, they profess and doubtless genuinely feel a profound moral indignation. Meanwhile, they have begun to address themselves, reluctantly but with determination, to the task of beating the Fascist powers at their own game. Like the Fascist states, they are preparing for war. But modern war cannot be waged or even prepared except by a highly centralized executive wielding absolute power over a docile people. Most of the planning which is going on in the democratic countries is planning designed to transform these countries into the likeness of totalitarian communities organized for slaughter and rapine. Hitherto this transformation has proceeded fairly slowly. Belief in our ideal postulates has acted as a brake on fascization, which has had to advance gradually and behind a smoke screen. But if war is declared, or even if the threat of war becomes more serious than at present, the process will become open and rapid. "The defence of democracy against Fascism" entails inevitably the transformation of democracy into Fascism.

Most of the essays in large-scale planning attempted by the democratic powers have been dictated by the desire to achieve military efficiency. Thus, the attempt to co-ordinate the British Empire into a self-sufficient economic unit was a piece of planning mainly dictated by military considerations. Still more specifically military in character have been the plans applied to the armament industries, not only in Great Britain, but also in France and the other democratic countries, for the purpose of increasing production. Like the Fascist plans for heightening military efficiency, such essays in planning are bound to make matters worse, not better. By transforming the British Empire from a Free Trade area into a private property protected by tariff walls, the governments concerned have made it absolutely certain that foreign hostility to the Empire shall be greatly increased. While the English possessed undisputed command of the sea, they conciliated world opinion by leaving the doors of their colonies wide open to foreign trade. Now that command of the sea has been lost, those doors are closed. In other words, England invites the world's hostility at the very moment when it has ceased to be in a position to defy that hostility. Greater folly could scarcely be imagined. But those who think in terms of militarism inevitably commit such follies.

Consider the second case. Re-armament at the present rate and on the present enormous scale must have one of two results. Either there will be general war within a very short time; for *si vis bellum, para bellum*. Or, if war is postponed for a few years, the present rate of re-armament will have to be slowed down and an economic depression at least as grave as that of 1929 will descend upon the world. Economic depression will create unrest; unrest will speed up the fascization of the democratic countries; the fascization of the democratic countries will increase the present probability of war to an absolute certainty. So much for planning undertaken for specifically military purposes.

Many pieces of planning, however, have not been specifically military in character. They have been devised by governments primarily for the purpose of counteracting the effects of economic depression. But, unfortunately, under the present dispensation, such plans must be conceived and carried out in the context of militarism and nationalism. This context imparts to every plan in the international field, a quality that, however good the intentions of the planners, is essentially militaristic. (Here it is worth while to enunciate a general truth, which the older anthropologists, such as Frazer, completely failed to grasp—the truth that a given habit, rite, tradition takes on its peculiar significance from its context. Two peoples may have what is, according to Frazerian ideas, the same custom; but this does not mean that the custom in question will signify the same thing to these two peoples. If the contexts in which this "identical" custom is placed happen to be different—as in fact they generally are—then it will carry widely different significances for the two peoples. Applying this generalization to our particular problem, we see that a non-militaristic plan carried out in a militaristic context is likely to have a significance and results quite different from the significance and results of the same plan in a non-militaristic context.)

Owing to the fact that even the democratic peoples are to some extent militarists and devotees of the idolatry of exclusive nationalism, almost all the economic planning undertaken by their governments has seemed to foreign observers imperialistic in character and has in fact resulted in a worsening of the international situation. Governments have used tariffs, export bounties, quotas and exchange devaluation as devices for improving the lot of their subjects; in the context of the world as it is today, these plans have seemed to other nations acts of deliberate ill will meriting reprisals in kind. Reprisals have led to counter-reprisals. International exchanges have become more and more difficult. Consequently yet further planning has had to be resorted to by each of the governments concerned for the protection of its own subjects—yet further planning which arouses yet bitterer resentment abroad and so brings war yet a little nearer.

We are confronted here by the great paradox of contemporary planning. Comprehensive planning by individual nations results in international chaos, and the degree of international chaos is in exact proportion to the number, completeness and efficiency of the separate national plans.

During the nineteenth and the first years of the twentieth century economic exchanges between the nations were carried on with remarkable smoothness. National economies were everywhere unplanned. The individuals who carried on international trade were forced in their own interest to conform to the rules of the game, as developed in the City of London. If they failed to conform, they were ruined and that was an end of it. Here we have the converse of the paradox formulated above. National planlessness in economic matters results in international economic co-ordination.

We are on the horns of a dilemma. In every country large numbers of people are suffering privations owing to defects in the economic machine. These people must be helped, and if they are to be helped effectively and permanently, the economic machine must be re-planned. But economic planning undertaken by a national government for the benefit of its own people inevitably disturbs that international economic harmony which is the result of national planlessness. In the process of planning for the benefit of their respective peoples, national governments impede the flow of international trade, enter into new forms of international rivalry and create fresh sources of international discord. During the last few years most of the governments of the world have had to choose between two almost equal evils. Either they could abandon the victims of economic maladjustment to their fate; but such a course was shocking to decent sentiment and, since the sufferers might vote against the government or even break out into violent revolt, politically dangerous. Or else they might help the sufferers by imposing a governmental plan upon the economic activity of their respective countries; but in this case they reduced the system of international exchanges to chaos and increased the probability of general war.

Between the horns of this dilemma a way lies obviously and invitingly open. The various national governments can take counsel together and co-ordinate their activities, so that one national plan shall not interfere with the workings of another. But, unfortunately, under the present dispensation, this obvious and eminently sensible course cannot be taken. The Fascist states do not pretend to want peace and international co-operation, and even those democratic governments which make the loudest professions of pacifism are at the same time nationalistic, militaristic and imperialistic. Twentieth-century political thinking is incredibly primitive. The nation is personified as a living being with passions, desires, susceptibilities. The National Person is superhuman in size and energy but completely sub-human in morality. Ordinarily decent behaviour cannot be expected of the National Person, who is thought of as incapable of patience, forbearance, forgiveness and even of common-sense and enlightened self-interest. Men, who in private life behave as reasonable and moral beings, become transformed as soon as they are acting

[45]

as representatives of a National Person into the likeness of their stupid, hysterical and insanely touchy tribal divinity. This being so, there is little to be hoped for at the present time from general international conferences. No scheme of co-ordinated international planning can be carried through, unless all nations are prepared to sacrifice some of their sovereign rights. But it is in the highest degree improbable that all or even a majority of nations will consent to this sacrifice.

In these circumstances the best and most obvious road between the horns of our dilemma must be abandoned in favour of roads more devious and intrinsically less desirable. National planning results, as we have seen, in disorder in the field of international exchanges and political friction. This state of things can be remedied, at least partially, in one or both of two ways. In the first place, schemes of partial international co-ordination can be arranged between such governments as can agree upon them. This has already been done in the case of the Sterling Bloc, which is composed of countries whose rulers have decided that it is worth while to co-ordinate their separate national plans so that they shall not interfere with one another. There is a possibility that, in due course, other governments might find it to their interest to join such a confederation. On this point, however, it is unwise to be too optimistic. Time may demonstrate the advantages of international co-operation; but meanwhile time is also fortifying the vested interests which have been created under the various national plans. To participate in a scheme of international co-operation may be to the general advantage of a nation; but it is certainly not to the advantage of each one of the particular interests within the nation. If those particular interests are politically powerful, the general advantage of the nation as a whole will be sacrificed to their private advantages.

The second way of reducing international economic disorder and political friction is more drastic. It consists in making nations as far as possible economically independent of one another. In this way the number of contacts between nations would be minimized. But since, in the present state of nationalistic sentiment, international contacts result only too frequently in international friction and the risk of war, this reduction in the number of international contacts would probably mean a lessening of the probability of war.

To the orthodox Free Trader such a suggestion must seem grotesque and most criminal. "The facts of geography and geology are unescapable. Nations are differently endowed. Each is naturally fitted to perform a particular task; therefore it is right that there should be division of labour among them. Countries should exchange the commodities they produce most easily against the commodities which they cannot produce or can produce only with difficulty, but which can be easily produced elsewhere." So runs the Free Trader's argument; and an eminently sensible argument it is—or, perhaps it would be truer to say, it was. For those who now make use of it fail to take account of two things: namely, the recent exacerbation of nationalistic feeling and the progress of technology. For the sake of prestige and out of fear of what might happen during war-time, most governments now desire, whatever the cost and however great the natural handicaps, to produce within their own territory as many as possible of the commodities produced more easily elsewhere. Nor is this all: the progress of technology has made it possible for governments to fulfil such wishes, at any rate to a considerable extent, in practice. To the orthodox Free Trader the ideal of national self-sufficiency is absurd. But it can already be realized in part and will be more completely realizable with every advance in technology. A single national government may be able to prevent technological discoveries from being developed in its territories. But it cannot prevent them from being developed elsewhere; and when they have been developed, such advantages accrue that even the most conservative are forced to adopt the new technique. There can thus be no doubt that, sooner or later, the devices which already make it possible for poorly endowed countries to achieve a measure of self-sufficiency will come into general use. This being so, it is as well to make a virtue of necessity and exploit the discoveries of technology systematically and, so far as possible, for the benefit of all. At present these technological discoveries are being used by the dictators solely for war purposes. But there is no reason why the idea of national self-sufficiency should be associated with ideas of war. Science makes it inevitable that all countries shall soon attain to a considerable degree of self-sufficiency. This inevitable development should be so directed as to serve the cause of peace. And, in effect, it can easily be made to serve the cause of peace. The influence of nationalistic idolatry is now so strong that every contact

[48]

between nations threatens to produce discord. Accordingly, the less we have to do with one another, the more likely are we to keep the peace. Thanks to certain technological discoveries, it is unnecessary henceforward that we should have much to do with one another. The more rapidly and the more systematically we make use of these discoveries, the better for all concerned.

Let us consider by way of example the problem of food supply. Many governments, including the English, German, Italian and Japanese, excuse their preparation for war, their possession of colonies or their desire, if they do not possess colonies, for new conquests, on the ground that their territories are insufficient to supply the inhabitants with food. At the present time this "natural" food shortage is intensified by an artificial shortage, due to faulty monetary policies, which prevent certain countries from acquiring food stuffs from abroad. These faulty monetary policies are the result of militarism. The governments of the countries concerned choose to spend all the available national resources for the purchase of armaments—on guns rather than butter. Food cannot be bought because the country is preparing to go to war; the country must go to war because food cannot be bought. As usual, it is a vicious circle.

Faulty monetary policy may prevent certain nations from buying food from abroad. But even if this policy were altered, it would still remain true that food must be obtained from foreign sources. In relation to existing home supplies, such countries as Great Britain, Germany and Japan are over-populated. Hence, according to the rulers of these countries, the need for new aggression or, where aggression was practised in the past, for the maintenance of long-established empires. To what extent is over-population a valid excuse for militarism and imperialism? According to experts trained in the techniques of modern agro-biology, imperialism has now lost one of its principal justifications. Readers are referred to Dr. Willcox's book, *Nations Can Live at Home,* for a systematic exposition of the agro-biologist's case. According to Dr. Willcox, any country which chooses to apply the most advanced methods to the production of food plants, including grasses for live-stock, can support a population far in excess of the densest population existing anywhere on the earth's surface at the present time. The methods outlined by Dr. Willcox have already been used commercially. The novel system of "dirtless farming" devised by Professor Gericke of California is still in the experimental stage; but if it turns out to be satisfactory, it promises a larger supply of food, produced with less labour and on a smaller area, than any other method can offer. It seems probable, indeed, that this "dirtless farming" will produce an agricultural revolution compared to which the industrial revolution of the eighteenth and nineteenth centuries will seem the most trifling of social disturbances.* Profitable technological inventions cannot be suppressed. If Professor Gericke's discovery turns out to be commercially useful, it will certainly be used. Solely in the interests of the farming community, governments will be forced to control the

* In the report of the commission appointed by President Roosevelt to consider probable future trends, "dirtless farming" was listed among the thirteen inventions likely to cause important social changes in the near future. The report was published in July 1937.

commercial exploitation of this revolutionary discovery. In the process of controlling it for the sake of the farm, ers, they can also control it in the interests of world peace. Even if "dirtless farming" should not turn out to be a commercial proposition, nations, in Dr. Willcox's phrase, can still "live at home," and live (if the birth-rate does not sharply rise) in a hitherto unprecedented plenty. It is profoundly significant that no government has hitherto made any serious effort to apply modern agro-biological methods on a large scale for the purpose of raising the standard of material well-being among its subjects and of rendering imperialism and foreign conquest superfluous. This fact alone would be a sufficient demonstration of the truth that the causes of war are not solely economic, but psychological. People prepare for war, among other reasons, because war is in the great tradition; because war is exciting and gives them certain personal or vicarious satisfactions; because their education has left them militaristically minded; because they live in a society where success, however achieved, is worshipped and where competition seems more "natural" (because, under the present dispensation, it is more habitual) than co-operation. Hence the general reluctance to embark on constructive policies, directed towards the removal at least of the economic causes of war. Hence, too, the extraordinary energy which rulers and even the ruled put into such destructive and war-provoking policies as re-armament, the centralization of executive power and the regimentation of the masses.

I have spoken hitherto, of the international consequences of national planning and of the measures which
planners should take in order to minimize such consequences. In the ensuing paragraphs I shall deal with
planning in its domestic aspects. Others have written,
at great length and in minute detail, about the strictly
technical problems of planning, and for a discussion of
these problems I must refer the readers to the already
enormous literature of the subject.* In this place I
propose to discuss planning in relation to our ideal
postulates and to set forth the conditions which must be
fulfiled if the plans are to be successful in contributing
towards the realization of those ideals.

In the section on Social Reform and Violence I made
it clear that most human beings are conservative, that
even desirable changes beget opposition, and that no
plan which has to be imposed by great and prolonged
violence is ever likely to achieve the desirable results
expected of it. From this it follows, first, that only strictly
necessary reforms should be undertaken; second, that no
change to which there is likely to be wide-spread and
violent opposition should be imposed, however intrinsically desirable it may be, except gradually and by in-
stalments; and, thirdly, that desirable changes should
be made, wherever possible, by the application to wider
fields of methods with which people are already familiar and of which they approve.

Let us apply these general principles to particular

* "Planned Society," by thirty-five authors (New York, 1937), contains
authoritative summaries of almost all aspects of planning, together with
full bibliographies.

examples of social planning, and first of all to the great arch-plan of all reformers: the plan for transforming a capitalist society, in which the profit motive predominates, into a socialist society, in which the first consideration is the common good.

Our first principle is that only strictly necessary changes shall be carried out. If we wish to transform an advanced capitalist society, what are the changes that we cannot afford not to make? The answer is clear: the necessary, the indispensable changes are changes in the management of large-scale production. At present the management of large-scale production is in the hands of irresponsible individuals seeking profits. Moreover, each large unit is independent of all the rest; there is a complete absence of co-ordination between them. It is the unco-ordinated activity of large-scale production that leads to those periodical crises and depressions which inflict such untold hardship upon the working masses of the people in industrialized countries. Small-scale production carried on by individuals who own the instruments with which they personally work is not subject to periodical slumps. Furthermore, the ownership of the means of small-scale, personal production has none of the disastrous political, economic and psychological consequences of large-scale production—loss of independence, enslavement to an employer, insecurity of the tenure of employment. The advantages of socialism can be obtained by making changes in the management of large-scale units of production. Small units of production need not be touched. In this way, many of the advantages of individualism can be preserved and at the same time opposition to indispensable reforms will be minimized.

Our second principle is that no reform, however intrinsically desirable, should be undertaken if it is likely to result in violent opposition. For example, let us assume (though it may not in fact be true) that collectivized agriculture is more productive than individualized agriculture and that the collectivized farm worker is, socially speaking, a better individual than the small farmer who owns his own land. This granted, it follows that the collectivization of agriculture is an intrinsically desirable policy. But though intrinsically desirable it is not a policy that should be carried out, except perhaps by slow degrees. Carried out at one stroke, it would inevitably arouse violent opposition, which would have to be crushed by yet greater violence. In Russia the rapid collectivization of agriculture could not be effected except by the liquidation, through imprisonment, execution and wholesale starvation, of a very large number of peasant proprietors. It is probable that a part, at least, of what is now (1937) called the Trotskyite opposition is composed of individuals who bear the government a grudge for this and other pieces of terrorism. To put down opposition, the government has had to resort to further violence, has had to make itself (to use Professor Lasky's euphemistic metallurgical metaphor) even more of an "iron dictatorship" than it was before. This further violence and this, shall we call it, high-speed steel dictatorship can only produce the ordinary results of brutality and tyranny—servitude, militarism, passive obedience, irresponsibility. Among the highly industrialized peoples of the West the collectivization of agriculture would have even more serious results than in Russia. Instead of being in an overwhelming majority, the peasants and farmers of Western Europe and America are less numerous than the town dwellers. Being less numerous, they are more precious. To liquidate, even to antagonize, any large number of this indispensable minority would be fatal to the people of the towns. A few millions of peasants could be starved in Russia and still, because there were so many millions of other peasants, the urban population could be fed. In countries like France or Germany, England or the United States, a policy of starving even quite a few peasants and farmers would inevitably result in the starving of huge numbers of urban workers.

The last of the three general principles of action enunciated above is to the effect that desirable changes should be made, wherever possible, by the application to wider fields of methods with which people are already familiar and of which they approve. A few concrete examples of the way in which existing institutions might be developed so as to bring about desirable changes in capitalistic societies are given below. The principle of the limitation of profit and of supervision by the state in the public interest has already been admitted and applied in such public utility corporations as the Port of London Authority, the Port of New York Authority, the London Passenger Transport Board, the Electricity

Board, the B.B.C.* There should be no insuperable difficulty in extending the application of this already accepted principle to wider fields. Similarly there should be no great difficulty in extending the application of the popularly approved principles of consumer co-operation and producer co-operation. Again, consider the existing forms of taxation. In almost all countries the rich have accepted the principle of income tax and death duties. By any government which so desires, such taxation can be used for the purpose of reducing economic inequalities between individuals and classes, for imposing a maximum wage and for transferring control over large-scale production and finance from private hands to the state. One last example: the investment trust is a well known and widely patronized financial convenience. Under the present dispensation the investment trust is a private, profit-making concern. There would, however, be no great technical or political obstacle in the way of transforming it into a publicly controlled corporation, having as its function the rational direction of the flow of investment.

I have spoken of intrinsically desirable reforms; but the phrase is crude and needs qualifying. In practice, no reform can be separated from its administrative, governmental, educational and psychological contexts. The tree is known by its fruits, and the fruits of any given reform depend for their quantity and quality at least as much on the contexts of the reform as upon the reform itself.

* In some cases these corporations have had to take responsibility for over-capitalized concerns. In others the minimum interest rate was fixed too high. These mistakes do not invalidate the principle involved.

For example, collective ownership of the means of production does not have as its necessary and unconditional result the liberation of those who have hitherto been bondsmen. Collective ownership of the means of production is perfectly compatible, as we see in contemporary Russia, with authoritarian management of factories and farms, with militarized education and conscription, with the rule of a dictator, supported by an oligarchy of party men and making use of a privileged bureaucracy, a censored press and a huge force of secret police. Collective ownership of the means of production certainly delivers the workers from their servitude to many petty dictators—landlords, money lenders, factory owners and the like. But if the contexts of this intrinsically desirable reform are intrinsically undesirable, then the result will be, not responsible freedom for the workers, but another form of passive and irresponsible bondage. Delivered from servitude to many small dictators, they will find themselves under the control of the agents of a single centralized dictatorship, more effective than the old, because it wields the material powers and is backed by the almost divine prestige of the national state.

The contexts of reform are more desirable in the democratic than in the totalitarian states; therefore the results of reform are likely to be better in the democratic states. Unhappily, contemporary circumstances are such that, unless the process is intelligently and actively resisted by men of good will, it is all but inevitable that these desirable contexts shall rapidly deteriorate. The reasons for this are simple. First of all, even the democratic peoples are imperialists and desire to beat the

Fascist states at their own game of war. In order to prepare effectively for modern war, political power will have to be more highly centralized, self-governing institutions progressively abolished, opinion more strictly controlled and education militarized. In the second place, the democratic countries are still suffering to some extent from the economic depression which started in 1929. The various governments concerned have resorted to a measure of economic planning in order to mitigate the hardships suffered by their peoples. Economic planning has given these governments an opportunity for strengthening their position. In England, for example, the central executive, the bureaucracy and the police are probably more powerful today than they have ever been. But the more powerful these forces become the less are they able to tolerate democratic liberty—even the small amount of it which exists among the so-called democratic peoples. Another point: economic planning inevitably leads to more economic planning, for the simple reason that the situation is so complex that planners cannot fail to make mistakes. Mistakes have to be remedied by the improvization and rapid enforcement of new plans. It is probable that these new plans will also contain mistakes, which must in turn be remedied by yet other plans. And so on. Now, where planning has come to be associated with an increase in the power of the executive (and unfortunately this has been the case in all the democratic countries), every fresh access of planning activities, necessitated by mistakes in earlier plans, takes the country yet another step towards dictatorship. At the same time, as we have seen, comprehensive national planning leads to international chaos and consequent discord. In other words national planning increases the risk of war; but war cannot be waged, or even prepared for, except by a highly centralized government. It will thus be seen that both directly and indirectly economic planning leads to a deterioration of the contexts in which desirable reform can be carried out.

In the chapters that follow I shall concentrate almost exclusively on the desirable contexts of reform. My reasons for this are simple. "Advanced thinkers" have talked and written at endless length about the desirable reforms, especially economic reforms. All of us have heard of the public ownership of the means of production; production for use and not for profit; public control of finance and investment, and all the rest. All of us, I repeat, have heard of these ideas and most of us are agreed that they ought to be transferred from the realm of theory to that of fact. But how few of us ever pay any attention to the administrative, educational and psychological contexts in which the necessary reforms are to be carried out! How few of us ever stop to consider the means whereby they shall be enforced! And yet our personal experience and the study of history make it abundantly clear that the means whereby we try to achieve something are at least as important as the end we wish to attain. Indeed, they are even more important. For the means employed inevitably determine the nature of the result achieved; whereas, however good the end aimed at may be, its goodness is powerless to counteract the effects of the bad means we use to reach it. Similarly, a reform may be in the highest degree desirable; but if the contexts in which that reform is enacted are undesirable, the results will inevitably be disappointing. These are simple and obvious truths. Nevertheless they are almost universally neglected. To illustrate these truths and to show how we might profitably act upon them will be my principal task in the ensuing pages.

A Note on Planning for the Future

Communities in which technological progress is being made are subject to continuous social change. Social changes caused by the advance of technology are often accompanied by much suffering and inconvenience. Can this be avoided?

A committee was recently appointed by the President of the United States to consider this question. Its report (referred to above) was made public in the summer of 1937 and is a very valuable document.

In the field of industry, the authors point out, technological progress never leads to any social changes which cannot be foreseen a good many years in advance. In most cases the first discovery of a new process is separated from its large-scale commercial application by at least a quarter of a century. (Often this period is considerably greater.) Any community which chooses to make use of the intelligence and imagination of its best scientific minds can foresee the probable social consequences of a given technological advance long years before they actually develop. Up to the present social changes due to technological progress have taken communities by surprise, not because they came suddenly, out of the blue, but because nobody in authority ever took the trouble to think out in advance what such changes were likely to be, or what were the best methods of preventing them from causing avoidable suffering. President Roosevelt's commission has pointed out what are the recent inventions most likely to cause important social changes in the immediate future, and has suggested a design for the administrative machinery required to minimize their ill effects. The problem, in this case, is purely a problem for technicians.

There is one field in which very small technological advances may produce disproportionately great effects upon society; I refer to the field of armament manufacture. A slight change, for example, in the design of internal combustion engines—so slight as to have no appreciable effect on the numbers of men employed in their construction—may bring (and indeed has actually brought) millions of innocent men, women and children a long step nearer to death by fire, poison and explosion. In this case, of course, the problem is not one for technicians; it is a problem that can be solved only when sufficient numbers of men of good will are prepared to make use of the methods by which, and by which alone, it can be solved. For the nature of these methods I must refer the reader to the chapters on War and Individual Work for Reform.

Rises and falls in the birth-rate are likely to produce social changes even more far-reaching than those produced by technological advances. It is about as certain as any future contingency can be that, half a century

from now, the population of the industrialized countries of Western Europe will have declined, both absolutely and in relation to that of the countries of Eastern
Europe. Thus, when Great Britain has only thirty-five
million inhabitants, of whom less than a tenth will be
under fifteen and more than a sixth over sixty, Russia
will have about three hundred millions. Will a country
so (relatively speaking) sparsely inhabited as the Britain
of 1990 be able to keep up its position as a "First-class,
Imperial Power"? In the past Sweden, Portugal and
Holland attempted to keep up the status of a Great
Power on the basis of a population that was absolutely
and relatively small. All of them failed in the attempt.
If only for demographical reasons, Britain should take
all possible steps to avoid a struggle for imperial power
which, if not immediately fatal, will almost certainly
prove fatal a couple of generations hence. In a militaristic world, relatively under-populated countries cannot hope (unless protected by more powerful neighbours) to retain exclusive possession of large empires.
British imperialism was all very well when Britain was,
relatively, highly populous and, thanks to being an island, invulnerable. For an exceedingly vulnerable and
relatively under-populated Britain, imperialism is the
policy of a lunatic. (See Griffin's "An Alternative to
Re-armament." London, 1936.)

Here again the problem raised by a declining birth
rate is not a problem for technicians. It is part of the
general problem of international politics and war, and
can be solved only when sufficient numbers of people
genuinely desire to solve it and are ready to take the
appropriate steps for doing so.

VI

Nature of the Modern State

FOR our present purposes, the significant facts about the governments of contemporary nations are these. There are a few rulers and many ruled. The rulers are generally actuated by love of power; occasionally by a sense of duty to society; more often and bewilderingly, by both at once. Their principal attachment is to pride, with which are often associated cruelty and avarice. The ruled, for the most part, quietly accept their subordinate position and even actual hardship and injustice. In certain circumstances it happens that they cease to accept and there is a revolt. But revolt is the exception; the general rule is obedience.

The patience of common humanity is the most important, and almost the most surprising, fact in history. Most men and women are prepared to tolerate the intolerable. The reasons for this extraordinary state of things are many and various. There is ignorance, first of all. Those who know of no state of affairs other than the intolerable are unaware that their lot might be improved. Then there is fear. Men know that their life is intolerable, but are afraid of the consequences of revolt. The existence of a sense of kinship and social solidarity constitutes another reason why people tolerate the intolerable. Men and women feel attached to the society of which they are members—feel attached even when the rulers of that society treat them badly. It is worthy of remark that, in a crisis the workers (who are the ruled) have always fought for their respective nations (i.e. for their rulers) and against other workers.

Mere habit and the force of inertia are also extremely powerful. To get out of a rut, even an uncomfortable rut, requires more effort than most people are prepared to make. In his *Studies in History and Jurisprudence*, Bryce suggests that the main reason for obedience to law is simply indolence. "It is for this reason," he says, "that a strenuous and unwearying will sometimes becomes so tremendous a power . . . almost a hypnotic force." Because of indolence, the disinherited are hardly less conservative than the possessors; they cling to their familiar miseries almost as tenaciously as the others cling to their privileges. The Buddhist and, later, the Christian moralists numbered sloth among the deadly sins. If we accept the principle that the tree is to be judged by its fruits, we must admit that they were right. Among the many poisonous fruits of sloth are dictatorship on the one hand and passive, irresponsible obedience on the other. Reformers should aim at delivering men from the temptations of sloth no less than from the temptations of ambition, avarice and the lust for power and position. Conversely, no reform which leaves the masses of the people wallowing in the slothful irresponsibility of passive obedience to authority can be counted as a genuine change for the better.*

Reinforcing the effect of indolence, kindliness and fear, rationalizing these emotions in intellectual terms, is philosophical belief. The ruled obey their rulers be-

* For the relation existing between energy and sexual continence, see Chapter XV.

cause, in addition to all the other reasons, they accept as true some metaphysical or theological system which teaches that the state ought to be obeyed and is intrinsically worthy of obedience. Rulers are seldom content with the brute facts of power and satisfied ambition; they aspire to rule *de jure* as well as *de facto*. The rights of violence and cunning are not enough for them. To strengthen their position in relation to the ruled and at the same time to satisfy their own uneasy cravings for ethical justification, they try to show that they rule by right divine. Most theories of the state are merely intellectual devices invented by philosophers for the purpose of proving that the people who actually wield power are precisely the people who ought to wield it. Some few theories are fabricated by revolutionary thinkers. These last are concerned to prove that the people at the head of their favourite political party are precisely the people who ought to wield power—to wield it just as ruthlessly as the tyrants in office at the moment. To discuss such theories is mainly a waste of time; for they are simply beside the point, irrelevant to the significant facts. If we wish to think correctly about the state, we must do so as psychologists, not as special pleaders, arguing a case for tyrants or would-be tyrants. And if we want to make a reasonable assessment of the value of any given state, we must judge it in terms of the highest morality we know—in other words, we must judge it in the light of the ideal postulates formulated by the prophets and the founders of religions. Hegel, it is true, regarded such judgments as extremely "shallow." But if profundity leads to Prussianism, as it did in Hegel's

[65]

case, then give me shallowness. Let those who will, be *tief*; I prefer superficiality and the common decencies. We shall understand nothing of the problems of gov ernment, unless we come down to psychological facts and ethical first principles.

To a greater or less degree, then, all the civilized communities of the modern world are made up of a small class of rulers, corrupted by too much power, and of a large class of subjects, corrupted by too much passive and irresponsible obedience. Participation in a social order of this kind makes it extremely difficult for individuals to achieve that non-attachment in the midst of activity, which is the distinguishing mark of the ideally excellent human being; and where there is not at least a considerable degree of non-attachment in activity, the ideal society of the prophets cannot be realized. A desirable social order is one that delivers us from avoidable evils. A bad social order is one that leads us into temptation which, if matters were more sensibly arranged, would never arise. Our present business is to discover what large-scale social changes are best calculated to deliver us from the evils of too much power and of too much passive and irresponsible obedience. It has been shown in the preceding chapter that the economic reforms, so dear to "advanced thinkers," are not in themselves sufficient to produce desirable changes in the character of society and of the individuals composing it. Unless carried out by the right sort of means and in the right sort of governmental, administrative and educational contexts, such reforms are either fruitless or actually fruitful of evil. In order to create the

proper contexts for economic reform we must change
our machinery of government, our methods of public
administration and industrial organization, our system
of education and our metaphysical and ethical beliefs.
With education and beliefs I shall deal in a later section
of this book. Our concern here is with government and
the administration of public and industrial affairs. In
reality, of course, these various topics are inseparable
parts of a single whole. Existing methods of government
and existing systems of industrial organization are not
likely to be changed except by people who have been
educated to wish to change them. Conversely, it is unlikely that governments composed as they are today
will change the existing system of education in such a
way that there will be a demand for a complete overhaul
of governmental methods. It is the usual vicious circle
from which, as always, there is only one way of escape—
through acts of free will on the part of morally enlightened, intelligent, well-informed and determined individuals, acting in concert. Of the necessity for the
voluntary association of such individuals and of the
enormously important part that they can play in the
changing of society I shall speak later. For the moment,
let us consider the machinery of government and industrial administration.

VII

Centralization and Decentralization

WE HAVE found agreement in regard to the ideal society and the ideal human being. Among the political reformers of the last century we even find a measure of agreement about the best means of organizing the state so as to achieve the ends which all desire. Philosophic Radicals, Fourierists, Proudhonian Mutualists, Anarchists, Syndicalists, Tolstoyans—all agree that authoritarian rule and an excessive concentration of power are among the main obstacles in the way of social and individual progress. Even the Communists express at least a theoretical dislike of the centralized, authoritarian state. Marx described the state as a "parasite on society" and looked forward to the time, after the revolution, when it would automatically "wither away." Meanwhile, however, there was to be the dictatorship of the proletariat and an enormous increase in the powers of the central executive. The present Russian state is a highly centralized oligarchy. Its subjects, children and women as well as men, are regimented by means of military conscription, and an efficient secret police system takes care of people when they are not actually serving in the army. There is a censorship of the press and the educational system, liberalized by Lenin, has now reverted to the authoritarian, militaristic type, familiar in Tsarist Russia, in the Italy of Mussolini, in Germany before the war and again under Hitler. We are asked by the sup-

[68]

porters of Stalin's government to believe that the best and shortest road to liberty is through military servitude; that the most suitable preparation for responsible self-government is a tyranny employing police espionage, delation, legalized terrorism and press censorship; that the proper education for future freemen and peace-lovers is that which was and is still being used by Prussian militarists.

Our earth is round, and it is therefore possible to travel from Paris to Rouen via Shanghai. Our history, on the contrary, would seem to be flat. Those who wish to reach a specific historical goal must advance directly towards it; no amount of walking in the opposite direction will bring them to their destination.

The goal of those who wish to change society for the better is freedom, justice and peaceful co-operation between non-attached, yet active and responsible individuals. Is there the smallest reason to suppose that such a goal can be reached through police espionage, military slavery, the centralization of power, the creation of an elaborate political hierarchy, the suppression of free discussion and the imposition of an authoritarian system of education? Obviously and emphatically, the answer is: No.

Marx believed that, after the revolution, the state would, in due course, automatically wither away. This is a point worth considering in some detail. In any given society, as Marx himself pointed out, the state exists, among other reasons, for the purpose of ensuring to the ruling class the continuance of its privileges. Thus, in a feudal community the state is the instrument by means of which the landed nobility keeps itself in power. Under capitalism, the state is the instrument by means of which the bourgeoisie retains its right to rule and to be rich. Similarly, under a hierarchical system of state socialism, the state is the instrument by means of which the ruling bureaucracy defends the position to which it has climbed. The more firmly you consolidate your hierarchy, the more tenaciously will its members cling to their privileges. A highly centralized dictatorial state may be smashed by war or overturned by a revolution from below; there is not the smallest reason to suppose that it will wither. Dictatorship of the proletariat is in actual fact dictatorship by a small privileged minority; and dictatorship by a small privileged minority does not lead to liberty, justice, peace and the co-operation of non-attached, but active and responsible individuals. It leads either to more dictatorship, or to war, or to revolution, or (more probably) to all three in fairly rapid succession.

No, the political road to a better society (and do not let us forget that, if we would reach the goal, we must advance along many other roads as well as the political) is the road of decentralization and responsible self-government. Dictatorial short cuts cannot conceivably take us to our destination. We must march directly towards the goal; if we turn our backs to it we shall merely increase the distance which separates us from the place to which we wish to go.

The political road to a better society is, I repeat, the road of decentralization and responsible self-government. But in present circumstances it is extremely improbable that any civilized nation will take that road. It is extremely improbable for a simple reason which I have stated before and which I make no excuse for repeating. No society which is preparing for war can afford to be anything but highly centralized. Unity of command is essential, not only after the outbreak of hostilities, but also (in the circumstances of contemporary life) before. A country which proposes to make use of modern war as an instrument of policy must possess a highly centralized, all-powerful executive. (Hence the absurdity of talking about the defence of democracy by force of arms. A democracy which makes or even effectively prepares for modern, scientific war must necessarily cease to be democratic. No country can be really well prepared for modern war unless it is governed by a tyrant, at the head of a highly trained and perfectly obedient bureaucracy.)

I have said that a country which proposes to make use of modern war as an instrument of policy must possess a highly centralized, all-powerful executive. But, conversely, a country which possesses a highly centralized, all-powerful executive is more likely to wage war than a country where power is decentralized and the population genuinely governs itself. There are several reasons for this. Dictatorships are rarely secure. Whenever a tyrant feels that his popularity is waning, he is tempted to exploit nationalistic passion in order to consolidate his own position. Pogroms and treason trials are the ordinary devices by means of which a dictator revives the flagging enthusiasm of his people. When these fail, he may be driven to war. Nor must we forget that the more absolute the ruler, the more completely does he tend to associate his own personal prestige with the prestige of the nation he rules. *"L'Etat c'est moi"* is an illusion to which kings, dictators and even such minor members of the ruling clique as bureaucrats and diplomats succumb with a fatal facility. For the victims of this illusion, a loss of national prestige is a blow to their private vanity, a national victory is a personal triumph. Extreme centralization of power creates opportunities for individuals to believe that the state is themselves. To make or to threaten war becomes, for the tyrant, a method of self-assertion. The state is made the instrument of an individual's manias of persecution and grandeur. Thus we see that extreme centralization of power is not only necessary if war is to be waged successfully; it is also a contributory cause of war.

In existing circumstances the ruling classes of every nation feel that they must prepare for war. This means that there will be a general tendency to increase the power of the central executive. This increase of power of the central executive tends to make war more likely. Hence there will be demands for yet more intensive centralization. And so on, *ad infinitum*—or, rather until the crash comes.

So long as civilized countries continue to prepare for war, it is enormously improbable that any of them will pursue a policy of decentralization and the extension of the principle of self-government. On the contrary, power will tend to become more narrowly concentrated than at present, not only in the totalitarian states, but also in the democratic countries, which will therefore tend to become less and less democratic. Indeed, the movement away from democratic forms of government and towards centralization of authority and military tyranny is already under way in the democratic countries. In England such symptoms as the Sedition Bill, the enrolment of an army of "air raid wardens," the secret but systematic drilling of government servants in the technique of "air raid precautions," are unmistakable. In France the executive has already taken to itself the power to conscribe everybody and everything in the event of war breaking out. In Belgium, Holland and the Scandinavian countries, as well as in the more powerful democracies, huge sums are being spent on re-armament. But re-armament is not a mere accumulation of ironmongery. There must be men trained to use the new weapons, a supply of docile labour for their manufacture. An increase in the amount of a country's armaments implies a corresponding increase in the degree of its militarization. The fire-eaters of the Left who, for the last two years, have been calling for a "firm stand" (i.e. military action) on the part of the democratic countries against fascist aggression have in effect been calling for an acceleration of the process by which the democratic countries are gradually, but systematically, being transformed into the likeness of those fascist states they so much detest.

Nothing succeeds like success—even success that is merely apparent. The prevalence of centralization in the contemporary world creates a popular belief that centralization is not what in fact it is—a great evil, imposed upon the world by the threat of war and avoidable only with difficulty and at the price of enormous effort and considerable sacrifices—but intrinsically sound policy. Because in fact political power is being more and more closely concentrated, people have come to be persuaded that the way to desirable change lies through the concentration of power. Centralization is the order of the day; the *zeitgeist* commands it; therefore, they argue, centralization must be right. They forget that the *zeitgeist* is just as likely to be a spirit of evil as a spirit of good and that the fact that something happens to exist is in no way a guarantee that it ought to exist.

Every dictatorship has its own private jargon. The vocabularies are different; but the purpose which they serve is in all cases the same—to legitimate the local despotism, to make a *de facto* government appear to be a government by divine right. Such jargons are instruments of tyranny as indispensable as police spies and a press censorship. They provide a set of terms in which the maddest policies can be rationalized and the most monstrous crimes abundantly justified. They serve as moulds for a whole people's thoughts and feelings and desires. By means of them the oppressed can be persuaded, not only to tolerate, but actually to worship their insane and criminal oppressors.

Significantly enough, one word is common to all the dictatorial vocabularies and is used for purposes of justification and rationalization by Fascists, Nazis and Communists alike. That word is "historical."

Thus, the dictatorship of the proletariat is an "historical necessity." The violence of Communists is justified because, unlike Fascist violence, it is being used to forward an ineluctable "historical" process.

In the same way, Fascism is said by its supporters to possess a quality of "historical" inevitableness. The Italians have a great "historical mission," which is to create an empire, in other words to gas and machine-gun people weaker than themselves.

No less "historically" necessary and right are the brutalities of men in brown shirts. As for the "historical" importance of the Aryan race, this is so prodigious that absolutely any wickedness, any folly is permitted to men with fair hair and blue eyes—even to *nachgedunkelte schrumpf-Germanen*, like Hitler himself and the swarthy little Goebbels.

The appeal to history is one which the dictators find particularly convenient; for the assumption which underlies it is that, in Hegelian language, the real is the rational—that what happens is ultimately the same as what ought to happen.

For example, it very often happens that might triumphs over right; therefore might is "historical" and deserves to conquer.

Again, absolute power is intoxicatingly delightful. In consequence, those who have seized absolute power are prepared, as a rule, to make use of any means, however disgraceful, in order to retain it. Spying, delation, torture, arbitrary imprisonment and execution—in every dictatorial country these are the ordinary instruments of domestic policy. They occur; they are therefore "historical." Being historical they are, in some *tief*, Hegelian way, reasonable and right.

[75]

That such a doctrine should be believed and taught by tyrants is not surprising. The odd, the profoundly depressing fact is that it should be accepted as true by millions who are not tyrants, nor even the subjects of tyrants. For ever increasing numbers of men and women, "historicalness" is coming to be accepted as one of the supreme values. This implicit identification of what ought to be with what is effectively vitiates all thinking about morals, about politics, about progress, about social reform, even about art. In those who make the identification it induces a kind of busy, Panglossian fatalism. Looking out upon the world, they observe that circumstances seem to be conspiring to drive men in a certain direction. This movement is "historical," therefore possesses value—exists and therefore ought to exist. They accept what is. Indeed, they do much more than accept; they applaud, they give testimonials. If the real is the rational and the right, then it follows that a "historical" action must have the same results as an action dictated by reason and the loftiest idealism.

Let us return, for a concrete example, to this matter of the centralization of power. The particular circumstances of our time (nationalistic sentiment, economic imperialism, threats of war and so forth) conspire to create a tendency towards the concentration and centralization of authority. The consequence of this is a curtailment of individual liberties and a progressive regimentation of the masses, even in countries hitherto enjoying a democratic form of government. The rational idealist deplores this tendency towards tyranny and enslavement and is convinced that its results can only be bad. Not so the man who is *tief* enough to regard historicalness as a value. His ultimate aim is probably the same as that of the rational idealist. But, believing as he does that the real is the rational, he persuades himself that the road which circumstances conspire to impose upon him must necessarily lead him to the desired goal. He believes that tyranny will somehow result in democracy, enslavement in the liberation of the individual, concentration of political and economic power in self-government all round. He is ready, in a word, to tolerate or even actively engage in any wickedness or any imbecility, because he is convinced that there is some "historical" providence which will cause bad, inappropriate means to result in good ends.

The sooner we convince ourselves that "historicalness" is not a value and that what we allow circumstances to make us do has no necessary connexion with what we ought to do, the better it will be for ourselves and for the world we live in. At the present moment of time, the "historical" is almost unmitigatedly evil. To accept the "historical" and to work for it is to co-operate with the powers of darkness against the light.

VIII

Decentralization and Self-Government

THE Anarchists propose that the state should be abolished; and in so far as it serves as the instrument by means of which the ruling class preserves its privileges; in so far as it is a device for enabling paranoiacs to satisfy their lust for power and carry out their crazy dreams of glory, the state is obviously worthy of abolition. But in complex societies like our own the state has certain other and more useful functions to perform. It is clear, for example, that in any such society there must be some organization responsible for co-ordinating the activities of the various constituent groups; clear, too, that there must be a body to which is delegated the power of acting in the name of the society as a whole. If the word "state" is too unpleasantly associated with ideas of domestic oppression and foreign war, with irresponsible domination and no less irresponsible submission, then by all means let us call the necessary social machinery by some other name. For the present there is no general agreement as to what that name should be; I shall therefore go on using the bad old word, until some better one is invented.

From what has been said in the preceding chapters it is clear that no economic reform, however intrinsically desirable, can lead to desirable changes in individuals and the society they constitute, unless it is carried through in a desirable context and by desirable meth-

[78]

ods. So far as the state is concerned, the desirable context for reform is decentralization and self-government all round. The desirable methods for enacting reform are the methods of non-violence.

Passing from the general to the particular and the concrete, the rational idealist finds himself confronted by the following questions. First, by what means can the principle of self-government be applied to the daily lives of men and women? Second, to what extent is the self-government of the component parts of a society compatible with its efficiency as a whole? And, thirdly, if a central organization is needed to co-ordinate the activities of the self-governing parts, what is to prevent this organization from becoming a ruling oligarchy of the kind with which we are only too painfully familiar?

The technique for self-government all round, self-government for ordinary people in their ordinary avocations, is a matter which we cannot profitably discuss unless we have a clear idea of what may be called the natural history and psychology of groups. Quantitatively, a group differs from a crowd in size; qualitatively, in the kind and intensity of the mental life of the constituent individuals. A crowd is a lot of people; a group is a few. A crowd has a mental life inferior in intellectual quality and emotionally less under voluntary control than the mental life of each of its members in isolation. The mental life of a group is not inferior, either intellectually or emotionally, to the mental life of the individuals composing it and may, in favourable circumstances, actually be superior.

The significant psychological facts about the crowd

are as follows. The tone of crowd emotion is essentially orgiastic and dionysiac. In virtue of his membership of the crowd, the individual is released from the limitations of his personality, made 'free of the sub-personal, sub-human world of unrestrained feeling and uncriticized belief. To be a member of a crowd is an experience closely akin to alcoholic intoxication. Most human beings feel a craving to escape from the cramping limitations of their ego, to take periodical holidays from their all too familiar, all too squalid little selves. As they do not know how to travel upwards from personality into a region of super-personality and as they are unwilling, even if they do know, to fulfil the ethical, psychological and physiological conditions of self-transcendence, they turn naturally to the descending road, the road that leads down from personality to the darkness of sub-human emotionalism and panic animality. Hence the persistent craving for narcotics and stimulants, hence the never failing attraction of the crowd. The success of the dictators is due in large measure to their extremely skilful exploitation of the universal human need for escape from the limitations of personality. Perceiving that people wished to take holidays from themselves in sub-human emotionality, they have systematically provided their subjects with the occasions for doing so. The Communists denounce religion as the opium of the people; but all they have done is to replace this old drug by a new one of similar composition. For the crowd round the relic of the saint they have substituted the crowd at the political meeting; for religious processions, military reviews and May Day parades. It is the same with Fascist dictators. In all the totalitarian states the masses are persuaded, and, even compelled, to take periodical holidays from themselves in the sub-human world of crowd emotion. It is significant that while they encourage and actually command the descent into sub-humanity, the dictators do all they can to prevent men from taking the upward road from personal limitation, the road that leads towards non-attachment to the "things of this world" and attachment to that which is super-personal. The higher manifestations of religion are far more suspect to the tyrants than the lower—and with reason. For the man who escapes from egotism into super-personality has transcended his old idolatrous loyalty, not only to himself, but also to the local divinities—nation, party, class, deified boss. Self-transcendence, escape from the prison of the ego into union with what is above personality, is generally accomplished in solitude. That is why the tyrants like to herd their subjects into those vast crowds, in which the individual is reduced to a state of intoxicated sub-humanity.

It is time now to consider the group. The first question we must ask ourselves is this: when does a group become a crowd? This is not a problem in verbal definition; it is a matter of observation and experience. It is found empirically that group activities and characteristic group feeling become increasingly difficult when more than about twenty or less than about five individuals are involved. Groups which come together for the purpose of carrying out a specific job of manual work can afford to be larger than groups which meet for the purpose of pooling information and elaborating a common policy, or which meet for religious exercises, or for mutual comfort, or merely for the sake of convivially "getting together." Twenty or even as many as thirty people can work together and still remain a group. But these numbers would be much too high in a group that had assembled for the other purposes I have mentioned. It is significant that Jesus had only twelve apostles; that the Benedictines were divided into groups of ten under a dean (Latin *decanus* from Greek δέκα ten); that ten is the number of individuals constituting a Communist cell. Committees of more than a dozen members are found to be unmanageably large. Eight is the perfect number for a dinner party. The most successful Quaker meetings are generally meetings at which few people are present. Educationists agree that the most satisfactory size for a class is between eight and fifteen. In armies, the smallest unit is about ten. The witches' "coven" was a group of thirteen. And so on. All evidence points clearly to the fact that there is an optimum size for groups and that this optimum is round about ten for groups meeting for social, religious or intellectual purposes and from ten to thirty for groups engaged in manual work. This being so, it is clear that the units of self-government should be groups of the optimum size. If they are smaller than the optimum, they will fail to develop that emotional field which gives to group activity its characteristic quality, while the available quantity of pooled information and experience will be inadequate. If they are larger than the optimum, they will tend to split into sub-groups of the optimum size or, if the constituent individuals remain together in a crowd there will be a danger of their relapsing into the crowd's sub-human stupidity and emotionality.

The technique of industrial self-government has been discussed with a wealth of concrete examples in a remarkable book by the French economist Hyacinthe Dubreuil, entitled, *A Chacun sa Chance*. Among the writers on industrial organization Dubreuil occupies a place apart; for he is almost the only one of them who has himself had experience of factory conditions as a workman. Accordingly, what he writes on the subject of industrial organization carries an authority denied to the utterances of those who rely on second-hand information as a basis for their theories. Dubreuil points out that even the largest industries can be organized so as to consist of a series of self-governing, yet co-ordinated, groups of, at the outside, thirty members. Within the industry each one of such groups can act as a kind of sub-contractor, undertaking to perform so much of such and such a kind of work for such and such a sum. The equitable division of this sum among the constituent members is left to the group itself, as is also the preservation of discipline, the election of representatives and leaders. The examples which Dubreuil quotes from the annals of industrial history and from his own experience as a workman tend to show that this form of organization is appreciated by the workers, to whom it gives a measure of independence even within the largest manufacturing concern, and that in most cases it results in increased efficiency of working. It possesses, as he points out, the further merit of being a form of organization that edu-

cates those who belong to it in the practice of co-operation and mutual responsibility.

Under the present dispensation, the great majority
of factories are little despotisms, benevolent in some
cases, malevolent in others. Even where benevolence
prevails, passive obedience is demanded of the workers,
who are ruled by overseers, not of their own election,
but appointed from above. In theory, they may be the
subjects of a democratic state; but in practice they
spend the whole of their working lives as the subjects
of a petty tyrant. Dubreuil's scheme, if it were generally
acted upon, would introduce genuine democracy into
the factory. And if some such scheme is not acted upon,
it is of small moment to the individual whether the
industry in which he is working is owned by the state,
by a co-operative society, by a joint stock company or
by a private individual. Passive obedience to officers
appointed from above is always passive obedience, whoever the general in ultimate control may be. Conversely,
even if the ultimate control is in the wrong hands, the
man who voluntarily accepts rules in the making of
which he has had a part, who obeys leaders he himself
has chosen, who has helped to decide how much and in
what conditions he himself and his companions shall be
paid, is to that extent the free and responsible subject of
a genuinely democratic government, and enjoys those
psychological advantages which only such a form of
government can give.

Of modern wage-slaves, Lenin writes that they "remain to such an extent crushed by want and poverty
that they 'can't be bothered with democracy,' have 'no

time for politics,' and in the ordinary peaceful course of events, the majority of the population is debarred from participating in public political life." This statement is only partially true. Not all those who can't be bothered with democracy are debarred from political life by want and poverty. Plenty of well-paid workmen and, for that matter, plenty of the wealthiest beneficiaries of the capitalistic system, find that they can't be bothered with politics. The reason is not economic, but psychological; has its source, not in environment, but in heredity. People belong to different psycho-physiological types and are endowed with different degrees of general intelligence. The will and ability to take an effective interest in large-scale politics do not belong to all, or even a majority of, men and women. Preoccupation with general ideas, with things and people distant in space, with contingent events remote in future time, is something which it is given to only a few to feel. "What's Hecuba to him or he to Hecuba?" The answer in most cases is: Nothing whatsoever. An improvement in the standard of living might perceptibly increase the number of those for whom Hecuba meant something. But even if all were rich, there would still be many congenitally incapable of being bothered with anything so far removed from the warm, tangible facts of everyday experience. As things are at present, millions of men and women come into the world disfranchised by nature. They have the privilege of voting on long-range, large-scale political issues; but they are congenitally incapable of taking an intelligent interest in any but short-range, small-scale problems. Too often the framers of democratic constitutions have acted as though man were made for democracy, not democracy for man. The vote has been a kind of bed of Procrustes upon which, however long their views, however short their ability, all human beings were expected to stretch themselves. Not unnaturally, the results of this kind of democracy have proved disappointing. Nevertheless, it remains true that democratic freedom is good for those who enjoy it and that practice in self-government is an almost indispensable element in the curriculum of man's moral and psychological education. Human beings belong to different types; it is therefore necessary to create different types of democratic and self-governing institutions, suitable for the various kinds of men and women. Thus, people with short-range, small-scale interests can find scope for their kind of political abilities in self-governing groups within an industry, within a consumer or producer co-operative, within the administrative machinery of the parish, borough or county. By means of comparatively small changes in the existing systems of local and professional organization it would be possible to make almost every individual a member of some self-governing group. In this way the curse of merely passive obedience could be got rid of, the vice of political indolence cured and the advantages of responsible and active freedom brought to all. In this context it is worth remarking on a very significant change which has recently taken place in our social habits. Materially, this change may be summed up as the decline of the community; psychologically, as the decline of the community sense. The reasons for this double change are

[86]

many and of various kinds. Here are a few of the more important.

Birth control has reduced the size of the average family and, for various reasons which will be apparent later, the old habits of patriarchal living have practically disappeared. It is very rare nowadays to find parents, married children, and grandchildren living together in the same house or in close association. Large families and patriarchal groups were communities in which children and adults had to learn (often by very painful means) the art of co-operation and the need to accept responsibility for others. These admittedly rather crude schools of community sense have now disappeared.

New methods of transport have profoundly modified the life in the village and small town. Up to only a generation ago most villages were to a great extent self-sufficing communities. Every trade was represented by its local technician; the local produce was consumed or exchanged in the neighbourhood; the inhabitants worked on the spot. If they desired instruction or entertainment or religion, they had to mobilize the local talent and produce it themselves. Today all this is changed. Thanks to improved transport, the village is now closely bound up with the rest of the economic world. Supplies and technical services are obtained from a distance. Large numbers of the inhabitants go out to work in factories and offices in far-off cities. Music and the drama are provided, not by local talent, but over the ether and in the picture theatre. Once all the members of the community were always on the spot; now, thanks to cars, motor cycles and buses the villagers are rarely in their village. Community fun, community worship, community efforts to secure culture have tended to decline for the simple reason that, in leisure hours, a large part of the community's membership is always somewhere else. Nor is this all. The older inhabitants of Middletown, as readers of the Lynds' classical study of American small-town life will remember, complained that the internal combustion engine had led to a decline of neighbourliness. Neighbours have Fords and Chevrolets, consequently are no longer there to be neighbourly; or if by chance they should be at home, they content themselves with calling up on the telephone. Technological progress has reduced the number of physical contacts, and thus impoverished the spiritual relations between the members of a community.

Centralized professionalism has not only affected local entertainment; it had also affected the manifestations of local charity and mutual aid. State-provided hospitals, state-provided medical and nursing services are certainly much more efficient than the ministrations of the neighbours. But this increased efficiency is purchased at the price of a certain tendency on the part of neighbours to disclaim liability for one another and throw their responsibilities entirely upon the central authority. Under a perfectly organized system of state socialism charity would be, not merely superfluous, but actually criminal. Good Samaritans would be prosecuted for daring to interfere in their bungling amateurish way with what was obviously a case for state-paid professionals.

DECENTRALIZATION AND SELF-GOVERNMENT

The last three generations have witnessed a vast increase in the size and number of large cities. Life is more exciting and more money can be earned in the cities than in villages and small towns. Hence the migration from country to city. In the van of this migrating host have marched the ambitious, the talented, the adventurous. For more than a century, there has been a tendency for the most gifted members of small rural communities to leave home and seek their fortune in the towns. Consequently what remains in the villages and country towns of the industrialized countries is in the nature of a residual population, dysgenically selected for its lack of spirit and intellectual gifts. Why is it so hard to induce peasants and small farmers to adopt new scientific methods? Among other reasons, because almost every exceptionally intelligent child born into a rural family for a century past has taken the earliest opportunity of deserting the land for the city. Community life in the country is thus impoverished; but (and this is the important point) the community life of the great urban centres is not correspondingly enriched. It is not enriched for the good reason that, in growing enormous, cities have also grown chaotic. A metropolitan "wen," as Cobbett was already calling the relatively tiny London of his day, is no longer an organic whole, no longer exists as a community, in whose life individuals can fruitfully participate. Men and women rub shoulders with other men and women; but the contact is external and mechanical. Each one of them can say, in the words of the Jolly Miller of the song, "I care for nobody, no, not I, and nobody cares

[89]

for me." Metropolitan life is atomistic. The city, as a
city, does nothing to correlate its human particles into
a pattern of responsible, communal living. What the
country loses on the swings, the city loses all over again
on the roundabouts.

In the light of this statement of the principal reasons
for the recent decline of the community and of the
community sense in individuals, we can suggest certain
remedies. Schools and colleges can be transformed into
organic communities and used to offset, during a short
period of the individual's career, the decay in family and
village life. (A very interesting experiment in this
direction is being made at Black Mountain College in
North Carolina.) To some extent, no doubt, the old,
"natural" life of villages and small towns, the life that
the economic, technological and religious circumstances
of the past conspired to impose upon them, can be
replaced by a consciously designed synthetic product—a
life of associations organized for local government, for
sport, for cultural activities and the like. Such associations already exist, and there should be no great difficulty in opening them to larger numbers and, at the
same time, in making their activities so interesting that
people will wish to join them instead of taking the line
of least resistance, as they do now, and living unconnected, atomistic lives, passively obeying during their
working hours and passively allowing themselves to be
entertained by machinery during their hours of leisure.
The existence of associations of this kind would serve
to make country life less dull and so do something to
arrest the flight towards the city. At the same time, the

decentralization of industry and its association with agriculture should make it possible for the countryman to earn as much as the city dweller. In spite of the ease with which electric power can now be distributed, the movement towards the decentralization of industry is not yet a very powerful one. Great centres of population, like London and Paris, possess an enormous power of attraction to industries. The greater the population, the greater the market; and the greater the market, the stronger the gravitational pull exercised upon the manufacturer. New industries establish themselves on the outskirts of large cities and make them become still larger. For the sake of slightly increased profits, due to lower distributing costs, the manufacturers are busily engaged in making London chaotically large, hopelessly congested, desperately hard to enter or leave, and vulnerable to air attacks as no other city of Europe is vulnerable. To compel a rational and planned decentralization of industry is one of the legitimate, the urgently necessary functions of the state.

Life in the great city is atomistic. How shall it be given a communal pattern? How shall the individual be incorporated in a responsible, self-governing group? In a modern city, the problem of organizing responsible community life on a local basis is not easily solved. Modern cities have been created and are preserved by the labours of highly specialized technicians. The massacre of a few thousands of engineers, administrators and doctors would be sufficient to reduce any of the great metropolitan centres to a state of plague-stricken, starving chaos. Accordingly, in most of its branches, the local government of a great city has become a highly technical affair, a business of the kind that must be centrally planned and carried out by experts. The only department in which there would seem to be a possibility of profitably extending the existing institutions of local self-government is the department concerned with police-work and the observance of laws. I have read that in Japan, the cities were, and perhaps still are, divided into wards of about a hundred inhabitants apiece. The people in each ward accepted a measure of liability for one another and were to some extent responsible for good behaviour and the observance of law within their own small unit. That such a system lends itself to the most monstrous abuses under a dictatorial government is obvious. Indeed, it is reported that the Nazis have already organized their cities in this way. But there is no governmental institution that cannot be abused. Elected parliaments have been used as instruments of oppression; plebiscites have served to confirm and strengthen tyranny; courts of justice have been transformed into Star Chambers and military tribunals. Like all the rest, the ward system may be a source of good in a desirable context and a source of unmitigated evil in an undesirable context. It remains in any case a device worth considering by those who aspire to impose a communal pattern upon the atomistic, irresponsible life of modern city dwellers. For the rest, it looks as though the townsman's main experience of democratic institutions and responsible self-government would have to be obtained, not in local administrations, but in the fields of industry and economics, of religious and cultural activity, of athletics and entertainment.

In the preceding paragraphs I have tried to answer the first of our questions and have described the methods by which the principle of self-government can be applied to the daily lives of ordinary men and women. Our second question concerns the compatibility of self-government all round with the efficiency of industry in particular and society as a whole. In Russia self-government in industry was tried in the early years of the revolution and was abandoned in favour of authoritarian management. Within the factory discipline is no longer enforced by elected representatives of the Soviet or worker's committee, but by appointees of the Communist Party. The new conception of management current in Soviet Russia was summed up by Kaganovitch in a speech before the seventeenth congress of the Communist Party. "Management," he said, "means the power to distribute material things, to appoint and discharge subordinates, in a word, to be master of the particular enterprise." This is a definition of management to which every industrial dictator in the capitalist countries would unhesitatingly subscribe.

By supporters of the present Russian government it is said that the change over from self-government to authoritarian management had to be made in the interests of efficiency. That extremely inexperienced and ill-educated workers should have been unable to govern themselves and keep up industrial efficiency seems likely enough. But in Western Europe and the United States such a situation is not likely to arise. Indeed, Dubreuil has pointed out that, as a matter of historical fact, self-government within factories has often led to increased efficiency. It would seem, then, that in countries where all men and women are relatively well educated and have been accustomed for some time to the working of democratic institutions, there is no danger that self-government will lead to a breakdown of discipline within the factory or a decline in output. But, like "liberty" the word "efficiency" covers a multitude of sins. Even if it should be irrefragably demonstrated that self-government in industry invariably led to greater contentment and increased output, even if it could be proved experimentally that the best features of individualism and collectivism could be combined if the state were to co-ordinate the activities of self-governing industries, there would still be complaints of "inefficiency." And by their own lights, the complainers would be quite right. For to the ruling classes, not only in the totalitarian, but also in the democratic countries, "efficiency" means primarily "military efficiency." Now, a society in which the principle of self-government has been applied to the ordinary activities of all its members, is a society which, for purely military purposes, is probably decidedly inefficient. A militarily efficient society is one whose members have been brought up in habits of passive obedience and at the head of which there is an individual exercising absolute authority through a perfectly trained hierarchy of administrators. In time of war, such a society can be manipulated as a single unit and with extraordinary rapidity and precision. A society composed of men and women habitu-

[94]

ated to working in self-governing groups is not a perfect war-machine. Its members may think and have wills of their own. But soldiers must not think nor have wills. "Theirs not to reason why; theirs but to do and die." Furthermore a society in which authority is decentralized, a society composed of co-ordinated but self-governing parts, cannot be manipulated so swiftly and certainly as a totalitarian society under a dictator. Self-government all round is not compatible with military efficiency. So long as nations persist in using war as an instrument of policy, military efficiency will be prized above all else. Therefore schemes for extending the principle of self-government will either not be tried at all or, if tried, as in Russia, will be speedily abandoned. Inevitably, we find ourselves confronted, yet once more, by the central evil of our time, the overpowering and increasing evil of war. In the next chapter I shall discuss possible methods for dealing with this evil. In what remains of the present chapter, I must try to answer our questions concerning the efficiency of a society made up of co-ordinated self-governing units and the nature of the co-ordinating body.

Dubreuil has shown that even the largest industrial undertakings can be organized so as to consist of a number of co-ordinated but self-governing groups; and he has produced reasons for supposing that such an organization would not reduce the efficiency of the businesses concerned and might even increase it. This small-scale industrial democracy is theoretically compatible with any kind of large-scale control of the industries concerned. It can be (and in certain cases actually has been) applied to industries working under the capitalist system; to businesses under direct state control; to co-operative enterprises; to mixed concerns, like the Port of London Authority, which are under state supervision, but have their own autonomous, functional management. In practice this small-scale industrial democracy, this self-government for all, is intrinsically most compatible with business organizations of the last two kinds—co-operative and mixed. It is almost equally incompatible with capitalism and state socialism. Capitalism tends to produce a multiplicity of petty dictators, each in command of his own little business kingdom. State socialism tends to produce a single, centralized, totalitarian dictatorship, wielding absolute authority over all its subjects through a hierarchy of bureaucratic agents.

Co-operatives and mixed concerns already exist and work extremely well. To increase their numbers and to extend their scope would not seem a revolutionary act, in the sense that it would probably not provoke the violent opposition which men feel towards projects involving an entirely new principle. In its effects, however, the act would *be* revolutionary; for it would result in a profound modification of the existing system. This alone is a sufficient reason for preferring these forms of ultimate industrial control to all others. The intrinsic compatibility of the co-operative enterprise and mixed concern with small-scale democracy and self-government all round constitutes yet another reason for the preference. To discuss the arrangements for co-ordinating the activities of partially autonomous co-operative and mixed concerns is not my business in this place. For technical details, the reader is referred once again to the literature of social and economic planning. I will confine myself here to quoting a relevant passage from the admirable essay contributed by Professor David Mitrany to the Yale Review in 1934. Speaking of the need for comprehensive planning, Professor Mitrany writes that "this does not necessarily mean more centralized government and bureaucratic administration. Public control is just as likely to mean decentralization—as, for instance, the taking over from a nation-wide private corporation of activities and services which could be performed with better results by local authorities. Planning, in fact, if it is intelligent, should allow for a great variety of organization, and should adapt the structure and working of its parts to the requirements of each case.

A striking change of view on this point is evident in the paradox that the growing demand for state action comes together with a growing distrust of the state's efficiency. Hence, even among socialists, as may be seen from the more recent Fabian tracts, the old idea of the nationalization of an industry under a government department, responsible to Parliament for both policy and management, has generally been replaced by schemes which even under public ownership provide for autonomous functional managements. After describing the constitution of such mixed concerns as the Central Electricity Board (set up in England by a Conservative government) the British Broadcasting Corporation and the London Transport Board, Professor Mitrany concludes that it is only "by some such means that the influence both of politics and of money can be eliminated. Radicals and conservatives now agree on the need for placing the management of such public undertakings upon a purely functional basis, which reduces the rôle of Parliament or of any other representative body to a distant, occasional and indirect determination of general policy."

Above these semi-autonomous "functional managers" there will have to be, it is clear, an ultimate co-ordinating authority—a group of technicians whose business it will be to manage the managers. What is to prevent the central political executive from joining hands with these technical managers of managers to become the ruling oligarchy of a totalitarian state? The answer is that, so long as nations continue to prepare for the waging of scientific warfare, there is nothing whatever to prevent this from happening—there is every reason, indeed, to suppose that it will happen. In the context of militarism, even the most intrinsically desirable changes inevitably become distorted. In a country which is preparing for modern war, reforms intended to result in decentralization and genuine democracy will be made to serve the purpose of military efficiency—which means in practice that they will be used to strengthen the position of a dictator or a ruling oligarchy.

Where the international context is militaristic, dictators will use the necessity for "defence" as their excuse for seizing absolute power. But even where there is no threat of war, the temptation to abuse a position of authority will always be strong. How shall our hypothetical managers of managers and the members of the central political executive be delivered from this evil? This point is discussed at some length in the last paragraphs of the chapter on "Inequality," to which the reader is referred. Ambition may be checked, but cannot be suppressed by any kind of legal machinery. If it is to be scotched, it must be scotched at the source, by education in the widest sense of the word. In our societies men are paranoiacally ambitious, because paranoiac ambition is admired as a virtue and successful climbers are adored as though they were gods. More books have been written about Napoleon than about any other human being. The fact is deeply and alarmingly significant. What must be the day-dreams of people for whom the world's most agile social climber and ablest bandit is the hero they most desire to hear about? Duces and Fuehrers will cease to plague the world only when the majority of its inhabitants regard such adventurers with the same disgust as they now bestow on swindlers and pimps. So long as men worship the Caesars and Napoleons, Caesars and Napoleons will duly rise and make them miserable. The proper attitude towards the "hero" is not Carlyle's, but Bacon's. "He doth like the ape," wrote Bacon of the ambitious tyrant, "he doth like the ape that, the higher he clymbes, the more he shewes his ars." The hero's qualities are brilliant; but so is the mandril's rump. When all concur in the great Lord Chancellor's judgment of Fuehrers, there will be no more Fuehrers to judge. Meanwhile we must content ourselves by putting merely legal and administrative obstacles in the way of the ambitious. They are a great deal better than nothing; but they can never be completely effective.

[99]

IX

War

EVERY road towards a better state of society is blocked, sooner or later, by war, by threats of war, by preparations for war. That is the truth, the odious and unescapable truth, that emerges, plain for all to see, from the discussions contained in the preceding chapters.

Let us very briefly consider the nature of war, the causes of war and the possible alternatives to war, the methods of curing the mania of militarism afflicting the world at the present time.*

I. NATURE OF WAR

(i) War is a purely human phenomenon. The lower animals fight duels in the heat of sexual excitement and kill for food and occasionally for sport. But the activities of a wolf eating a sheep or a cat playing with a mouse are no more war-like than the activities of butchers and fox-hunters. Similarly, fights between hungry dogs or rutting stags are like pot-house quarrels and have nothing in common with war, which is mass-murder organized in cold blood. Some social insects, it is true, go out to fight in armies; but their attacks are always directed against members of another species. Man is unique in organizing the mass murder of his own species.

*Certain passages in this chapter are reprinted with little alteration from articles contributed by the author to "An Encyclopaedia of Pacifism" (London, 1937).

(ii) Certain biologists, of whom Sir Arthur Keith is the most eminent, consider that war acts as "nature's pruning hook," ensuring the· survival of the fittest among civilized individuals and nations. This is obviously nonsensical. War tends to eliminate the young and strong and to spare the unhealthy. Nor is there any reason for supposing that people with traditions of violence and a good technique of war-making are superior to other peoples. The most valuable human beings are not necessarily the most warlike. Nor as a matter of historical fact is it always the most warlike who survive. We can sum up by saying that, so far as individuals are concerned, war selects dysgenically; so far as nations and peoples are concerned it selects purely at random, sometimes ensuring the domination and survival of the more warlike peoples, sometimes, on the contrary, ensuring their destruction and the survival of the unwarlike.

(iii) There exist at the present time certain primitive human societies, such as that of the Eskimos, in which war is unknown and even unthinkable. All civilized societies, however, are warlike. The question arises whether the correlation between war and civilization is necessary and unavoidable. The evidence of archaeology seems to point to the conclusion that war made its appearance at a particular moment in the history of early civilization. There is reason to suppose that the rise of war was correlated with an abrupt change in the mode of human consciousness. This change, as Dr. J. D. Unwin suggests,* may have been correlated with in-

* In "Sex and Culture" (Oxford, 1934).

creased sexual continence on the part of the ruling classes of the warlike societies. The archaeological symptom of the change is the almost sudden appearance of royal palaces and elaborate funerary monuments. The rise of war appears to be connected with the rise of self-conscious leaders, preoccupied with the ideas of personal domination and personal survival after death. Even today when economic considerations are supposed to be supreme, ideas of "glory" and "immortal fame" still ferment in the minds of the dictators and generals, and play an important part in the causation of war.

(iv) The various civilizations of the world have adopted fundamentally different attitudes towards war. Compare the Chinese and Indian attitudes towards war with the European. Europeans have always worshipped the military hero and, since the rise of Christianity, the martyr. Not so the Chinese. The ideal human being, according to Confucian standards, is the just, reasonable, humane and cultivated man, living at peace in an ordered and harmonious society. Confucianism, to quote Max Weber, "prefers a wise prudence to mere physical courage and declares that an untimely sacrifice of life is unfitting for a wise man." Our European admiration for military heroism and martyrdom has tended to make men believe that a good death is more important than a good life and that a long course of folly and crime can be cancelled out by a single act of physical courage. The mysticism of Lao Tsu (or whoever was the author of the Tao Teh Ching) confirms and completes the rationalism of Confucius. The Tao is an eternal cosmic principle that is, at the same time, the inmost root of

the individual's being. Those who would live in harmony with Tao must refrain from assertiveness, self-
importance and aggressiveness, must cultivate humility
and return good for evil.

Since the time of Confucius and Lao Tsu, Chinese
ideals have been essentially pacifistic. European poets
have glorified war; European theologians have found
justification for religious persecution and nationalistic
aggression. This has not been so in China. Chinese
philosophers and Chinese poets have almost all been
anti-militarists. The soldier was regarded as an inferior
being, not to be put on the same level with the scholar
or administrator. It is one of the tragedies of history
that the Westernization of China should have meant the
progressive militarization of a culture which, for nearly
three thousand years, has consistently preached the
pacifist ideal. Conscription was imposed on large numbers of Chinese in 1936, and the soldier is now held up
for admiration. Comic, but significant, is the following
quotation from the New York *Times* of June 17, 1937.
"Sin Wan Pao, Shanghai's leading Chinese language
newspaper, advised Adolf Hitler and Benito Mussolini
to-day to follow the examples of General Yang Sen . . .
war lord and commander of the Twentieth Army in
Szechwan Province. The general has twenty-seven wives.
'Only 40 years old, General Yang has a child for every
year of his life,' the newspaper said. 'General Yang has
established complete military training for his offspring.
It begins when a young Yang reaches the age of 7, with
strict treatment by the time the child is 14. The family
has an exclusive military camp. When visitors come,

the Yang children hold a military reception and march past the guests in strict review order.' " One laughs; but the unfortunate truth is that General Yang and the forty little Yangs in their strict review order are grotesquely symptomatic of the new, worse, Western spirit of a China that has turned its back on the wisdom of Confucius and Lao Tsu and gone whoring after European militarism. Japanese aggression is bound to intensify this new militaristic spirit in China. Within a couple of generations, it is possible that China will be an aggressive imperialist power.

Indian pacifism finds its completest expression in the teaching of Buddha. Buddhism, like Hinduism, teaches *ahimsa*, or harmlessness towards all living beings. It forbids even laymen to have anything to do with the manufacture and sale of arms, with the making of poisons and intoxicants, with soldiering or the slaughter of animals. Alone of all the great world religions, Buddhism made its way without persecution, censorship or inquisition. In all these respects its record is enormously superior to that of Christianity, which made its way among people wedded to militarism and which was able to justify the bloodthirsty tendencies of its adherents by an appeal to the savage Bronze-Age literature of the Old Testament. For Buddhists, anger is always and unconditionally disgraceful. For Christians, brought up to identify Jehovah with God, there is such a thing as "righteous indignation." Thanks to this possibility of indignation being righteous, Christians have always felt themselves justified in making war and committing the most hideous atrocities.

The fact that it should have been possible for the three principal civilizations of the world to adopt three distinct philosophic attitudes towards war is encouraging; for it proves that there is nothing "natural" about our present situation in relation to war. The existence of war and of our political and theological justifications of war is no more "natural" than were the sanguinary manifestations of sexual jealousy, so common in Europe up to the beginning of last century and now of such rare occurrence. To murder one's unfaithful wife, or the lover of one's sister or mother, was something that used to be "done." Being socially correct, it was regarded as inevitable, a manifestation of unchanging "human nature." Such murders are no longer fashionable among the best people, therefore no longer seem to us "natural." The malleability of human nature is such that there is no reason why, if we so desire and set to work in the right way, we should not rid ourselves of war as we have freed ourselves from the weary necessity of committing a *crime passionnel* every time a wife, mistress or female relative gets herself seduced. War is not a law of nature, nor even a law of human nature. It exists because men wish it to exist; and we know as a matter of historical fact, that the intensity of that wish has varied from absolute zero to a frenzied maximum. The wish for war in the contemporary world is widespread and of high intensity. But our wills are to some extent free; we can wish otherwise than we actually do. It is enormously difficult for us to change our wishes in this matter; but the enormously difficult is not the impossible. We must be grateful for even the smallest crumbs of comfort.

II. CAUSES OF WAR

War exists because people wish it to exist. They wish it to exist for a variety of reasons.

(i) Many people like war because they find their peace-time occupations either positively humiliating and frustrating, or just negatively boring. In their studies on suicide Durkheim and, more recently, Halbwachs have shown that the suicide-rate among non-combatants tends to fall during war-time to about two-thirds of its normal figure. This decline must be put down to the following causes: to the simplification of life during war-time (it is in complex and highly developed societies that the suicide rate is highest) ; to the intensification of nationalist sentiment to a point where most individuals are living in a state of chronic enthusiasm; to the fact that life during war-time takes on significance and purposefulness, so that even the most intrinsically boring job is ennobled as "war-work"; to the artificial prosperity induced, at any rate for a time, by the expansion of war industries; to the increased sexual freedom which is always claimed by societies, all or some of whose members live under the menace of sudden death. Add to this the fact that life in war-time is (or at least was in previous wars) extremely interesting, at least during the first years of the war. Rumour runs riot, and the papers are crammed every morning with the most thrilling news. To the influence of the press must be attributed the fact that, whereas during the Franco-Prussian War the suicide rate declined only in the belligerent countries, during the World War a considerable decline was registered even in the neutral states. In 1870 about half the inhabitants of Europe were unable to read, and newspapers were few and expensive. By 1914 primary education had everywhere been compulsory for more than a generation and the addiction to newspaper reading had spread to all classes of the population. Thus, even neutrals were able to enjoy, vicariously and at second hand, the exciting experience of war.

Up to the end of the last war non-combatants, except in countries actually subject to invasion, were not in great physical danger. In any future war it is clear that they will be exposed to risks almost, if not quite, as great as those faced by the fighting men. This will certainly tend to diminish the enthusiasm of non-combatants for war. But if it turns out that the effects of air bombardment are less frightful than most experts at present believe they will be, this enthusiasm may not be extinguished altogether, at any rate during the first months of a war. During the last war, a fair proportion of the combatants actually enjoyed some phases at least of the fighting. The escape from the dull and often stultifying routines of peace-time life was welcomed, even though that escape was bought at the price of physical hardship and the risk of death and mutilation. It is possible that conditions in any future war will be so appalling that even the most naturally adventurous and combative human beings will soon come to hate and fear the process of fighting. But until the next war actually breaks out, nobody can have experience of the new conditions of fighting. Meanwhile, all the governments are actively engaged in making a subtle kind of propaganda that is directed against potential enemies, but not against war. They warn their subjects that they will be bombarded from the air by fleets of enemy planes; they persuade or compel them to subject themselves to air-raid drills and other forms of military discipline; they proclaim the necessity of piling up enormous armaments for the purpose of counter-attack and retaliation and they actually build those armaments to the tune, in most European countries, of nearly or fully half the total national revenue. At the same time they do all in their power to belittle the danger from air raids. Millions of gas masks are made and distributed with assurances that they will provide complete protection. Those who make such assurances know quite well that they are false. Gas masks cannot be worn by infants, invalids or the old and give no protection whatsoever against vesicants and some of the poisonous smokes, which for this reason will be the chemicals chiefly used by the air navies of the world. Meanwhile warnings by impartial experts are either officially ignored or belittled. (The attitude of the government's spokesman at the British Medical Association meeting at Oxford in 1936 and that of the *Times* in 1937 towards the Cambridge scientists who warned the public against the probable effects of air bombardment are highly significant in this context.) The whole effort of all the governments is directed, I repeat, to making propaganda against enemies and in favour of war; against those who

[108]

try to tell the truth about the nature and effects of the new armaments and in favour of manufacturing such armaments in ever increasing quantities. There are two reasons why such propaganda is as successful as it is. The first, as I have explained in this paragraph, must be sought in the fact that, up to the present, many non-combatants and some combatants have found war a welcome relief from the tedium of peace. The second reason will be set forth in the following paragraph, which deals with another aspect of the psychological causation of war.

(ii) A principal cause of war is nationalism, and nationalism is immensely popular because it is psychologically satisfying to individual nationalists. Every nationalism is an idolatrous religion, in which the god is the personified state, represented in many instances by a more or less deified king or dictator. Membership of the *ex hypothesi* divine nation is thought of as imparting a kind of mystical pre-eminence. Thus, all "God's Englishmen" are superior to "the lesser breeds without the law" and every individual God's-Englishman is entitled to think himself superior to every member of the lesser breed, even the lordliest and wealthiest, even the most intelligent, the most highly gifted, the most saintly. Any man who believes strongly enough in the local nationalistic idolatry can find in his faith an antidote against even the most acute inferiority complex. Dictators feed the flames of national vanity and reap their reward in the gratitude of millions to whom the conviction that they are participants in the glory of the divine nation brings relief from the gnawing

[109]

consciousness of poverty, social unimportance and personal insignificance.

Self-esteem has as its complement disparagement of others. Vanity and pride beget contempt and hatred. But contempt and hatred are exciting emotions—emotions from which people "get a kick." Devotees of one national idolatry enjoy getting the kick of hatred and contempt for devotees of other idolatries. They pay for that enjoyment by having to prepare for the wars which hatred and contempt render almost inevitable. Another point. In the normal course of events most men and women behave tolerably well. This means that they must frequently repress their anti-social impulses. They find a vicarious satisfaction for these impulses through films and stories about gangsters, pirates, swindlers, bad bold barons and the like. Now, the personified nation, as I have pointed out already, is divine in size, strength and mystical superiority, but sub-human in moral character. The ethics of international politics are precisely those of the gangster, the pirate, the swindler, the bad bold baron. The exemplary citizen can indulge in vicarious criminality, not only on the films, but also in the field of international relations. The divine nation of whom he is mystically a part bullies and cheats, blusters and threatens in a way which many people find profoundly satisfying to their sedulously repressed lower natures. Submissive to the wife, kind to the children, courteous to the neighbours, the soul of honesty in business, the good citizen feels a thrill of delight when his country "takes a strong line," "enhances its prestige," "scores a diplomatic victory," "increases its territory"—

in other words when it bluffs, bullies, swindles and steals. The nation is a strange deity. It imposes difficult duties and demands the greatest sacrifices and, because it does this and because human beings have a hunger and thirst after righteousness, it is loved. But it is also loved because it panders to the lowest elements in human nature and because men and women like to have excuses to feel pride and hatred, because they long to taste even at second hand the joys of criminality.

So much for the psychological causes of war—or, to be more exact, the psychological background whose existence makes possible the waging of wars. We have now to consider the immediate causes of war. Ultimately, they also are psychological; but since they display special forms of human behaviour and since these special forms of behaviour manifest themselves in certain highly organized fields of activity, we prefer to call them "political" and "economic" causes. For the purposes of classification, this is convenient; but the convenience has its disadvantages. We are apt to think of "politics" and "economics" as impersonal forces outside the domain of psychology, working in some way on their own and apart from human beings. To the extent that human beings are habit-bound and conditioned by their social environment, politics and economics possess a certain limited autonomy; for wherever a social organization exists, individuals tend to submit themselves to the workings of its machinery. But man is not made for the Sabbath, nor is he invariably willing to believe that he is made for the Sabbath. To some extent his will is free, and from time to time he remembers the fact and alters the organizational machinery around him to suit his needs. When this happens the conception of politics and economics as autonomous forces, independent of human psychology, becomes completely misleading. It is convenient, I repeat, to class the economic and political causes of war under separate headings. But we must not forget that all such causes are ultimately psychological in their nature.

(iii) The first of the political causes of war is war itself. Many wars have been fought, among other reasons, for the sake of seizing some strategically valuable piece of territory, or in order to secure a "natural" frontier—that is to say, a frontier which it is easy to defend and from which it is easy to launch attacks upon one's neighbours. Purely military advantages are almost as highly prized by the rulers of nations as economic advantages. The possession of an army, navy and air force, is in itself a reason for going to war. "We must use our forces now," so runs the militarist's argument, "in order that we may be in a position to use them to better effect next time."

The part played by armaments in causing war may properly be considered under this heading. All statesmen insist that the armaments of their own country are solely for purposes of defence. At the same time, all statesmen insist that the existence of armaments in a foreign country constitutes a reason for the creation of new armaments at home. Every nation is perpetually taking more and more elaborate defensive measures against the more and more elaborate defensive measures of all other nations. The armament race would go on *ad infinitum*, if it did not inevitably and invariably lead to war. Armaments lead to war for two reasons. The first is psychological. The existence of armaments in one country creates fear, suspicion, resentment and hatred in neighbouring countries. In such an atmosphere, any dispute easily becomes envenomed to the point of being made a *casus belli*. The second is technical in character. Armaments become obsolete, and today the rate of obsolescence is rapid and accelerating. At the present rate of technological progress an aeroplane is likely to be out of date within a couple of years, or less. This means that, for any given country, there is likely to be an optimum moment of preparedness, a moment when its equipment is definitely superior to that of other nations. Within a very short time this superiority will disappear and the nation will be faced with the task of scrapping its now obsolescent equipment and building new equipment equal to, or if possible better than, the new equipment of its neighbours. The financial strain of such a process is one which only the richest countries can stand for long. For poorer nations it is unendurable. Hence there will always be a strong temptation for the rulers of the poor countries to declare war during the brief period when their own military equipment is superior to that of their rivals.

The fact that armaments are to a great extent manufactured by private firms and that these private firms have a financial interest in selling weapons of war to their own and foreign governments is also a contributory cause of war. This matter will be dealt with in a later section.

(iv) Wars may be made for the purpose of furthering a religious or political creed. The Mohammedan invasions, the Crusades, the Wars of Religion during the sixteenth and seventeenth centuries, the French Revolutionary Wars, the American Civil War, the Spanish Civil War are all examples of what may be called ideological wars. True, the makers of ideological wars were to some extent influenced by non-ideological considerations—by greed for wealth and dominion, by desire for glory, and the like. But in all cases the ideological motive was paramount. Unless there had been a desire to propagate a new creed or defend an old, these wars would not have been fought. Moreover, the fighting would not have been so bitter as in fact it generally was, if the fighters had not been inspired by religious or pseudo-religious faith. The aim of modern nationalistic propaganda is to transform men's normal affection for their home into a fiercely exclusive worship of the deified nation. Disputes between nations are beginning to take on that uncompromising, fanatical quality which, in the past, characterized the dealings between groups of religious or political sectaries. It looks as though all future wars will be as ferociously ideological as the old wars of religion.

(v) In the past, many wars were fought for the sake of the "glory" resulting from victory. The glory was generally thought of as belonging to the leader of the army, or the king his master. The Assyrian monarchs fought for glory; so did Alexander the Great; so did many mediaeval kings and lords; so did Louis XIV and the dynasts of eighteenth-century Europe; so did Napoleon; so perhaps will the modern dictators. Where countries are ruled by a single individual at the head of a military oligarchy, there is always a danger that personal vanity and the thirst for glory may act as motives driving him to embroil his country in war.

(vi) Glory is generally regarded as the perquisite of the general or king; but not always or exclusively. In a country whose people are moved by strong nationalistic feelings, glory can be thought of as pertaining in some degree to every member of the community. All Englishmen shared in the glory of their Tudor monarchs; all Frenchmen in that of Louis XIV. During the French Revolution, a deliberate attempt was made to popularize glory by means of written and spoken propaganda. The attempt was fully successful. Similar attempts are being made all over the world today. The press, the radio and the film bring national glory within the reach of all. When things go badly at home and his people start to complain, the dictator is always tempted to manufacture a little compensatory glory abroad. Glory was a good deal cheaper in the past than it is today. Moreover, the dictatorial war lord of earlier times did not have to consider public opinion to the same extent that even the most absolute of his modern counterparts must do. The reason is simple. In the past, the glory-making machine was a small professional army. So long as the battles were being fought at a reasonable distance from their homes, people did not feel much concern about this professional army; its sufferings did not affect them personally and when it won a victory, they got the glory vicariously and free of charge. Today, every man must

serve as a conscript and the aeroplane has made war almost as dangerous for non-combatants as for front-line
fighters. Glory must be paid for by all; war is now the
affair of every man, woman and child in the community.
The cost of modern war in life and money is so enormous and must be so widely distributed, its possible
effects on public opinion and the structure of society so
incalculable, that even dictators hesitate to make their
people fight except where "national honour" and "vital
interests" are concerned. Twentieth-century armaments
are an insurance against small and trivial wars. On the
other hand, they are an absolute guarantee that when
"vital interests" and "national honour" are at stake,
the resulting war shall be unprecedentedly destructive.

(vii) Of the economic causes of war the first in historical importance is the desire of one nation to possess
itself of fertile territory belonging to another nation.
Hitler, for example, has stated that the Germans need
new territory in which to accommodate their surplus
population. If Germany goes to war with Russia it will
be, in part at least, to satisfy this real or imaginary craving for more and better land.

In modern times wars have been fought not so much
for fertile lands as for the possession or control of raw
materials indispensable to industry. The iron ore of
Lorraine has been a bone of contention between France
and Germany. Japan's activities in Manchuria and
Northern China can be explained, at least in part, by
need for minerals. Italian and German participation in
the Spanish Civil War has not been exclusively moti-
vated by ideological considerations. The two Fascist dic-

tators have their eyes on the copper of Rio Tinto, the iron of Bilbao, which before the outbreak of war were under English control.

(viii) Under capitalism, all highly industrialized countries need foreign markets. The reason for this is that, where production is carried on for profit, it is difficult or impossible to distribute enough purchasing power to enable people to buy the things they themselves have produced. Defects in domestic purchasing power have to be made up by finding foreign markets. The imperialistic activities of the great powers during the nineteenth century were directed in large measure towards securing markets for their productions. But— and this is one of the strangest paradoxes of the capitalist system—no sooner has a market been secured either by conquest, or peaceful penetration, than the very industrialists who manufacture for that market proceed to equip the conquered or peacefully penetrated country with the machinery that will enable it to dispense with their goods. Most of the industrially backward countries have been equipped to provide for themselves, and even to export a surplus, by those very capitalists who originally used them as markets for their own productions. Such a policy seems and, on a long view, actually is completely lunatic. On a short view, however, it is sensible enough. Capitalists are concerned not only to sell their production, but also to invest their savings. Savings invested in industrial concerns newly established in backward countries, where the standard of living is low and labour can be sweated, generally bring enormous returns, at any rate during the first years. For the sake of these huge temporary profits capitalists are prepared to sacrifice the smaller but more lasting profits to be derived from using these same backward countries as markets for their productions. In course of time the profits of oversea investment diminish and meanwhile the markets have been lost for ever. But in the interval capitalists have earned a huge return on their investments.

(ix) This brings us to an extremely important cause of war—the pursuit by politically powerful minorities within each nation of their own private interests. The worst, or at any rate the most conspicuous, offenders in this respect are the manufacturers of armaments. It is unnecessary for me to cite facts and figures; they are available in a number of well-documented, easily accessible books and pamphlets.* It is enough to state the following simple generalizations. War and the preparation for war are profitable to the arms manufacturer. The more heavily the nations arm, the greater his profits. This being so, he is tempted to foment war scares, to pit government against government, to use every means in his power, from bribery to "patriotic" propaganda, in order to stultify all efforts at disarmament. The historical records show that the manufacturers of armaments have only too frequently succumbed to these temptations.

One of the measures common to the programs of all the world's left-wing parties is the nationalization of the arms industry. To a certain extent all states are

* See the works of Seldes, Noel Baker and the pamphlets published by the Union for Democratic Control.

already in the armaments business. In England, for example, the government arsenals produce about five-twelfths of the nation's arms, private firms about seven-twelfths. Complete nationalization would thus be merely the wider application of a well-established principle.

Now, the complete nationalization of the arms industry would certainly achieve one good result: it would liberate governments from the influence of socially irresponsible capitalists, interested solely in making large profits. So far, so good. But the trouble is that this particular reform does not go far enough—goes, in fact, hardly anywhere at all. Armaments are armaments, whoever manufactures them. A plane from a government factory can kill just as many women and children as a plane from a factory owned by a private capitalist. Furthermore the fact that armaments were being manufactured by the state would serve in some measure to legalize and justify an intrinsically abominable practice. The mass of unthinking public opinion would come to feel that an officially sanctioned arms industry was somehow respectable. Consequently the total abolition of the whole evil business would become even more difficult than it is at present. This difficulty would be enhanced by the fact that a central executive having complete control of the arms industry would be very reluctant to part with such an effective instrument of tyranny. For an instrument of tyranny is precisely what a nationalized armaments industry potentially is. The state is more powerful than any private employer, and the personnel of a completely nationalized arms industry could easily be dragooned and bribed into becoming a kind of technical army under the control of the executive. Finally, we must consider the effect of nationalization upon international affairs. Under the present dispensation adventurers like the late Sir Basil Zaharoff are free (within the limits imposed by the licensing system) to travel about, fanning the flames of international discord and peddling big guns and submarines. This is a state of things which should certainly be changed. But the state of things under a regime of nationalization is only a little better. Once in business, even governments like to make a profit; and the arms business will not cease to be profitable because it has been nationalized. Then, as now, industrially backward states will have to buy arms from the highly industrialized countries. All highly industrialized states will desire to sell armaments, not only for the sake of profits, but also in order to exercise control over the policy of their customers. Inevitably, this will result in the growth of intense rivalry between the industrialized powers—yet another rivalry, yet another potential cause of international discord and war. It would seem, then, that the nationalization of the armaments industry is merely the substitution of one evil for another. The new evil will be less manifest, less morally shocking than the old; but it is by no means certain that, so far as war is concerned, the results of nationalization will be perceptibly better than the results of private manufacture. What is needed is not the nationalization of the arms industry, but its complete abolition. Abolition will come when the majority wish it to come. The process of persuading the majority to wish it will be described in the next chapter.

The manufacturers of armaments are not the only "merchants of death." To some extent, indeed, we all deserve that name. For in so far as we vote for governments that impose tariffs and quotas, in so far as we support policies of re-armament, in so far as we consent to our country's practice of economic, political and military imperialism, in so far even as we behave badly in private life, we are all doing our bit to bring the next war nearer. The responsibility of the rich and the powerful, however, is greater than that of ordinary men; for they are better paid for what they do to bring war closer and they know more clearly what they are about. Less spectacularly mischievous than the armament makers, but in reality hardly less harmful, are the speculative investors who preach imperialism because they can derive such high returns on their capital in backward countries. To the nation as a whole its colonies may be unprofitable, and actually costly. But to the politically powerful minority of financiers with capital to invest, of industrialists with surplus goods to dispose of, these same colonies may be sources of handsome profits.

The small, but politically powerful, minority of financiers and industrialists is also interested in various forms of economic imperialism. By a judicious use of their resources, the capitalists of highly industrialized nations stake out claims for themselves within nominally independent countries. Those claims are then represented as being the claims of their respective nations and the quarrels between the various financial interests concerned become quarrels between states. The peace of the world has frequently been endangered, in order that oil magnates might grow a little richer.

In the press, which is owned by rich men, the interests of the investing minority are always identified (doubtless in perfectly good faith) with those of the nation as a whole. Constantly repeated statements come to be accepted as truths. Innocent and ignorant, most newspaper readers are convinced that the private interests of the rich are really public interests and become indignant whenever these interests are menaced by a foreign power, intervening on behalf of *its* investing minority. The interests at stake are the interests of the few; but the public opinion which demands the protection of these interests is often a genuine expression of mass emotion. The many really feel and believe that the dividends of the few are worth fighting for.

(x) Remedies and Alternatives. So much for the nature and causes of war. We must now consider, first, the methods for preventing war from breaking out and for checking it once it has begun and, second, the political alternatives and psychological equivalents to war.

It will be best to begin with the existing methods of war prevention. These methods are not conspicuously successful for two good reasons: first, they are in many cases of such a nature that they cannot conceivably produce the desired results and, second, even when intrinsically excellent, they are not calculated to eliminate the existing causes of war or to provide psychologically equivalent substitutes for war. Accordingly, after describing and discussing the methods at present in use, I shall go on to outline the methods which should be used, if the causes of war are to be eliminated and suitable alternatives to war created.

The hopes which so many men and women of good will once rested in the League of Nations have been disappointed. The failure of the League of Nations to secure the pacification of the world is due in part to historical accident, but mainly to the fact that it was based on entirely wrong principles. The historical accident which stultified the League's ability to do good was the refusal of the Americans to join it and the exclusion for many years of the "enemy powers" and Russia. But even if America, Germany and Russia had all been original members, it is still as certain as any contingency can be that the League would not have produced the good results expected of it. The League admits to membership any community, however small, which possesses an army of its own. No community, however large, which does not possess an army is eligible. In practice and by implication the League defines a nation as "a society organized for war." And effectively this is the only definition of a nation that applies to all the existing members of the class. Every other definition, in terms of race, of colour, of language, of culture and even of simple topography is proved to be inadequate by the existence of exceptions. Formally and in fact, the League of Nations is a league of societies organized for war.

The militarism which is built into the very definition of the League finds expression in the means whereby, under its present constitution, it is proposed to secure peace. The framers of the League Covenant did what many of the framers of the American Constitution desired to do, but were fortunately dissuaded by Alexander Hamilton from doing: they inserted a clause decreeing first economic and then military sanctions against an "aggressor."

Sanctions are objectionable for exactly the same reasons as war is objectionable. Military sanctions *are* war. Economic sanctions, if applied with vigour, must inevitably lead to war-like reactions on the part of the nation to which they are applied, and these war-like reactions can only be countered by military sanctions. Sanctionists call their brand of war by high-sounding names. We must not allow ourselves to be deceived by mere words. In the actual circumstances of the present day, "collective security" means a system of military alliances opposed to another system of military alliances. The first system calls itself the League; the second is nominated in advance "the Aggressor."

Once war has broken out, nations will consult their own interests whether to fight or remain neutral; they will not permit any international agreement to dictate their course of action. Speaking on November 20, 1936, Mr. Eden stated that "our armaments may be used in bringing help to a victim of aggression in any case where, in our judgment, it would be proper under the provision of the Covenant to do so. I use the word 'may,' deliberately, since in such an instance there is no automatic obligation to take military action. It is, moreover, right that this should be so, for nations cannot be expected to incur automatic military obligations save for areas where their vital interests are concerned." Upholding the League Covenant is not regarded as a

vital interest by any nation. Nor, so far as Article XVI
is concerned, ought to be so regarded. Justice, like
charity, begins at home, and no government has the
moral right gratuitously to involve its subjects in war.
War is so radically wrong that any international agreement which provides for the extension of hostilities
from a limited area to the whole world is manifestly
based upon unsound principles. Modern war destroys
with the maximum of efficiency and the maximum of
indiscrimination, and therefore entails the'commission
of injustices far more numerous and far worse than any
it is intended to redress. It is worth remarking in this
context that it is now possible to be an orthodox Catholic and a complete pacifist. To condemn war as such and
to refuse, as the Quakers and other Protestant sects
have done, to participate in any war whatsoever, is
heretical. St. Thomas has laid down that war is justified
when waged in defence of the vital interests of a community. Starting from the Thomist position, certain
Catholic thinkers, notably in Holland and England,
have reached the conclusion that, though it may be
heretical to condemn war as war, one can be a complete
pacifist in relation to war in its contemporary form and
still remain orthodox. War is justified when it is waged
in defence of the vital interests of the community. But
the nature of modern war is such that the vital interests
of the community cannot be defended by it; on the contrary, they must inevitably suffer more from the waging
of war than they would suffer by non-resistance to violence. Therefore, in the circumstance of the present
time, complete pacifism is reasonable, right and even

orthodox. Bertrand Russell's pacifism is based upon exactly the same considerations of expediency as that of these neo-Thomists. His and their arguments are peculiarly relevant to the problem of sanctions. For what the sanctionists demand is that wars which, in the very nature of things, cannot do anything except destroy the vital interests of the communities concerned in them, should be automatically transformed from wars between two or a few nations into universal combats, bringing destruction and injustice to all the peoples of the world.

To this contention sanctionists reply by asserting that the mere display of great military force by League members will be enough to deter would-be aggressors. The greater your force, the slighter the probability that you will have to use it; therefore, they argue, re-arm for the sake of peace. The facts of history do not bear out this contention. Threats do not frighten the determined nor do the desperate shrink before a display of overwhelming force. Moreover, in the contemporary world, there is no reason to suppose that the force mustered against an aggressor will be overwhelming. "The League" and "the Aggressor" will be two well-matched sets of allied powers. Indeed, the composition of these two alliances is already pretty well settled. France, Russia, and probably England are booked to appear as "The League"; Italy, Germany and Japan as "the Aggressor." The smaller nations will remain neutral, or back whichever side they think is likely to win. As for the sanctionist's exhortation to re-arm for the League and for peace, this is merely a modern version of *si vis pacem, para bellum.*

[126]

Those who prepare for war start up an armament race and, in due course, get the war they prepare for.

According to sanctionist theory, the League is to take military action in order to bring about a just settlement of disputes. But the prospects of achieving a just settlement at the end of a League war are no better than at the end of any other kind of war. Wars result in just settlements only when the victors behave with magnanimity, only when they make amends for violence by being just and humane. But when wars have been fierce and prolonged, when the destruction has been indiscriminate and on an enormous scale, it is extraordinarily difficult for the victor to behave magnanimously, or even with justice. Passions ran so high in the last war that it was psychologically impossible for the conquerors to make a just and humane settlement. In spite of Wilson and his Fourteen Points, they imposed the Treaty of Versailles—the treaty which made it inevitable that a Hitler should arise and that Germany should seek revenge for past humiliations. A war waged by League members allied to impose military sanctions on an aggressor will probably be at least as destructive as the war of 1914-1918—possibly far more destructive. Is there any reason to suppose that the victorious League— that is, if it is victorious—will be in a more magnanimous mood than were the Allies in 1918? There is no such reason. The sanctionists are cherishing the old illusion of "the war to end war." But wars do not end war; in most cases they result in an unjust peace that makes inevitable the outbreak of a war of revenge.

In this context it is worth mentioning the project for

an "international police force" sponsored by the New Commonwealth and approved, so far as the international air police force is concerned, by the British Labour Party. First, we must point out that the phrase, "international police force" is completely misleading. Police action against an individual criminal is radically different from action by a nation or group of nations against a national criminal. The police act with the maximum of precision; they go out and arrest the guilty person. Nations and groups of nations act through their armed forces, which can only act with the maximum of imprecision, killing, maiming, starving and ruining millions of human beings, the overwhelming majority of whom have committed no crime of any sort. The process, which all self-righteous militarists, from plain jingo to sanctionist and international policemen, describe as "punishing a guilty nation," consists in mangling and murdering innumerable innocent individuals. To draw analogies between an army and a police force, between war (however "righteous" its aims) and the prevention of crime, is utterly misleading. An "international police force" is not a police force and those who call it by that name are trying, consciously or unconsciously, to deceive the public. What they assimilate to the, on the whole, beneficent policeman is in fact an army and air force, equipped to slaughter and destroy. We shall never learn to think correctly unless we call things by their proper names. The international police force, if it were ever constituted, would not be a police force; it would be a force for perpetrating indiscriminate massacres. If you approve of indiscriminate massacre, then you must say so. You have no right to deceive the unwary by calling your massacre-force by the same name as the force which controls traffic and arrests burglars.

This International Massacre-Force does not yet exist and, quite apart from any question of desirability, it seems almost infinitely improbable that it ever will exist. How is such a force to be recruited? how officered? how armed? where located? Who is to decide when it is to be used and against whom? To whom will it owe allegiance and how is its loyalty to be guaranteed? Is it likely that the staff officers of the various nations will draw up plans for the invasion and conquest of their own country? or that aviators will loyally co-operate in the slaughter of their own people? How can all nations be persuaded to contribute men and materials towards the international force? Should the contributions be equal? If they are not equal and a few great powers supply the major part of the force, what is to prevent these powers from establishing a military tyranny over the whole world? The project sponsored by the New Commonwealth and the Labour Party combines all the moral and political vices of militarism with all the hopeless impracticability of a Utopian dream. In the language of the stud book, the International Police Force may be described as by Machiavelli out of News from Nowhere.

Morality and practical common sense are at one in demanding that efforts to create an "International Police Force" shall be strenuously resisted and that Article XVI shall be removed from the Covenant. The effort to stop war, once it has broken out, by means of military sanctions or the action of an international army and air force is foredoomed to failure. War cannot be stopped by more war. All that more war can do is to widen the area of destruction and place new obstacles in the way of reaching a just and humane settlement of international disputes. It should be the business of the League to concentrate all its energies on the work of preventing wars from breaking out. This it can do by developing existing machinery for the peaceable settlement of international disputes; by extending the field of international co-operation in the study and solution of outstanding social problems; and finally, by devising means for eliminating the causes of war.

About the machinery of peaceful settlement and international co-operation it is unnecessary to say very much. A machine may be exquisitely ingenious and of admirable workmanship but if people refuse to use it, or use it badly, it will be almost or completely useless. This is the case with the machinery of peaceful change and international co-operation. It has been in existence for a long time and if the governments of the various nations had always wished to make use of it, it would have served its purpose—the preservation of peace—with admirable efficiency. But governments have not always wished to make use of it. Wherever "national honour" and "vital interests" were concerned, they have preferred to threaten or actually make use of violence. Even in cases where they have consented to employ the machinery of peaceful settlement, they have sometimes displayed such bad will that the machine has been un-

able to function. A good example of the way in which
bad will can prevent even the best arbitral machinery
from producing the results it is meant to produce is
supplied by the history of the dispute between Chile
and Peru over the provinces of Tacna and Arica. The
dispute began in 1883, when the Treaty of Ancon provided that the two provinces should remain in the possession of Chile for a period of ten years, after which a
plebiscite should be held, to decide whether the territory should remain Chilean or revert to Peruvian sov-
ereignty. The treaty was ambiguous inasmuch as it did
not specify whether the plebiscite should be held immediately after the expiry of the ten-year period, nor by
which power and under whose laws it should be organized. The Chileans made use of this ambiguity to
delay the holding of the plebiscite until such time as,
by intimidating and expelling the Peruvian inhabitants
and importing Chileans, they should be sure of securing a majority. Direct negotiations were tried and
failed. An appeal to the League of Nations in 1920
proved abortive. Finally, arbitration by the President
of the United States was accepted in 1925 and it was
agreed that a plebiscite should be held under the aus-
pices of a commission, presided over by General Pershing. But the Chileans still had no intention of allowing
the machine to work. Pershing retired in 1926 and his
successor, General Lassiter, had to declare that the commission must be dissolved without fulfilling its mission.
Finally, in 1928, under friendly pressure from the
United States, the two countries resumed diplomatic
relations (they had been interrupted for nearly twenty

years) and, in 1929, agreed to accept the arbitration of President Hoover, who finally settled the matter by assigning Tacna to Peru and Arica to Chile. This international quarrel lasted for forty-six years. From the first both sides had agreed to make use of the machinery of peaceful change (a plebiscite and the payment of a monetary compensation). But from the first one of the parties refused to allow the machine to work as it should. In the end sheer boredom took the place of good will. The Chileans couldn't be bothered to persist any longer in their intransigence. The machine was permitted to function and within a few months turned out the peaceful solution which it had been expressly contrived to produce.

The case of the Anglo-American dispute over the boundary between Maine and New Brunswick is very similar to that of the more recent dispute between Chile and Peru. After years of bickering, the arbitration of the King of the Netherlands was accepted in 1827; but when, in 1831, he made his award, the United States rejected it. The dispute dragged on, becoming progressively more acrimonious, for another eleven years. Then, growing weary of the whole matter, both sides decided that it was time to make a settlement. Lord Ashburton was sent to Washington to negotiate with the Secretary of State, Daniel Webster, and in a very short time the Maine boundary and a number of other outstanding differences between the two countries were amicably settled. Here again the machinery of peaceful change produced the results it was designed to produce only when the parties concerned were willing to use it as it was meant to be used. Another significant point is that the negotiations between the two countries were greatly facilitated by the fact that the two negotiators, Webster and Ashburton, were personal friends and enjoyed, in their respective countries, a high reputation for integrity and good sense. Consequently the process of negotiation was easy and its results, though attacked by extremists on both sides of the Atlantic, were acceptable to the majority of ordinary, moderate men, who trusted in the judgment and honesty of the negotiators. For the arbitrator even more, perhaps, than for the negotiator, character is the supreme asset. Any suspicion that the judge in an international dispute is partial, corrupt or merely injudicious is enough to imperial the success of the arbitration. Here again we see that the machine itself is of secondary importance; what matters is the will, the intelligence and the moral character of the men who use the machine. That machinery should exist and that it should be the best that legal and administrative ingenuity can devise is essential. The mere fact that the machinery is there is a hint to the disputants that they ought to use it, rather than resort to armed violence. Opportunity helps to make the good man as well as the thief. It is important, as we have seen, to deliver men from evil by reducing the number of opportunities for behaving badly. It is equally important to create new opportunities for behaving well, to provide desirable alternatives to the evil courses prescribed by tradition. Such institutions as the Hague Court and, in its arbitral and co-operative capacity, the League of Nations, are merely pieces of judicial and administrative machinery and can do nothing of themselves to preserve peace or cure the world of its militaristic insanity. Their existence, however, is an invitation and an opportunity to use peaceful instead of violent methods; and the better the machinery, the more effectively will men be able to exploit the opportunity, once it has been seized.

All the existing methods of preventing war are characterized by one or other of two principal defects. Either they are, like military sanctions, intrinsically bad and so incapable of producing any but bad results. (The results of using unlimited violence and cunning are exactly the same, whether you call the process plain war or employ such charming euphemisms as "Sanctions," "Collective Security," "International Police Action.") Or else they are merely pieces of more or less well designed machinery, incapable by themselves of affecting the fundamental causes of war. This is true even of the special pieces of machinery set up from time to time since the War for the special purpose of eliminating some at least of the economic, political and military causes of war. The Naval Conference of 1927 and the general Disarmament Conference of 1932-1934 were excellent pieces of machinery. But unfortunately none of the parties concerned showed the smallest desire to make use of them. During the 1927 conference the Bethlehem Shipbuilding Corporation, the Newport News Shipbuilding and Drydock Company and the American Brown Boveri Corporation employed a Mr. Shearer to make anti-British propaganda both at Geneva and in the United States, with a view to preventing any agreement on a reduction in naval armaments from being reached. Mr. Shearer was extremely active and, feeling that he had been inadequately remunerated, sued the three companies in 1929 for a quarter of a million dollars, "for services rendered." The companies could probably have saved their money. Even without Mr. Shearer's intervention, it is pretty certain that the negotiations would have resulted in no serious diminution of the British and American navies. At the general Disarmament Conference the determination not to use the machine was manifested even more clearly than in 1927. No government was willing so much as to consider unilateral disarmament and even the Soviet suggestion of complete disarmament all round was ruled out of order before the Conference had begun. The discussions dragged on for two years—discussions concerned not with disarmament, but with the kind of weapons to be used in the next war. Finally the Conference was adjourned *sine die* and the various powers set to work to rearm on a scale unprecedented in human history.

The same obstinate refusal to make use of intrinsically excellent machinery has been displayed at the various conferences on economic and monetary problems. All the economists are agreed that international trade cannot become normal unless tariff barriers are lowered, the quota system abolished and some satisfactory medium of international exchange established. Nor is this all. Everyone knows that economic warfare, carried on by competitive currency devaluations, by tariffs, quotas and export bounties, is bound to lead sooner or later to military warfare. Nevertheless, no government has shown itself ready to make use of any of the excellent machinery specially designed for the purpose of solving the world's economic problems.

It is the same with the Mandate System. The Mandate System is a machine which makes it possible for backward peoples to be placed under the control of an international authority, not under the exclusive rule of a single nation. In regard to colonies the world is at present divided into two camps of Haves and Have-nots. The Haves adopt the motto of the British Nàvy League: What I have I hold. The Have-nots demand a place in the sun, or in more vulgar language, a share in the loot. In recent years these demands have become particularly insistent and menacing. The Haves have consequently found it necessary to rearm, among other reasons, in order to defend their colonies. In the days when sea-power was all important the defence of a "far-flung empire" was relatively easy. Today it is, to say the least of it, exceedingly difficult. It has been repeatedly suggested that the imperial powers should renounce their claim to exclusive ownership of colonies and, using the machinery of the Mandate System, place their colonial territories under international control. By doing this they would allay the envy and resentment of the Have-not countries, appreciably lessen the problem of war and solve the, at present, almost insoluble problem of imperial defence. This suggestion has not been acted upon by any colony-owning country. On the contrary, it has been indignantly rejected. All the governments concerned, from that of Great Britain to that of Portugal, have expressed the determination to shed the last drop of their subjects' blood before yielding a foot of colonial territory. The British government has done more than refuse to transfer its colonies to the League of Nations: it has chosen the moment when it no longer possesses command of the seas and when, even if it did possess it, such command would be of little use, to reverse the free-trade policy by means of which its predecessors (though at the head of a country incomparably stronger and less vulnerable than contemporary Britain) thought fit to placate the envy of other powers. It has closed the doors of its colonies to the trade of other nations, thus forcibly reminding them of their own poverty and giving them new grievances against the British Empire. It is one of the absurd paradoxes of the present situation that those Englishmen who are most anxious to establish friendly relations with the dictatorships, especially Germany and Italy, are precisely those who are loudest in their denunciations of the only scheme by means of which these Have-not States might be placated. Being militarists, they want to make friends with other militarists; being jingos, they cannot accept the conditions upon which such a friendship might be formed —the conditions upon which, incidentally, it might be possible to get rid of militarism altogether. The machinery of the Mandate System is there, ready to be used; but nobody is willing to extend its present operations, and, even in the existing mandated territories, the mandatory powers are tending to disregard their international obligations and to treat their mandates as plain unvarnished colonies.

Machinery has been devised by the League for the

purpose of securing the elementary rights of individuals belonging to minorities, racially or linguistically distinct from the majority of the inhabitants of their country. From the first the governments in control of countries containing such minorities have shown themselves reluctant to make use of this machinery, and recently the reluctance has been transformed, in a number of cases, into downright refusal. It is known by all concerned that maltreatment of minorities begets bad feeling, both at home and abroad. Nevertheless, the governments concerned refuse to use the machinery of conciliation and obstinately persist in oppressing those of their unhappy subjects who have noses of the wrong shape or speak the wrong language.

The machinery for peaceful change is ready and waiting; but nobody uses it, because nobody wants to use it. Wherever we turn we find that the real obstacles to peace are human will and feeling, human convictions, prejudices, opinions. If we want to get rid of war we must get rid first of all its psychological causes. Only when this has been done will the rulers of the nations even desire to get rid of the economic and political causes.

By definition and in fact the League of Nations is, as we have seen, a league of societies prepared for war. That those who rule such essentially militaristic societies should take the initiative in eliminating the causes of war is, of course, enormously improbable. One cannot be the ruler of a militaristic society, unless one is oneself a militarist, unless one accepts the beliefs and cherishes the sentiments which result in a militaristic

policy. This being so, it is perfectly clear that most of
the work of transforming the modern militaristic community into a community that desires peace and that
proves the genuineness of its desire by pursuing only
such policies as make for peace, will have to be done by
private individuals, acting either alone or in association.
Reforms are seldom initiated by the rulers of a nation.
They have their source at the periphery and work gradually inwards towards the centre, till at last the strength
of the reforming movement is so great that its leaders
either become the government or the existing government adopts its principles and carries out its policies.
With the work which will have to be done by private
individuals and associations, I shall speak in the next
chapter. In what remains of the present chapter I shall
consider one by one the psychological causes of war, as
outlined in earlier paragraphs, and point out how they
might be eliminated.

(i) War, as we have seen, is tolerated, and by some
even welcomed, because peace-time occupations seem
boring, humiliating and pointless.

The application of the principle of self-government
to industry and business should go far to deliver men
and women in subordinate positions from the sense of
helpless humiliation which is induced by the need of
obeying the arbitrary orders of irresponsible superiors;
and the fact of being one of a small co-operative group
should do something to make the working life of its
members seem more interesting. Heightened interest
can also be obtained by suitably rearranging the individual's tasks. Fourier insisted long ago on the de-

sirableness of variety in labour, and in recent years his suggestion has been acted upon, experimentally, in a number of factories in Germany, America, Russia and elsewhere. The result has been a diminution of boredom, and in many cases, an increase in the volume of production. Tasks may be varied slightly, as when a worker in a cigarette factory is shifted from the job of feeding tobacco into a machine to the job of packing and weighing. Or they may be varied radically and fundamentally, as when workers alternate between industrial and agricultural labour. In both cases the psychological effects seem to be good.

(ii) It was suggested that the war-time decline in the suicide rate was due, among other things, to the heightened significance and purposefulness of life during a national emergency. At such a time the end for which all are striving is clearly seen; duties are simple and explicit; the vagueness and uncertainty of peace-time ideals gives place to the sharp definition of the war-time ideal, which is: victory at all costs; the bewildering complexities of the peace-time social patterns are replaced by the beautifully simple pattern of a community fighting for its existence. Danger heightens the sense of social solidarity and quickens patriotic enthusiasm. Life takes on sense and meaning and is lived at a high pitch of emotional intensity.

The apparent pointlessness of modern life in time of peace and its lack of significance and purpose are due to the fact that, in the western world at least, the prevailing cosmology is what Mr. Gerald Heard has called the "mechanomorphic" cosmology of modern science. The universe is regarded as a great machine pointlessly grinding its way towards ultimate stagnation and death; men are tiny offshoots of the universal machine, running down to their own private death; physical life is the only real life; mind is a mere product of body; personal success and material well-being are the ultimate measures of value, the things for which a reasonable person should live. Introduced suddenly to this mechanomorphic cosmology, many of the Polynesian races have refused to go on multiplying their species and are in process of dying of a kind of psychological consumption. Europeans are of tougher fibre than the South Sea Islanders and besides they have had nearly three hundred years in which to become gradually acclimatized to the new cosmology. But even they have felt the effects of mechanomorphism. They move through life hollow with pointlessness, trying to fill the void within them by external stimuli— newspaper reading, day-dreaming at the films, radio music and chatter, the playing and above all the watching of games, "good times" of every sort. Meanwhile any doctrine that offers to restore point and purpose to life is eagerly welcomed. Hence the enormous success of the nationalistic and communistic idolatries which deny any meaning to the universe as a whole, but insist on the importance and significance of certain arbitrarily selected parts of the whole—the deified nation, the divine class.

Nationalism first became a religion in Germany, during the Napoleonic wars. Communism took its rise some fifty years later. Those who did not become devotees of the new idolatries either remained Christians, clinging to doctrines that became intellectually less and less acceptable with every advance of science, or else accepted mechanomorphism and became convinced of the pointlessness of life. The World War was a product of nationalism and was tolerated and even welcomed by the great masses of those who found life pointless. War brought only a passing relief to the victims of mechanomorphic philosophy. Disillusion, fatigue and cynicism succeeded the initial enthusiasm and when it was over, the sense of pointlessness became a yawning abyss that demanded to be filled with ever more and intenser distractions, ever better "good times." But good times are not a meaning or a purpose; the void could never be filled by them. Consequently when the nationalists and communists appeared with their simple idolatries and their proclamation that, though life might mean nothing as a whole, it did at least possess a temporary and partial significance, there was a powerful reaction away from the cynicism of the post-war years. Millions of young people embraced the new idolatrous religions, found a meaning in life, a purpose for their existence and were ready, in consequence, to make sacrifices, accept hardships, display courage, fortitude, temperance and indeed all the virtues except the essential and primary ones, without which all the rest may serve merely as the means for doing evil more effectively. Love and awareness— these are the primary, essential virtues. But nationalism and communism are partial and exclusive idolatries that inculcate hatred, pride, hardness, and impose that intolerant dogmatism that cramps intelligence and narrows the field of interest and sympathetic awareness.

The "heads" of pointlessness has as its "tails" idolatrous nationalism and communism. Our world oscillates from a neurasthenia that welcomes war as a relief from boredom to a mania that results in war being made. The cure for both these fearful maladies is the same—the inculcation of a cosmology more nearly corresponding to reality than either mechanomorphism or the grotesque philosophies underlying the nationalistic and communistic idolatries. This cosmology and the ethical consequences of its acceptance will be discussed in detail in a later chapter. My next task is to deal with the part that can and must be played by private individuals in the carrying through of desirable changes.

X

Individual Work for Reform

WE HAVE seen that the only effective methods for carrying out large-scale social reforms are non-violent methods. Violence produces only the results of violence and the attempt to impose reforms by violent methods is therefore foredoomed to failure. The only cases in which violent methods succeed are those where initial violence is rapidly followed by compensatory acts of justice, humaneness, sympathetic understanding and the like. This being so, mere common sense demands that we shall begin with non-violence and not run the risk of stultifying the whole process of reform by using violence, even as an initial measure.

Non-violent methods of reform are likely to succeed only where a majority of the population is either actively in favour of the reform in question, or at least not prepared actively to oppose it. Where the majority is not either favourable or passively neutral to the reform, violent attempts to impose it are certain to lead to failure.

In communities ruled by hereditary monarchs it has sometimes happened that an exceptionally enlightened king has tried to make reforms which, though intrinsically desirable, did not happen to be desired by the mass of his people. Akhnaton's is a case in point. Such efforts at reform made by rulers too far advanced to be understood by their subjects are likely to meet with partial or complete failure.

[144]

In countries where rulers are chosen by popular vote there is no likelihood that startlingly novel and unacceptable reforms will be initiated by the central authority. In such countries the movement for reform must always start at the periphery and move towards the centre. Private individuals, either alone or in groups, must formulate the idea of reform and must popularize it among the masses. When it has become sufficiently popular, it can be incorporated into the legislation of the community.

In the modern world, as we have seen, the great obstacle to all desirable change is war. The cardinal, the indispensable reform is therefore a reform in the present policy of national communities in regard to one another. Today all nations conduct their foreign policy on militaristic principles. Some are more explicitly, more noisily and vulgarly militaristic than others; but all, even those that call themselves democratic and pacific, consistently act upon the principles of militarism. It is hardly conceivable that any desirable reform in this direction should be initiated by those who now hold political power. The movement of reform must therefore come from private individuals. It is the business of these private individuals to persuade the majority of their fellows that the policy of pacifism is preferable to that of militarism. When and only when they have succeeded, it will become possible to change those militaristic national policies which make the outbreak of another war all but inevitable and which, by doing this, hold up the whole process of desirable change.

It may be objected that the majority of men and

women all over the world ardently desire peace and that therefore there is no need for private individuals to make propaganda in favour of peace. In reply to this I may quote a profoundly significant phrase from "The Imitation." "All men desire peace, but very few desire those things which make for peace." The truth is, of course, that one can never have something for nothing. The voters in every country desire peace. But hardly any of them are prepared to pay the price of peace. In the modern world the "things that make for peace" are disarmament, unilateral if necessary; renunciation of exclusive empires; abandonment of the policy of economic nationalism; determination in all circumstances to use the methods of non-violence; systematic training in such methods. How many of the so-called peace-lovers of the world love these indispensable conditions of peace? Few indeed. The business of private individuals is to persuade their fellows that the things that make for peace are not merely useful as means to certain political ends, but are also valuable as methods for training individuals in the supreme art of non-attachment.

Individuals can work either alone or in association with other like-minded individuals. The work of the solitary individual is mainly preliminary to the work of the individuals in association. The solitary individual can undertake one or both of two important tasks: the task of intellectual clarification; the task of dissemination. He can be a theorist, a sifter of ideas, a builder of systems; or he can be a propagandist either of his own or others' ideas. To put it crudely, he can be either a writer or a public speaker. Both these tasks are useful and even indispensable, but both, I repeat, are preliminary to the greater and more difficult task which must be accomplished by individuals in association. Their task is to act upon the ideas of the solitary writer or speaker, to make practical applications of what were merely theories, to construct here and now small working-models of the better society imagined by the prophets; to educate themselves here and now into specimens of those ideal individuals described by the founders of religions. Success in such a venture is doubly valuable. If the success is on a large scale, the existing social and economic order will have undergone a perceptible modification for the better. At the same time the demonstration that the new theories may be made to produce desirable results in practice will act as the best possible form of propaganda on their behalf. Most people find example more convincing than argument. The fact that a theory has actually worked is a better recommendation for its soundness than any amount of ingenious dialectic.

At almost every period and in almost every country private individuals have associated for the purpose of initiating desirable change and of working out for themselves a way of life superior to that of their contemporaries. In the preservation and development of civilization these groups of devoted individuals have played a very important part and are destined, I believe, to play a part no less important in the future. Let us briefly consider the lessons to be drawn from their history.

The first condition of success is that all the members of such associations should accept the same philosophy of life and should be whole-heartedly determined to take their full share in the work for whose accomplishment the association was founded. This condition was fulfilled, on many occasions and for considerable stretches of time, in the history of Christian and Buddhist monasticism. It was not fulfilled in the case of many of the political and religious communities founded in America during the nineteenth century. The experiment of New Harmony, for example, was foredoomed to failure, because the founder of the community, Robert Owen, made no attempt to exclude unsuitable collaborators. New Harmony was colonized by people of the most diverse opinions, a large proportion of whom were either failures, cranks or swindlers. Its life was consequently short and squalid; its conclusion ignominious. John Humphrey Noyes, on the other hand, was always careful to admit into his fold only those who had successfully undergone a long period of probation. That was one of the reasons why the Oneida Community prospered, materially and spiritually.

The next essential is that such associations should be founded for the pursuit of noble ends and in the name of a high ideal. The fact that a community demands considerable sacrifices from its members, imposes a strict discipline and exacts unremitting effort is not a disadvantage. On the contrary, if the goal is felt to be worth achieving, men and women are glad to make sacrifices. The Trappist Rule attracted the greatest number of postulants at the time when, under the abbacy of Dom Augustine de Lestrange, its observances had been made unprecedentedly strict. For those who accepted the

Christian cosmology, the practice of such austerities as were imposed by the Trappist Rule was logical enough. For those with a different conception of ultimate reality, it would make no sense whatever. La Trappe is not cited here as an example to be imitated, but merely to show that even unnecessary and supererogatory hardships may be cheerfully accepted for God's sake. And not for God's sake only. In the contemporary world every political cause, from Communism to Nazism, has attracted its army of devotees—men and women who are ready to accept poverty and discomfort, incessant labour and the risk of imprisonment and sometimes even death. By those who are convinced that their cause is good, suffering is not feared and avoided; it is even welcomed.

All over the world and at all times associations of devoted individuals have exhibited one common characteristic: property has been held in common and all members have been vowed to personal poverty. In some communities, Hindu, Buddhist and Christian, it has been the custom for members to beg their bread. Others have preferred to work for their living. Associations of devoted individuals command attention and admiration; and where the devoted individuals are attached to the cause of the locally accepted religion, admiration is tinged with superstitious awe. People give expression to their feelings of admiration and awe by making gifts of property and money. Most religious communities have begun poor and have ended with large endowments. Great wealth is incompatible with non-attachment and this is true, not only of individuals, but also (though the process of corruption is less rapid) of communities. Nothing fails like success. Successful religious orders have always tended to sink into complacency, bogged in the morass of their endowments. Luckily, however, there have always been adventurous spirits ready and able to start afresh with great enthusiasm and little money. In due course, they too achieve success, and the movement for reform has to start all over again.

All effective communities are founded upon the principle of unlimited liability. In small groups composed of members personally acquainted with one another, unlimited liability provides a liberal education in responsibility, loyalty and consideration. It was upon the principle of unlimited liability that Raiffeisen based his system of co-operative agricultural banking, a system which worked successfully even among a population so illiterate, so desperately poverty-stricken as that of the barren Westerwald district of Prussia in the later forties of last century.

Summed up in a couple of sentences, the economic conditions of effective community living would seem to be as follows. Groups must accept the principle of unlimited liability. Individual members should possess nothing and everything—nothing as individuals, everything as joint owners of communally held property and communally produced income. Property and income should not be so large as to become ends in themselves, nor so small that the entire energies of the community have to be directed to procuring tomorrow's dinner.

We come next to the problem of discipline. History shows that it is possible for associations of devoted individuals to survive under disciplinary systems as radically different from one another as those, respectively, of the Society of Jesus and of the Society of Friends. Loyola was a soldier, and the order he founded was organized on military principles. His famous letter on obedience is written in the spirit of what may be called the Higher Militarism. The General of the order is clothed not merely with the powers of a commander-in-chief in time of war; he is also to be regarded by his inferiors as one who stands in the place of God, and must be obeyed as such without reference to his personal qualities as a human being. "Theirs not to reason why; theirs but to do and die." This doctrine so dear to the ordinary mundane militarist, is reaffirmed by Loyola in the theological language of the Higher Militarism. "The sacrifice of the Intellect" is the third and highest grade of obedience, particularly pleasing to God. The inferior must not only submit his will to that of the superior; he must also submit his intellect and judgment, must think the superior's thoughts and not his own.

Between the Higher Militarism of Loyola and the complete democracy of a Quaker committee, in which resolutions are not even put to the vote but discussed until at last there emerges a general "sense of the meeting," lies the constitutional monarchy of Benedictine monasticism. Gregory the Great characterized the Benedictine Rule as "conspicuous for its discretion." He was right. Discretion is the outstanding characteristic of almost every one of St. Benedict's seventy chapters. The monk's time is discreetly divided between practical work and devotion; he is discreetly clothed and discreetly fed—not too well, but also not too ill. Life in the

[151]

monastery is ascetic, but discreetly so. Discretion is no less conspicuous in the chapters dealing with the functions of the abbot. The abbot is king of the monastery and in the last resort his authority is absolute. But before giving an order it is his duty, if the question at issue is an important one, to consult the whole community and hear what even its humblest member has to say. In matters of less moment, he is to confer with a cabinet of the older monks. Furthermore, his authority is not personal. He reigns; but his reign is a reign of law. His monks are subject to the Rule and to him only in so far as he represents and applies the Rule.

Communities governed on Jesuit principles, communities governed on Benedictine principles, communities governed on Quaker principles—all three types, as history has demonstrated, are capable of surviving. Our choice between the various types will be determined partly by the nature of the tasks to be performed, but mainly by the nature of our conception of what human individuals and societies ought to be. Certain tasks demand a technical and therefore highly centralized direction. But even in these cases technical centralization is generally compatible, as we have seen, with self-government in execution. Loyola's choice of the Higher Militarism was dictated partly by his own experience as a soldier and partly by the fact that, during his day, the Church was at war, both spiritually and physically, with Protestantism. To fight this war, an army was needed. Loyola set out to recruit and train that army. In modern times the conception of sect-war has given place to that of class-war. Hence the essentially military organization of the Fascist and Communist parties, bodies in certain respects curiously similar to the Ignatian order. Neither Fascists nor Communists accept as valid the old ideal of the non-attached individual. In the light of their philosophies of life, they are doubtless quite right in organizing themselves as they do. But Loyola accepted the ideal of non-attachment. In the light of his philosophy, he was unquestionably wrong in his adoption of the Higher Militarism. Non-attachment is valueless unless it is the non-attachment of a fully responsible individual. A corpse is not malignant or ambitious or lustful; but it is not for that reason a practiser of non-attachment. The Jesuit postulant is bidden in so many words to model his behaviour on that of a corpse. He is to allow himself to be moved and directed by his superior as though he were a cadaver or a walking stick. Such passive obedience is incompatible with genuine non-attachment. If we believe in the value of non-attachment, we must avoid the Higher Militarism and devise some system of organization that shall be, not only efficient, but in the widest sense of the word educative. The constitutional monarchy of Benedictinism is more educative than Loyola's totalitarianism. Where the members of the community have already achieved a certain measure of responsibility, Quaker democracy is probably better than Benedictinism.

At all times and in all places communities have been formed for the purpose of making it possible for their members to live more nearly in accord with the currently accepted religious ideals than could be done "in the world." Such communities have always devoted a considerable proportion of their time and energy to study, to the performance of ceremonial acts of devotion and, in some cases at any rate, to the practice of "spiritual exercises." The nature and purpose of "spiritual exercises" will be discussed at length in the chapter on "Religious Practices." All that need be said here is that the best spiritual exercises provide a method by which the will may be strengthened and directed, and the consciousness heightened and enlarged. The Benedictine Rule prescribed no systematic course of spiritual exercises. Loyola's exercises were extremely effective in strengthening and directing the will, but tended to prevent the consciousness from rising to the highest level of mystical contemplation. The Quakers had stumbled upon a method which, when properly used, not only strengthened the will, but also heightened consciousness. Unfortunately, it often happened that the method was not used properly. Individual Christian mystics, like St. John of the Cross and the author of "The Cloud of Unknowing," have fully understood the psychological nature and the spiritual and educational value of the right kind of spiritual exercises. A similar understanding is to be found in the East, where Hindu and Buddhist communities make systematic use of spiritual exercises as a means to spiritual insight into ultimate reality and for the purpose of purifying, directing and strengthening the will.

Many communities have been content to seek salvation only for their own members and have considered that they did enough for the "world" by praying for it and providing it with the example of piety and purposeful living. Most Hindu and many Buddhist communities belong to this type. In some countries, Buddhist monks conceive it their duty to teach and schools are attached to the monasteries. In the West the majority of Christian communities have always regarded the performance of some kind of practical work as an indispensable part of their functions. Under the Benedictine Rule, monks were expected to spend about three hours at their devotions, and about seven at work. Cluny gave more time to devotion and less to work. But the Cistercian reform was a return to the letter of the Benedictine Rule. Much has been written on the civilizing influence of the monasteries in their practical, non-religious capacity. The early Benedictines revived agricultural life after the collapse of the Roman Empire —re-colonized the land that had been deserted, reintroduced industrial techniques in places where they had been almost lost. Seven hundred years later, the Cistercians were responsible for another great agricultural revival. Under their influence, swamps were drained and brought under the plough; the breeds of horses and cattle were greatly improved. In England they devoted themselves especially to sheep and were responsible for that great trade in wool which was one of the main sources of English prosperity during the Middle Ages. For many centuries education and the dissemination of knowledge through written books was mainly in the hands of the Benedictines. Poor relief and medical aid were also supplied by the monasteries and in most countries, almost up to the present day, there were no nurses except those who had been trained in a community of nuns. During the last two centuries most of the non-religious work performed by the religious communities has come to be done either by the state or by secular organizations in the way of ordinary business. Up till that time, however, neither the central authority nor the private business man was willing or able to undertake these jobs. We may risk a generalization and say that at any given moment of history, it is the function of associations of devoted individuals to undertake tasks which clear-sighted people perceive to be necessary, but which nobody else is willing to perform.

In the light of this brief account of the salient characteristics of past communities we can see what future communities ought to be and do. We see that they should be composed of carefully selected individuals, united in a common belief and by fidelity to a shared ideal. We see that property and income should be held in common and that every member should assume unlimited liability for all other members. We see that disciplinary arrangements may be of various kinds, but that the most educative form of organization is the democratic. We see that it is advisable for communities to undertake practical work in addition to study, devotion and spiritual exercises, and that this practical work should be of a kind which other social agencies, public or private, are either unable or unwilling to perform.

Religious and philosophical beliefs and the methods by which the will can be trained and the mind enlightened will be dealt with in later chapters. Here I am concerned with the question of practical, mundane work.

INDIVIDUAL WORK FOR REFORM

All of us desire a better state of society. But society cannot become better before two great tasks are performed. Unless peace can be firmly established and the prevailing obsession with money and power profoundly modified, there is no hope of any desirable change being made. Governments are not willing to undertake these tasks; indeed, in many countries they actively persecute those who even express the opinion that such tasks are worth performing. Private individuals are not prepared to undertake them in the ordinary way of business. If the work is to be done at all—and it is clear that, unless it is done, the state of the world is likely to become progressively worse—it must be done by associations of devoted individuals. To tend the sick, to relieve the poor, to teach without charge—these are all intrinsically excellent tasks. But for associations of devoted individuals to perform such tasks is now a work of supererogation and, in a certain sense, an anachronism. It was right that they should undertake them when nobody else was prepared to do so. If they undertake them now, when such tasks are being performed, very efficiently, by other agencies, they are wasting the energy of their devotion. They should use this energy to do what nobody else will do, to break the new ground that nobody else will break.

The function of the well-intentioned individual, acting in isolation, is to formulate or disseminate theoretical truths. The function of well-intentioned individuals in association is to live in accordance with those truths, to demonstrate what happens when theory is translated into practice, to create small-scale working models of the better form of society to which the speculative idealist looks forward. Let us consider the sort of things that would have to be done by associations of individuals devoted to the tasks of establishing peace and a new form of economic and social organization, in which the present obsession with money and power should not be given the opportunity of coming into existence. The two tasks are, of course, closely related. Both capitalism and nationalism are fruits of the obsession with power, success, position. Economic competition and social domination are fundamentally militaristic. Within a society the various classes have their private imperialisms, just as the society as a whole has its own, essentially similar, public imperialism. And so on. Any association which tried to create a working model of a society unobsessed by the lust for power and success would at the same time be creating a working model of a society living in peace and having no reasons for going to war. For the sake of convenience, I shall deal separately with the pacifistic and economic activities of our hypothetical association. In reality, however, the two classes of activity are closely related and complementary.

"All men desire peace, but very few desire those things that make for peace." The thing that makes for peace above all others is the systematic practice in all human relationships, of non-violence. For full and recent discussions of the subject the reader is referred to Richard Gregg's book, "The Power of Non-Violence," and to works by Barthélemy de Ligt, notably *"Pour Vaincre sans Violence"* and *"La Paix Créatrice."* In the paragraphs that follow I have tried to give a brief, but tolerably complete summary of the argument in favour of non-violence.

The inefficiency of violence has been discussed in an earlier chapter; but the subject is such an important one that I make no apology for repeating the substance of what was said in that place.

If violence is answered by violence, the result is a physical struggle. Now, a physical struggle inevitably arouses in the minds of those directly and even indirectly concerned in it emotions of hatred, fear, rage and resentment. In the heat of conflict all scruples are thrown to the winds, all the habits of forbearance and humaneness, slowly and laboriously formed during generations of civilized living, are forgotten. Nothing matters any more except victory. And when at last victory comes to one or other of the parties, this final outcome of physical struggle bears no necessary relation to the rights and wrongs of the case; nor, in most cases, does it provide any lasting settlement to the dispute.

The cases in which victory in war provides a more or less lasting settlement may be classified as follows. (1) Victory results in a final settlement when the vanquished are completely or very nearly exterminated. This happened to the Red Men in North America and to the Protestant heretics in sixteenth-century Spain. That "the blood of the martyrs is the seed of the church" is true only when a good many people survive martyrdom. If the number of martyrs is equal to the total number of the faithful (as it was in the case of the Japanese Christians during the seventeenth century), then no church will spring from their blood and the dispute between orthodox and heretic will have been settled once and for all. Modern wars are generally waged between densely populated countries. In such cases extermination is unlikely. One war tends therefore to beget another.

(2) Where the fighting forces are so small that the mass of the rival populations is left physically unharmed and psychologically unembittered by the conflict, the victory of one or other army may result in a permanent settlement. Today entire populations are liable to be involved in their country's battles. The relatively harmless wars waged according to an elaborate code of rules by small professional armies are things of the past.

(3) Victory may lead to a permanent peace, where the victors settle down among the vanquished as a ruling minority and are, in due course, absorbed by them. This does not apply to contemporary wars.

(4) Finally, victory may be followed by an act of reparation on the part of the victors. Reparation will disarm the resentment of the vanquished and lead to a permanent settlement. This was the policy pursued by the English after the Boer War. Such a policy is essentially an application of the principles of non-violence. The longer and more savage the conflict, the more difficult is it to make an act of reparation after victory. It was relatively easy for Campbell Bannerman to be just after the Boer War; for the makers of the Versailles Treaty, magnanimity was psychologically all but impossible. In view of this obvious fact, common sense demands that the principles of non-violence should be applied, not after a war, when their application is supremely difficult, but before physical conflict has broken out and as a sub-

stitute for such a conflict. Non-violence is the practical consequence that follows from belief in the fundamental unity of all being. But, quite apart from the validity of its philosophical basis (which I shall discuss in a later chapter), non-violence can prove its value pragmatically —by working. That it can work in private life we have all had occasion to observe and experience. We have all seen how anger feeds upon answering anger, but is disarmed by gentleness and patience. We have all known what it is to have our meannesses shamed by somebody else's magnanimity into an equal magnanimity; what it is to have our dislikes melted away by an act of considerateness; what it is to have our coldnesses and harshnesses transformed into solicitude by the example of another's unselfishness. The use of violence is accompanied by anger, hatred and fear, or by exultant malice and conscious cruelty. Those who would use non-violence must practise self-control, must learn moral as well as physical courage, must pit against anger and malice a steady good will and a patient determination to understand and to sympathize. Violence makes men worse; non-violence makes them better. In the casual relations of social life the principles of non-violence are systematized, crudely, no doubt, and imperfectly, by the code of good manners. The precepts of religion and morality represent the systematization of the same principles in regard to personal relations more complex and more passionate than those of the drawing-room and the street.

Men of exceptional moral force and even ordinary people, when strengthened by intense conviction, have demonstrated over and over again in the course of history the power of non-violence to overcome evil, to turn aside anger and hatred. The hagiographies of every religion are full of accounts of such exploits and similar stories can be found in the records of modern missionaries and colonial administrators, of passive resisters and conscientious objectors. Such sporadic manifestations of non-violence might be put down as exceptional and of no historical importance. To those who raise such an objection we would point out that, in the course of the last century and a half, the principles of non-violence have been applied, ever more systematically and with a growing realization of their practical value, to the solution of social and medical problems regarded before that time as completely insoluble. It was only in the eighteenth and nineteenth centuries that it began to be realized that such problems—the problem of the insane, the problem of the criminal, the problem of the "savage"—were insoluble only because violence had made them so. Thus, the cruel treatment of the insane resulted in their disease being aggravated and becoming incurable. It was not until 1792 that Pinel struck the chains from the unhappy inmates of the Salpêtriere. In 1815 a committee of the House of Commons investigated the state of Bethlehem Hospital and found it appalling. Bedlam was a place of filth and squalor, with dungeons, chains and torture chambers. As late as 1840 the great majority of asylums in Western Europe were still prisons and their inmates were still being treated as though they were criminals. Towards the middle of the century a considerable effort at reform was made and, since then, doctors have come to rely in their treatment more and more upon kindness and intelligent sympathy, less and less upon harshness and constraint. For a full and very vivid account of life in a well-run modern hospital for the insane, W. B. Seabrook's "Asylum" may be recommended. Compare this testimony with the description of life in the Salpêtrière before Pinel's day or in unreformed Bedlam. The difference is the difference between organized violence and organized non-violence.

The story of prison reform is essentially similar to that of the reform of asylums. When John Howard began his investigations in the middle of the seventies of the eighteenth century the only decent prisons in Europe were those of Amsterdam. (Significantly enough, there was much less crime in Holland than in other countries.) Prisons were houses of torture in which the innocent were demoralized and the criminal became more criminal. In spite of Howard, no serious attempts were made even in England to reform the monstrous system until well into the nineteenth century. Thanks to the labours of Elizabeth Fry and the Prison Discipline Society (yet another example of the good work that can be done by associations of devoted individuals) the English Parliament was at last induced to pass two acts in 1823 and 1824, acts which enunciated the principle of a new and better system. It is unnecessary to describe the further course of reform. Suffice it to say that in all democratic countries, at least, the movement has been in the direction of greater humaneness. There has been general agreement among all those best qualified to speak that if criminals are to be reformed or even prevented from becoming worse, organized violence must give place to organized and intelligent non-violence. This humanitarian movement has always been opposed by those who say that "criminals should not be pampered." The motives of such opposition always turn out upon investigation to be thoroughly discreditable. People need scapegoats on whom to load their own offences and in comparison to whom they may seem to themselves entirely virtuous; furthermore, they derive a certain pleasure from the thought of the suffering of others. Still, in spite of much concealed sadism and much openly displayed self-righteousness, the humanitarian movement has gone steadily forward. Only in the dictatorial countries has it received a check. Here, the idea of reformation has been abandoned and the old notion of retaliatory punishment has been revived. This is a significant symptom of that regression from charity which is characteristic of so much contemporary activity.

Like the alienist and the gaoler, the colonial administrator and the anthropologist have discovered that organized and intelligent non-violence is the best, the most practical policy. For some time the Dutch and the English, like the Romans before them, have known that it was wise, wherever possible, to "leave the natives alone." During the last thirty years professional anthropologists have left the libraries in which their older colleagues fitted together their mosaics of travellers' tales and missionary gossip, and have actually taken to living with the objects of their study. In order to be able to do this with safety, they have found it essential to apply the principles of non-violence with a truly Tolstoyan thoroughness. In consequence, they have won the friendship of their "savages" and have learned incomparably more about their ways of thinking and feeling than had ever been discovered before. During recent years, the administration of the Belgian, Dutch, English and French colonies has become on the whole more humane and, at the same time, more efficient. This double improvement is mainly due to the anthropologists, with their doctrine of intelligent and sympathetic non-violence. The hideous methods employed in the conquest of Abyssinia are unhappily symptomatic of the new, worse spirit that is now abroad.

So much for the power of non-violence in the relations of individuals with individuals. We have now to consider mass movements in which the principles of non-violence are applied to the relations between large groups or entire populations and their governments. Before citing examples of these it will be as well to reconsider briefly a matter already touched upon in an earlier chapter, namely, the results which follow attempts to carry through intrinsically desirable social changes by violent methods. History seems to demonstrate very clearly that, when revolution is accompanied by more than a very little violence, it achieves, not the desirable results anticipated by its makers, but some or all of the thoroughly undesirable results that flow from the use of violence. During the French Revolution, for example, the transfer of power to the Third Estate was accomplished by the regularly elected National Assembly. The Terror was the fruit of sordid quarrels for power among the revolutionaries themselves and its results were the extinction of the republic and the rise, first, of the Directory, then of Napoleon's military dictatorship. Under Napoleon a revolutionary fervour that found its natural expression in acts of violence was easily transformed into military fervour. French imperialism resulted in the intensification of nationalistic feelings throughout Europe, in the almost universal imposition of military slavery, or conscription, and in the systematization of economic rivalry between national groups. It would be interesting to construct a historical "Uchronia" (to use Renouvier's useful word), based upon the postulate that Robespierre and the other Jacobin leaders were convinced pacifists. The "non-Euclidean" history deducible from this first principle would be a history, I suspect, innocent of Napoleon, of Bismarck, of British imperialism and the scramble for Africa, of the World War, of militant Communism and Fascism, of Hitler and universal rearmament. What follows is an Uchronian account of very recent history as it might have been if the Spanish Republic had been pacifist. "Even though we know well that pacifism was as impossible to the working-class psychology of 1931 Spain as to that of the United States in 1917, it is important to point out that, if the Spanish Republic had actually been pacifist in theory and practice, the present counter-revolution could never have arisen. A pacifist republic would of course have immediately liberated the conquered Moors and transformed them into friends; it would have dismissed the old régime generals and returned their armies to civil life. It would have done

[166]

away with the fears of Church and peasants by requiring from Communists and Anarcho-Syndicalists the renunciation of violence during the period of the Popular Front." (From "What About Spain?" by Jessie Wallace Hughan, Ph.D., War Resisters League, New York.)

Returning from Uchronic speculations to a consideration of actuality, we find that in Russia the original aim of the revolutionaries was the creation of a society enjoying the maximum possible amount of self-government in every field of activity. Unfortunately, the rulers of the country have persisted in making use of the violent methods inherited from the old Tsarist régime. With what results? Russia is now a highly centralized military and economic dictatorship. Its government is oligarchical and makes use of secret police methods, conscription, press censorship, and intensive propaganda or *bourrage de crâne*, for the purpose of keeping the people in unquestioning subjection.

By way of contrast, let us now consider a few examples of non-violent revolution. Of these, the movements best known to English-speaking readers are those organized by Gandhi in South Africa and later in India. The South African movement may be described as completely successful. The discriminatory legislation against the Hindus was repealed in 1914, entirely as the result of non-violent resistance and non-co-operation on the part of the Indian population. In India several important successes were recorded and it was shown that very large groups of men and women could be trained to respond to the most brutal treatment with a quiet courage and equanimity that profoundly impressed their per-

[167]

secutors, the spectators in the immediate vicinity and, through the press, the public opinion of the entire world. The task of effectively training very large numbers in a very short time proved, however, too great and, rather than see his movement degenerate into civil war (in which the British, being better armed, would inevitably have won a complete victory) Gandhi suspended the activities of his non-violent army.

Among other non-violent movements crowned by partial or complete success we may mention the following. From 1901 to 1905 the Finns conducted a campaign of non-violent resistance to Russian oppression; this was completely successful and in 1905 the law imposing conscription on the Finns was repealed. The long campaign of non-violent resistance and non-co-operation conducted by the Hungarians under Deák was crowned with complete success in 1867. (It is significant that the name of Kossuth, the leader of the violent Hungarian revolution of 1848 was and still is far better known than that of Deák. Kossuth was an ambitious, power-loving militarist, who completely failed to liberate his country. Deák refused political power and personal distinction, was unshakably a pacifist and without shedding blood compelled the Austrian government to restore the Hungarian constitution. Such is our partiality for ambition and militarism that we all remember Kossuth, in spite of the complete failure of his policy, while few of us have ever heard of Deák, in spite of the fact that he was completely successful.) In Germany two campaigns of non-violent resistance were successfully carried out against Bismarck—the Kulturkampf by the Catholics and the working class campaign, after 1871, for the recognition of the Social-Democratic Party. More recently non-violent resistance and non-co-operation were successfully used in modern Egypt against British domination.

A special form of non-co-operation is the boycott, which has been used effectively on a number of occasions. For example, it was employed by the Persians to break the hated tobacco monopoly. The Chinese employed it against British goods, after the shooting of students by British troops. It was also used in India, by the followers of Gandhi. A striking example of the way in which even a threat of non-violent non-co-operation can avert war was provided by the British Labour Movement in 1920. The Council of Action formed on August 9th of that year warned the government that if it persisted in its scheme of sending British troops to Poland for an attack upon the Russians, a general strike would be called, labour would refuse to transport munitions or men, and a complete boycott of the war would be declared. Faced by this ultimatum, the Lloyd George government abandoned its plans for levying war on Russia. (This episode proves two things: first, that if enough people so desire and have sufficient determination, they can prevent the government of their country from going to war; second, that this condition is fulfilled only in rare and exceptional circumstances. In most cases the great majority of a country's inhabitants do not, when the moment comes, desire to prevent their government from going to war. They are swept off their feet by the flood of nationalistic sentiment which is always released in a moment of crisis and which a skilful government knows how to augment and direct by means of its instruments of propaganda. Once more we see that the machinery for stopping war is present, but that the will to use that machinery is generally lacking. To create and reinforce that will, first in themselves and then in others, is the task of devoted individuals associated for the purpose of establishing peace.)

I have given examples of the use of non-violence in the relations of individuals with individuals and of whole populations with governments. It is now time to consider the use of non-violence in the relations of governments with other governments. Examples of non-violence on the governmental level are seldom of a very heroic kind and the motives actuating the parties concerned are seldom unmixed. The tradition of politics is a thoroughly dishonourable tradition. The world sanctions two systems of morality—one for private individuals, another for national and other groups. Men who, in private life, are consistently honest, humane and considerate, believe that when they are acting as the representatives of a group, they are justified in doing things which, as individuals, they know to be utterly disgraceful. The nation, as we have seen, is personified in our imaginations as a being superhuman in power and glory, sub-human in morality. We never even expect it to behave in any but the most discreditable way. This being so, we must not be surprised if examples of genuine non-violent behaviour between governments are rare, except in the case of disputes involving matters so unimportant that the sub-human disputants don't feel it worth their while to fight. These can generally be settled easily enough by means of the existing machinery of conciliation. But wherever more important issues are at stake, national egotism is allowed free rein and the machinery of conciliation is either not used at all or used only reluctantly and with manifest bad will. In recent European history it is possible to find only one example of the completely non-violent settlement of a major dispute between two governments. In 1814 the Treaty of Kiel provided that Norway should be handed over to the kingdom of Sweden. Bernadotte invaded the country; but after a fortnight, during which no serious conflict took place, opened negotiations. The union of the two countries was agreed upon, being achieved, in the words of the preamble to the Act of Union, "not by force or arms, but by free conviction." Ninety years later the union was dissolved. By an overwhelming majority, the Norwegians decided to become independent. The Swedes accepted that decision. No violence was used on either side. The relations between the two countries have remained cordial ever since.

This has been a long digression, but a necessary one. Non-violence is so often regarded as impractical, or at best a method which only exceptional men and women can use, that it is essential to show, first, that even when used sporadically and unsystematically (as has been the case up till now), the method actually works, and, second, that it can be used by quite ordinary people and even, on occasion, by those morally sub-human beings, kings, politicians, diplomats and the other representatives of national groups, considered in their professional capacity. (Out of business hours these morally sub-human beings may live up to the most exacting ethical standards.)

Modern associations of devoted individuals will have as one of their principal functions the systematic cultivation of non-violent behaviour in all the common relationships of life—in personal relationships, in economic relationships, in relationships of groups with other groups and of groups with governments. The means by which communities can secure non-violent behaviour as between their members are essentially those which must be applied by all reformers. The social structure of the community can be arranged in such a way that individuals shall not be tempted to seek power, to bully, to become rapacious; and at the same time a direct attack can be made upon the sources of the individual will—in other words, the individual can be taught, and taught to teach himself, how to repress his tendencies towards rapacity, bullying, power-seeking and the like. Further training will be needed in the repression not only of fear—a consummation successfully achieved by military training—but also in the repression of anger and hatred. The member of our hypothetical association must be able to meet violence without answering violence and without fear of complaint—and he must be able to meet it in this way, not only in moments of enthusiasm, but also when the blood is cold, when there is no emotional support from friends and sympathizers. Non-violent resistance to violent oppression is relatively easy in times of great emotional excitement; but it is very difficult at other times. It is so difficult as to be practically

[172]

impossible except for those who have undergone systematic training for that very purpose. It takes three to four years of training to make a good soldier. It probably takes at least as long to make a good non-violent resister, capable of putting his principles into practice in any circumstances, however horrible. The question of group training has been fully discussed by Richard Gregg in his "Power of Non-Violence," and it is therefore unnecessary for me to repeat the discussion in this place. The psychological techniques for affecting the sources of the individual will—techniques developed by the devotees of every religion—are dealt with in a later chapter.

Trained individuals would perform two main functions. First, it would be their business to keep the life of the association at a higher level than the life of the surrounding society and in this way to hold up to that society a working model of a superior type of social organization. Second, they would have to "go out into the world," where their trained capacities would be useful in allaying violence once it had broken out and in organizing non-violent resistance to domestic oppression and the preparation for and waging of international war.

Groups of individuals pledged to take no part in any future war already exist (e.g. The War Resisters International, The Peace Pledge Union); but their organization is too loose and their membership too large and too widely scattered for them to be considered as associations, in the sense in which I have been using the word above. None the less they can and do render very important services to the cause for which all the reformers have always fought. They are propagandists, first of all. In private conversations, in speeches at public meetings, in pamphlets and newspaper articles, their members preach the gospel of non-violence, thus continuing and extending into non-sectarian fields the admirable work performed by the Society of Friends and other purely religious organizations. The result is that in England, in Holland, in the Scandinavian countries, in America and to some extent in Belgium and France, the public at large is beginning to become aware, if only dimly and still theoretically, that there exists a morally better and more effective alternative to revolution, to war, to violence and brutality of every kind.

Groups of war resisters, when sufficiently large and, in the moment of crisis, sufficiently unanimous, can prevent their government from going to war. This was clearly shown in 1920, when the Council of Action compelled Lloyd George to call off his threatened attack on the Soviets. It is unfortunately quite clear that the official leaders of the various left-wing parties of the world are not likely, in the immediate future, to call for similar passive resistance to any war which can be represented as "a war of defence," "a war to save democracy," "a war against Fascism," even a "war to end war." This means that, in the case of practically any war that is likely to break out in the near future, organized labour cannot be counted upon to work for peace. Without the aid of organized labour, war resisters have but the smallest chance of actually preventing their governments from waging a war. Nevertheless they can certainly do something to make the process morally and perhaps even physically more difficult than it would otherwise be. Peace can be secured and maintained only by the simultaneous adoption in many different fields of long-term policies, carefully designed with this end in view. Meanwhile, however, there is one short-term policy which every individual can adopt—the policy of war resistance.

People of "advanced views" often question this conclusion. The causes of war, they argue, are predominantly economic; these causes cannot be removed except by a change in the existing economic system; therefore a policy of war resistance by individuals is futile.

Those who use such arguments belong to two main classes: currency reformers and socialists.

Currency reformers, such as Major Douglas and his followers, point to the defects in our monetary system and affirm that, if these defects were remedied, prosperity could be spread over the whole world and every possible cause of war eliminated. This is surely over-optimistic. Defects in the monetary system may intensify economic conflicts in general. But by no means all economic conflicts are conflicts between nations. Many of the bitterest economic conflicts are between rival groups within the same nation; but, because these rival groups feel a sentiment of national solidarity, their conflicts do not result in war. It is only when monetary systems are organized in the interest of particular nations or groups of nations that they become a potential cause of war. So long as nationalism exists, scientifically managed currencies may actually make for war rather than peace. "Once the controllers of national monetary systems begin to apply their power self-consciously, for the betterment of their people, we have monetary conflicts arising on strictly national lines, such as we see today in competitive depreciation and exchange control." (Kenneth Boulding in "Economic Causes of War.") The greater the conscious scientific control exercised by national authorities, the greater the international friction, at least until such time as all nations agree to adopt the same methods of control. (See the relevant passages in the chapter on "Planned Society.")

The present economic system is unjust and inefficient and it is urgently desirable, as the socialists insist, that it should be changed. But such change would not lead immediately and automatically to universal peace. "In so far as the socialization of a single nation creates truly national monopolies in the exports of that nation, so the power of the government increases and the national character of economic conflicts becomes intensified. Thus, the socialization of a single nation, even though the rulers of that nation be most peaceably minded, is likely to intensify the fears of other nations in proportion as the control of the socialist government over its country's economic life is increased. . . . Unless they are supported by a strong conscious peace sentiment, they (the socialist regimes of individual nations) may be turned to purposes of war just as effectively—and indeed probably more effectively—than capitalist societies." (*Op. cit.*)

It will thus be seen that individual war resisters acting alone or in association have a very important part to play in the immediate future. That changes in the present economic and monetary systems must be made is evident; and it is also clear that, in the long run, these changes will make for the establishment of the conditions of permanent peace. But meanwhile, so long as nationalistic sentiment persists, reforms of the economic and monetary system may temporarily increase international ill feeling and the probability of war. The function of associations of individual war resisters is to prevent, if possible, necessary and intrinsically desirable changes in the economic and monetary systems from resulting in international discord and war.

In some countries the missionaries of non-violence can still preach their gospel without interference. In most of the world, however, they can only labour, if at all, in secret. Men of good will have always had to combine the virtues of the serpent with those of the dove. This serpentine wisdom is more than ever necessary today, when the official resistance to men of good will is greater and better organized than at any previous period. Progress in technology and in the science and art of organization has made it possible for governments to bring their police to a pitch of efficiency undreamed of by Napoleon, Metternich and the other great virtuosi of secret-police rule in previous ages. Before the Risorgimento the Austrians governed Italy by means of gendarmes, spies and *agents provocateurs*. Garibaldi fought to rid his country of these disgusting parasites. Today, Mussolini has a secret police far superior to anything that the Austrians could boast of. It is the same in contemporary Russia. Stalin's police is like the Tsar's—like the Tsar's but, thanks to telephones, wireless, fast cars and the latest filing systems, a good deal smarter. The same is true of every other country. All over the world the police are able to act with a rapidity, a precision and a foresight never matched in the past.* Moreover, they are equipped with scientific weapons, such as the ordinary person cannot procure. Against forces thus armed and organized, violence and cunning are unavailing. The only methods by which a people can protect itself against the tyranny of rulers possessing a modern police force are the non-violent methods of massive non-co-operation and civil disobedience. Such methods are the only ones which give the people a chance of taking advantage of its numerical superiority to the ruling caste and to discount its manifest inferiority in armaments. For this reason it is enormously important that the principles of non-violence should be propagated rapidly and over the widest possible area. For it is only by means of well and widely organized movements of non-violence that the populations of the world can hope to avoid that enslavement to the state which in so many countries is already an accomplished fact and which the threat of war and the advance of technology are in process of accomplishing elsewhere. In the circumstance of our age, most movements of revolutionary violence are likely to be suppressed instantaneously; in cases where the revolutionaries are well equipped with modern arms, the movement will probably turn into a long and stub-

* Like all instruments, the modern police force can be used either well or ill. Police trained in non-violence could use modern methods to forestall outbreaks of violence, to prevent potential hostilities from developing, to promote co-operation. A non-violent police force could be made a complete substitute for an army.

bornly disputed civil war, as was the case in Spain. The chances that any change for the better will result from such a civil war are exceedingly small. Violence will merely produce the ordinary results of violence and the last state of the country will be worse than the first. This being so, non-violence presents the only hope of salvation. But, in order to resist the assaults of a numerous and efficient police, or, in the case of foreign invasion, of soldiers, non-violent movements will have to be well organized and widely spread. The regression from humanitarianism, characteristic of our age, will probably result in manifestations of non-violent resistance being treated with a severity more ruthless than that displayed by most governments in recent times. Such severity can only be answered by great numbers and great devotion. Confronted by huge masses determined not to co-operate and equally determined not to use violence, even the most ruthless dictatorship is non-plussed. Moreover, even the most ruthless dictatorship needs the support of public opinion, and no government which massacres or imprisons large numbers of systematically non-violent individuals can hope to retain such support. Once dictatorial rule has been established, the task of organizing non-violent resistance to tyranny or war becomes exceedingly difficult. The hope of the world lies in those countries where it is still possible for individuals to associate freely, express their opinions without constraint and, in general, have their being at least in partial independence of the state.

A more efficient police force is not the only obstacle which technological progress has put in the way of desirable change. I have said that even the most ruthless dictatorship needs the support of public opinion; unhappily, modern technology has put into the hands of the ruling minorities new instruments for influencing public opinion incomparably more efficient than anything possessed by the tyrants of the past. The press and the radio are already with us and within a few years television will doubtless be perfected. Seeing is believing to an even greater extent than hearing; and a government which is able to fill every home with subtly propagandist pictures as well as speech and print, will probably be able, within wide limits, to manufacture whatever kind of public opinion it needs. Missionaries for our hypothetical associations are likely to find in this synthetic public opinion an enemy even more difficult to overcome or circumvent than the secret police. Part of their work will have to be a work of education—the building up in individual minds of intellectual and emotional resistance to suggestion. (See the relevant passages in the chapter on Education.)

So much for the first task of our associations—the establishment of peace through the doing and teaching of those things which make for peace. Their other task is to cure themselves and the world of the prevailing obsession with money and power. Once more, direct approach to the sources of the individual will must be combined with the "preventive ethics" of a social arrangement that protects from the temptations of avarice and ambition. What should be the nature of this social arrangement? It will be best to begin with a consideration of what it should not be. Most of those who in

INDIVIDUAL WORK FOR REFORM

recent years have actually founded associations of devoted individuals have not even attempted to solve the economic problems of our time: they have simply run away from them. Appalled by the complexities of life in an age of technological advance, they have tried to go backwards. Their communities have been little Red Indian Reservations of economic primitives, fenced away from the vulgar world of affairs. But the problem of modern industry and finance cannot possibly be solved by setting up irrelevant little associations of handicraftsmen and amateur peasants, incapable in most cases of earning their livelihood and dependent for their bread and butter upon income derived from the hated world of machines. We cannot get rid of machinery, for the simple reason that in the process of getting rid of it we should be forced to get rid of that moiety of the human race whose existence on this planet is made possible only by the existence of machines. The machine age in Erewhon had evidently led to no startling increase of population; hence the relative ease with which the Erewhonians were able to return to the horse and handicraft civilization. In the real world, machinery has resulted in the trebling of the population of the industrial countries within a century and a half. A return to horses and handicrafts means a return, through starvation, revolution, massacre and disease, to the old level of population. Obviously, then, such a return is outside the sphere of practical politics. Those who preach such a return and, in their communities of devoted individuals, actually practise it, are merely shirking the real issues. Machine production cannot be abolished; it is here to stay. The question is whether it is to stay as an instrument of slavery or as a way to freedom. A similar question arises in regard to the wealth created by machine production. Is this wealth to be distributed in such a way as to secure the maximum of social injustice, or the minimum? Governments and private companies in the ordinary way of business are not specially concerned to discover the proper solutions of these problems. The task, therefore, devolves upon associations of devoted individuals.

We see then, that if such associations are to be useful in the modern world, they must go into business—and go into business in the most scientific, the most unprimitive way possible.

Now, in order to engage in any advanced form of industrial or agricultural production, considerable quantities of capital are required. The fact is unfortunate; but in existing circumstances it cannot be otherwise. Good intentions and personal devotion are not enough to save the world; if they were, the world would have been saved long before this—for the supply of saints has never failed. But the good are sometimes stupid and very often ill-informed. Few saints have also been scientists or organizers. Conversely, few scientists and organizers have been saints. If the world is to be saved, scientific methods must be combined with good intentions and devotion. By themselves, neither goodness nor intelligence are equal to the task of changing society and individuals for the better.

Where modern industrial and agricultural production are concerned, scientific method cannot be applied *in vacuo.* It must be applied to machines, to workmen, to an office organization. But machines must be bought and supplied with their motive power, workmen and administrators must be paid. Hence the need of capital. In the circumstances of modern life, associations of devoted individuals cannot do much good unless they command the means to make a considerable investment.

Having made its investment and embarked upon production, the association will have to work out, by practical experiment, the most satisfactory solutions of such problems as the following:—To find the best way of combining workers' self-government with technical efficiency—responsible freedom at the periphery with advanced scientific management at the centre.

To find the best way of varying the individual's labours so as to eliminate boredom and multiply educative contacts with other individuals, working in responsible self-governing groups.

To find the best way of disposing of the wealth created by machine production. (Some form of communal ownership of property and income seems, as we have seen, to be a necessary condition of successful living in an association of devoted individuals.)

To find the best way of investing superfluous wealth and to determine the proportion of such wealth that ought to be invested in capital goods.

To find the best way of using the gifts of individual workers and the best way of employing persons belonging to the various psychological types. (See the chapter on "Inequality.")

To find the best form of community life and the best way of using leisure.

To find the best form of education for children and of self-education for adults. (See the chapters on "Education" and "Religious Practices.")

To find the best form of communal government and the best way to use gifts of leadership without subjecting the individuals so gifted to the temptation of ambition or arousing in their minds the lust for power. (See the chapter on "Inequality.")

Devoted and intelligent individuals living in association and working systematically along such lines as these should be able quite quickly to build up a working model of a more satisfactory type of society.

XI

Inequality

THE world which a poor man inhabits is not the same as the world a rich man inhabits. If there is to be intelligent co-operation between all members of a society, there must be agreement as to the things upon which they are to work together. People who are forced by economic inequality to inhabit dissimilar universes will be unable to co-operate intelligently.

To obtain complete equality of income for all is probably impossible and perhaps even undesirable. But certain steps in the direction of equalization can and undoubtedly ought to be taken.

Even in capitalist countries the principle not only of the minimum but also of the maximum wage has already been admitted. Within the last thirty years it has generally been agreed that there are limits beyond which incomes and personal accumulations of capital ought not to go. In such countries as England, France and, more recently, the United States, fortunes are diminished at every death by anything from a tenth to three quarters. Between deaths, the tax collector regularly takes away from the rich anything from a quarter to three-fifths of their incomes. Now that the principle of the limitation of wealth has been implicitly accepted, even by the wealthy, there should be no great difficulty in imposing an absolute maximum.

At what figure should the maximum wage be fixed?

[185]

A judge of the London Bankruptcy Court, retiring after half a life-time of service, made an interesting statement recently on the relation between income and happiness. He had observed, he said, that increase of income tended to result in increase of personal satisfaction up to a limit of about £5000 a year. After that figure, satisfaction seemed generally to decline. (Non-attachment, we might add, becomes difficult or impossible for most people at a point considerably below this figure. "It is harder for a rich man . . ." The possession of considerable wealth causes men to identify themselves with what is less than self—does so as effectively as the possession of means so small that the individual suffers hunger and continual anxiety. Extreme poverty can also be a needle's eye.)

The problem of the maximum wage can also be approached from another angle. The question may be posed in this way: in existing circumstances, how much does an individual require in order to live in the highest state of physical and intellectual efficiency, of which his organism is capable? It has been calculated that, if he is to be properly nourished, housed and educated, if he is to have adequate holidays, adequate medical attention and adequate educative travel, he will need an income of about £600 or £700 a year, or its equivalent in cash or communally provided services. Where several people are living together in a family group, this sum can doubtless be reduced without reducing each individual's opportunities for self-development. At the present time, the great majority of human beings receive only a fraction of this optimum income.

The degree of economic inequality is not the same in

all countries. In England, for example, inequality is greater, even among employees of the state, than in France. The highest government servant in England are paid forty or fifty times as much as the lowest. In France, the head of the department receives only about twenty times as much as the typist. Strangely enough, the degree of economic inequality would seem to be greater in Soviet Russia than in many capitalist countries. Max Eastman cites figures which show that, whereas the managing director of an American mining firm receives about forty times as much as one of his miners, the corresponding person in Russia may be earning up to eighty times the wage of the lowest-paid worker.

What is the degree of economic inequality that should be allowed to exist in any community? Clearly, there can be no universally valid answer, at any rate in existing circumstances. In a society where the minimum wage is very small, it may be necessary to fix the rate of inequality at a higher level than in one where the majority of people are earning something more nearly approaching the optimum income. This may seem unjust and (since poor and rich inhabit different worlds) inexpedient. And, in effect, it is unjust and inexpedient. But the inexpediency of reducing all incomes to a level far below the optimum is probably greater than the inexpediency of keeping a few incomes at or above the optimum level. No society can make progress unless at least some of its members are in receipt of an income sufficient to ensure their fullest development. This means that, where minimum wages are low, as they are in even the richest of contemporary communities, it may

[187]

be necessary to allow the best paid individuals to draw an income twenty or even thirty times as great as that of the worst-paid. If ever it becomes possible to distribute the optimum income to all, the inequality rate may be greatly reduced. There is no reason, in such a society, why the highest incomes should be more than two or three times as great as the lowest.

The economic is not the only kind of inequality. There is also the more formidable, the less remediable inequality which exists between individuals of different psychological types. "The fool sees not the same tree that the wise man sees." The universes of two individuals may be profoundly dissimilar, even though they may be in receipt of equal incomes. Pitt is to Addington as London is to Paddington. Nature as well as nurture has set great gulfs between us. Some of these gulfs are unbridged and seemingly unbridgeable; across them there is no communication. For example, I simply cannot imagine what it feels like to be a genius at chess, a great mathematician, a composer, who does his thinking in terms of melodies and progressions of harmonies. Some people are so clear-sighted that they can see the moons of Jupiter without a telescope; in some the sense of smell is so keen that, after a little training, they can enumerate all the constituent elements in a perfume composed of fifteen to twenty separate substances; some people can detect minute variations of pitch, to which the majority of ears are deaf.

Many attempts have been made to produce a scientific classification of human types in terms of their physical and psychological characteristics. For example, there was the Hippocratic classification of men according to the predominance of one or other of the four humours; this theory dominated European medicine for upwards of two thousand years. Meanwhile the astrologers and palmists were using five-fold classification in terms of planetary types. We still speak of sanguine or mercurial temperaments, describe people as jovial, phlegmatic, melancholic, saturnine. Aristotle wrote a treatise on physiognomy in which he attempted a classification of individuals in terms of the supposed characteristics of the animals they resembled. This pseudo-zoological classification of human beings kept cropping up in physiognomical literature until the time of Lavater.

In recent years we have had a number of new classifications. Stockard, in his "Physical Basis of Personality," uses a two-fold classification in terms of "linear" and "lateral" types of human beings. Kretschmer uses a three-fold classification. So does Dr. William Sheldon, whose classification in terms of somatotonic, viscerotonic and cerebrotonic I shall use in the present chapter. It seems probable that, with the latest work in this field, we may be approaching a genuinely scientific description of human types. Meanwhile, let us not forget that many of the old systems of classification, though employing strange terms and an erroneous explanatory hypothesis, were based firmly upon the facts of observation and personal experience.

It is worth remarking that there have been fashions in temperaments just as there have been fashions in clothes and medicine, theology and the female figure.

For example, the men of the eighteenth century admired above all the phlegmatic temperament—the temperament of the man who is naturally cautious, thoughtful, not easily moved. Voltaire gave place to Rousseau; admiration for a certain sagacious coolness, to the cult of sentimentality for sentimentality's sake. Phlegm lost its old prestige and the sanguine temperament—hot passion and wet tears—rose to a position of fashionable preeminence, from which it was driven a generation later by the Byronic temperament, which is a mixture of sanguine and melancholy, a strange hybrid of inconsistencies, warm and moist allied with cold and dry. Meanwhile, at the Gothic height of the Romantic Movement, the Philosophic Radicals were doing their best to revive the prestige of phlegm; and a little later it was the choleric temperament, the temperament of the pushful, energetic man of business, that came into fashion. With muscular Christianity even religion becomes choleric and (in Sheldon's phrase) somatotonic.

In view of the fact that membership of one or other of the psycho-physiological species is hereditary and inalienable, the habit of exalting one temperament at the expense of all the rest is manifestly silly. All the temperaments exist and something can be made of each of them. People have a right to be phlegmatic, just as they have a right to be plump. In our intolerant ignorance we demand that all shall conform to a fashionable ideal and be, say, melancholy or thin. There are times (such is our folly), when we demand that they shall have psychological characteristics which are to a great extent inconsistent with the physiological peculiarities that are

[190]

in fashion at the moment. Thus, until a year or two since, we insisted that women should be simultaneously good mixers and as thin as rakes. But the born good mixer is a person of lateral type, plump and well covered. Fashion in this case demanded the conjunction of incompatibles.

All the systems of classification are agreed that no individual belongs exclusively to one type; to some extent all men and women are of mixed type. But the amount of mixing may be small or great. Where it is small, the individual approximates to the pure type and is separated by great gulfs of psychological incommensurability from those in whom the characteristics of some other type predominate. Thus, it is all but impossible for the melancholy man to enter the universe inhabited by the choleric. The person who, if he went mad, would be a manic-depressive, cannot comprehend the potential victim of schizophrenia. The rotund and jolly "lateral" type is worlds apart from the unexpansive, inward-turning "linear." The "viscerotonic" man simply can't imagine why the "cerebrotonic" shouldn't be a "good mixer," like himself. The one "has a warm heart"; his "reins move" his "bowels yearn." The other is "a highbrow" and "has no guts." (Rich treasures of physiological psychology lie buried in the language of the Old Testament and even in schoolboys' slang!)

At this point an example from my own personal experience may not be out of place. My own nature, as it happens, is on the whole phlegmatic, and, in consequence, I have the greatest difficulty in entering into the experiences of those whose emotions are easily and violently aroused. Before such works of art as *Werther*, for example, or *Women in Love*, or the *Prophetic Books* of William Blake I stand admiring, but bewildered. I don't know why people should be shaken by such tempests of emotion on provocations, to my mind, so slight. Reading through the Prophetic Books not long ago, I noticed that certain words, such as "howling," "cloud," "stormy," "shriek" occurred with extraordinary frequency. My curiosity was aroused; I made a pencil mark in the margin every time one of these words occurred. Adding up the score at the end of a morning's reading, I found that the average worked out to something like two howls and a tempest to every page of verse. The Prophetic Books are, of course, symbolical descriptions of psychological states. What must have been the mentality of a man for whom thunder, lightning, clouds and screams seemed the most appropriate figures of speech for describing his ordinary thoughts and feelings? For my own part, I simply cannot imagine. I observe the facts, I record them—but only from the outside, only as a field naturalist. What they mean in terms of actual experience, I don't even pretend to know. There is a gulf here, an absence of communication. Nevertheless, if I had known Blake, I should certainly have found that there was a common ground between us, that there were ways in which we could have established satisfactory human relations. If, for example, I had behaved towards him with courtesy and consideration, he would almost undoubtedly have behaved towards me in the same manner. If I had treated him honourably, the chances are that he would have treated me honourably. If I had displayed confidence in him, it is highly probable that he would sooner or later have displayed an equal confidence in me. The solution of the problem of natural (and, where it exists, of acquired) inequality is moral and practical. The gulfs which separate human beings of unlike temperaments and different degrees of ability do not extend over the entire field of the personality. The inhabitants of the highlands of Arizona are cut off from one another by the mile-deep abyss of the Grand Canyon. But if they follow the Colorado River down towards its mouth they find themselves at last in the plains at a point where the stream can be conveniently bridged. Something analogous is true in the psychological world. Human beings may be separated by differences of intellectual ability as wide and deep as the Grand Canyon, may peer at one another, uncomprehending, across great gulfs of temperamental dissimilarity. But it is always in their power to move away from the territories in which these divisions exist; it is always possible for them, if they so desire, to find in the common world of action, the site for a broad and substantial bridge connecting even the most completely incommensurable of psychological universes. It is the business of the large-scale reformer so to arrange the structure of society that no impediment shall be put in the way of bridge-building. It is the business of educators and religious teachers to persuade individual men and women that bridge-building is desirable and to teach them at the same time how to translate mere theory and platonic good resolutions into actual practice.

Impediments to bridge-building will be most numerous in communities where inequalities of income (and, along with them, inequalities of education) are very great and where the social pattern is hierarchical and authoritarian. They will be fewest in communities where the principle of self-government is most widely applied, where responsible group-life is most intense, and where inequalities of income and education are small. Feudalism, capitalism and military dictatorship (whether accompanied by public ownership of the means of production or not) are almost equally unfavourable to bridge-building. Under these regimes natural inequalities are emphasized and new artificial inequalities created *ex nihilo*. The most propitious environment for equality is constituted by a society where the means of production are owned co-operatively, where power is decentralized, and where the community is organized in a multiplicity of small, interrelated but, as far as may be, self-governing groups of mutually responsible men and women.

Equality in action—in other words, reciprocal good behaviour—is the only kind of equality that possesses a real existence. But this equality in action cannot be fully realized except where individuals of different types and professions are given opportunities for associating freely and frequently with one another. It is the job of the large-scale reformer to arrange the social structure in such a way that existing obstacles to free and frequent contact between individuals shall be removed and new opportunities for contact created. The change-over from an authoritarian to a co-operative pattern of society would effectively get rid of most of the arbitrary caste barriers which at present make it so hard for individuals to come together freely. At the same time opportunities for the making of new contacts could be created in a variety of ways. For example, it would be possible to extend to a wider circle the advantages of the simultaneously academic and technical system of education developed by Dr. A. E. Morgan at Antioch College, Ohio. (I shall return to this example in the chapter on Education.)

It is not only during the period of formal education that opportunities for new contacts can be made. By arranging for individuals to change over from one job to another, the large-scale reformer can greatly increase the number of personal relationships entered into during any given working life. Such changes of job are valuable, not only because they bring the individual into contact with new groups of his fellow men and women, but also because they alleviate the boredom induced by monotony and the sight of all too familiar surroundings. (Boredom, as we have already seen, is one of the reasons for the persistent popularity of war; any change, whether in the structure of society or in the structure of the individual personality, that tends to reduce boredom tends also to reduce the danger of war.)

I have given only two examples; but many other methods could doubtless be devised for multiplying valuable contacts and so transforming the life of every individual man and woman into an education in responsibility and equal co-operation.

There are no bridges across the Grand Canyon. Those who live on opposite sides of the abyss must go down to the plains in order to find a crossing-place. But between those who live on the same side, communication is easy. They can come and go without hindrance, can mingle freely with their fellows. In other words men and women of different types can establish contact with one another only in action, and only on condition of reciprocal good behaviour. Men and women of the same type are psychologically commensurable. Communication between them is, of course, facilitated by reciprocal good behaviour; but even when the behaviour is bad, even when they dislike and mistrust, they can understand one another. Cerebrotonics who have had the same sort of education can come together on the intellectual plane. Viscerotonics will mingle in the loud and expansive good fellowship which all of them enjoy. Somatotonics will appreciate each other's delight in muscular activity for its own sake. And there are also the smaller subdivisions. Mathematicians will associate with other mathematicians. The musician speaks a language which all other musicians understand. People with the same kind of eccentric sexual habits meet on the common ground of their particular aberration. (Thus, the freemasonry of homosexuality brings together men of the most diverse types, intraverted intellectuals and bargees, emotional viscerotonic people and people of somatotonic type, professional boxers and able-bodied seamen.) In a word, there will always be a tendency for birds of a feather to flock together. This is inevitable and right.

What is not right is that flocking should be exclusively between birds of a feather. It is essential that society should be so arranged that there are opportunities for people of different types to co-operate. This, of course, will not prevent people of the same type from forming groups of their own. For it is fortunately possible for a human being to be a member of many groups simultaneously. Thus, a man may have a family and various sets of friends; may be a member of a professional association, a friendly society, a golf club, a church, a scientific association. It is worth remarking in this context that, so far as the concrete facts of human experience are concerned, "Society" is a meaningless abstraction. A man has no direct experience of his relations with "Society"; he has experience only of his relations with limited groups of similar or dissimilar individuals. Social theory and practice have often gone astray, because they have started out from such abstractions as "Society" instead of the facts of concrete experience—relationships within groups and of groups with one another. It is a significant historical fact that political philosophies which make great play with such large, abstract words as "Society" have generally been philosophies intended to justify a tyranny, either military-capitalist-feudal, like the tyranny of Hegel's Prussia and Hitler's Third Reich, or military-state-socialist-bureaucratic, like that of Russia after the death of Lenin. If we want to realize the good ends proposed by the prophets, we shall do well to talk less about the claims of "Society" (which have always, as a matter of brute fact, been identified with the claims of a ruling oligarchy) and more about the rights and duties of small co-operating groups.

Some individuals have more general intelligence than others; some possess special abilities which others lack; certain men and women have a temperament which unfits them to be leaders or administrators; in others, on the contrary, the configuration of the "humours" is such that they are admirably well adapted to take the direction of a common enterprise. The problem is, first, to see that round and square pegs get into the holes that fit them and, second, to prevent the born leader, when he is where his abilities entitle him to be, from exploiting his position in undesirable ways.

In his book, *A Chacun sa Chance,* Hyacinthe Dubreuil has pointed out that, where small groups are engaged on a particular job of work for which they are jointly responsible and for which they are rewarded, not as individuals, but as a group, the choice of a leader and the assignment of particular tasks to each individual, seldom present any special difficulty. Every man is a very shrewd judge of the professional competence of those who are in the same line of business as himself. Every man knows what fair dealing and consideration are, and generally knows well enough which person, in the particular group in which he happens at the moment to be working, is most likely to be considerate and fair as well as efficient. In most of the situations of working life the exigencies of the job may be relied upon to induce men and women, who are working together in small, co-operating, responsible groups, to elect as group leader and organizer the person who is on the whole best fitted for the post.* Nor is there any great danger that such a group leader will be tempted or, if tempted, be able to exploit his position to the detriment of his fellows. The problem of what may be called small-scale leadership is not a difficult one, except in societies of hierarchical pattern. In such societies (and where industrial organization is concerned, even the democratic states are hierarchical and dictatorial), the little leader is constantly tempted to revenge himself on those below him for all the indignities he has received from his superiors. Chickens in a poultry yard have a well defined "pecking order." Hen A pecks hen B, who pecks C, who pecks D and so on. It is the same in human societies under the present dispensation. The tyrannical jack-in-office is to a great extent the product of tyranny in higher places. Big dictators breed little dictators, just as surely as big scorpions breed little scorpions, as big dung-beetles breed little dung-beetles. A society organized, not hierarchically, but on co-operative lines, and in which the principle of self-government is applied wherever possible, should be tolerably immune from the plague of small-scale tyranny.

Bad leadership is undesirable at any social level. At the top, it may produce, not merely local discomfort, but general disaster. The body politic is subject to two grave diseases in the head, madness and imbecility. When people like Sulla or Napoleon assume the func-

---

* Dubreuil's findings are confirmed by Mr. Peter Scott, who has had wide experience in organizing co-operative groups among the unemployed in South Wales. Such groups, he found, always tended to elect the best men as leaders.

tions of the social brain, the community which they direct succumbs to some form of insanity. Most commonly the disease is paranoia; all the contemporary dictatorships, for example, suffer acutely from delusions of grandeur and of persecution. The alternative to mad King Stork is, only too frequently, a hopelessly inactive and deficient King Log who infects the body politic with his own imbecility. Imbeciles rise to power either by hereditary right or, if the system of choice is elective, because they possess certain demagogic talents, or very often, because it suits certain powerful interests within the community to have an imbecile in office. Most modern societies have abolished the hereditary principle in politics; idiots can no longer rule a country by right of blood. In the world of finance and industry, however, the hereditary principle is still admitted; morons and drunkards may be company directors by divine right. In the world of politics, the chances of getting imbecile leaders under an elective system could be considerably reduced by applying to politicians a few of those tests for intellectual, physical and moral fitness which we apply to the candidates for almost every other kind of job. Imagine the outcry if hotel keepers were to engage servants without demanding a "character" from their previous employers; or if sea captains were chosen from homes for inebriates; or if railway companies entrusted their trains to locomotive engineers with arteriosclerosis and prostate trouble; or if civil servants were appointed and doctors allowed to practice without passing an examination! And yet, where the destinies of whole nations are at stake, we do not hesitate to entrust

the direction of affairs to men of notoriously bad character; to men sodden with alcohol; to men so old and
infirm that they can't do their work or even understand
what it is about; to men without ability or even education. In practically every other sphere of activity we have
accepted the principle that nobody may be admitted to
hold responsible positions unless he can pass an examination, show a clean bill of health and produce satisfactory testimonials as to his moral character; and even then
the office is given, in most cases, only on the condition
that its holder shall relinquish it as soon as he reaches
the threshold of old age. By applying these rudimentary
precautions to politicians, we should be able to filter out
of our public life a great deal of that self-satisfied stupidity, that authoritative senile incompetence, that
downright dishonesty, which at present contaminate it.

To guard against the man of active, paranoid ambition, the potential King Stork of a political or industrial
society, is more difficult than to guard against the half-
wit, the dodderer and the petty crook. Political and legal
checks to ambition, such as those contained in the American Constitution, are effective up to a certain point, but
only up to a certain point. Legal checks and balances are
merely institutionalized mistrust; and mistrust, however
elaborately and ingeniously translated into terms of law,
can never be an adequate foundation for social life. If
people do not wish to play the political or industrial
game according to the prescribed rules, no amount of
surveillance will keep them from taking unfair advantages whenever they offer. "Over the mountains," runs
the old song, "and under the graves": avarice and the

lust for power will "find out the way" even more surely than love. They will find out the way for just so long as people are brought up to regard ambition as a virtue and the accumulation of money as man's most important business. At present, we choose to organize our political and economic life and to educate our children in such a way that we must inevitably suffer, as time goes on, more and more severely and chronically from the organized paranoia of dictatorship. But even if reforms were carried out today their full effects would not be felt until those brought up under the present dispensation had either died or sunk into impotent old age. Meanwhile, it may be asked, are there any changes in social organization which would make it more difficult for ambitious men to impose their wills upon society?

An examination system would rid our business and our politics of imbeciles and the more simple-minded types of crook. It would do little to keep out the individual of consuming ambition, and nothing at all, when he had passed his tests, to educate him into a more desirable, less greedily Napoleonic frame of mind. Something more is needed than examinations. Mere social machinery cannot give us the whole of that something more; but as much of it as social machinery *can* give could probably be provided by some institution akin to that of the Chartered Accountants. A self-governing union of professional men, who have accepted certain rules, assumed certain responsibilities for one another, and can focus the whole force of their organized public opinion, in withering disapproval, upon any delinquent member of the society—such an organization is one of the most powerful educative social devices ever invented. Leadership will never be made expert and responsible until there is an institute of chartered business managers, another of chartered politicians and yet another of chartered administrators. (In England the higher civil service is almost a caste, having its own rules and standards, which it enforces by distributing that most gratifying form of praise, that most unbearable form of blame, the praise and blame of fellow professionals. To the fact that it approximates so nearly to an institute of chartered administrators it owes its efficiency and its remarkable freedom from corruption.)

Examinations and membership of a professional order would unquestionably do a great deal to raise the standard of political and economic leadership and to check the tendency of ambitious individuals to exceed due bounds. To extend the application of an old is always easier than to introduce a new and unfamiliar principle, and as the examination system is almost universally in use and the chartered professional organization widely known and respected, there should be no great difficulty in merely widening their field of applicability. Only in some such way as this can we minimize the social dangers inherent in the fact of individual inequality.

XII

Education

PROFESSIONAL educationists and, along with them, certain psychologists, have been inclined to exaggerate the efficacy of childhood training and the accidents of early life. The Jesuits used to boast that, if they were given the child at a sufficiently early age, they could answer for the man. Similarly the Freudians attribute all men's spiritual ills to their experience during early childhood. But the Jesuits trained up free thinkers and revolutionaries as well as docile believers. And many psychologists are turning away from the view that all neuroses are due to some crucial experience in infancy. "Treatment in accordance with the trauma theory is often," writes Jung, "extremely harmful to the patient, for he is forced to search in his memory—perhaps over a course of years—for a hypothetical event in his childhood, while things of immediate importance are grossly neglected." The truth is that a man is affected, not only by his past, but also by his present and what he foresees of the future. The conditioning process which takes place during childhood does not completely predetermine the behaviour of the man. To some extent, at any rate, he can be re-conditioned by the circumstances of his adolescent and adult life; to some extent his will is free, and, if he so chooses and knows the right way to set about it, he can re-condition himself. This re-conditioning may be in a desirable direction; it may equally well be in an undesirable one. For example, the conditioning which children now receive in nursery schoois is generally excellent. That which they receive in more advanced schools is generally bad. In spite of the Jesuits and Freud, the bad conditioning during adolescence effectively neutralizes the results of good conditioning during childhood. In his "Anatomy of Frustration," Mr. H. G. Wells makes his hero comment upon the distressing difference between "the charm, the alert intelligence, the fearless freedom of the modern child of six or seven and the slouching mental futility of the ordinary youth in his later teens." The first is the product of the nursery school; the second of the elementary and secondary, the preparatory and public school. We educate young children for freedom, intelligence, responsibility and voluntary co-operation; we educate older children for passive acceptance of tradition and for either dominance or subordination. This fact is symptomatic of the uncertainty of purpose which prevails in the Western democracies. The old patriarchal tradition coexists in our minds with a newer and quite incompatible hankering for freedom and democracy. In our enthusiasm for the second, we train up our young children to be free, self-governing individuals; having done which, we take fright and, remembering that our society is still hierarchical, still in great measure authoritarian, we devote all our energies to teaching them to be rulers on the one hand and, on the other, acquiescent subordinates.

Here, in passing, it may be remarked that "modern" schools may be too "modern" by half. There is a danger that children may be given more freedom than they can

[205]

profitably deal with, more responsibility than they desire or know how to take. To give children too much freedom and responsibility is to impose a strain which many of them find distressing and even exhausting. Exceptional cases apart, children like to have security, like to feel the support of a firm framework of moral laws and even of rules of polite conduct. Within such a firmly established framework there is plenty of room for a training in independence, responsibility and co-operation. The important thing is to avoid extremes—the extreme of too much liberty and responsibility on the one hand and, on the other, of too much restriction, above all too much restriction of the wrong sort. For the fixed framework may just as well be a bad code as a good one. Children may derive just as comforting a sense of security from the moral code, say, of militarism as from that of non-attachment. But the results of an upbringing within a framework of militaristic morality will be quite different from the results of an upbringing in the ethic of non-attachment.

Coming back to the world as we know it, we have to ask ourselves an important question. Even if we were to prolong the nursery-school type of training—training, that is to say, for self-government and responsible co-operation—if we were to continue it far into adolescence, would we, in the existing world, succeed in making any conspicuous change for the better in society or the individuals composing it? Practical life is the most efficient of all teachers. Take adolescents trained for self-government and co-operation and turn them loose into a hierarchical, competitive, success-worshipping society: what will happen? Will the effects of the conditioning received in school survive? Probably not. Most likely, there will be a period of bewilderment and distress; then, in the majority of cases, re-adjustment to the circumstances of life. Which shows, yet once more, that life is a whole and that desirable changes in one department will not produce the results anticipated from them, unless they are accompanied by desirable changes in all other departments.

In the preceding paragraph I have suggested that a good education is not that infallible cure of all our ills which some enthusiasts have supposed to be. Or rather that it can become such a cure only when it is associated with good conditions in other departments of life. As usual it is not a question of simple cause and effect, but of complex interrelationship, of action and reaction. Good education will be fully effective only when there are good social conditions and, among individuals, good beliefs and feelings; but social conditions, and the beliefs and feelings of individuals will not be altogether satisfactory until there is good education. The problem of reform is the problem of breaking out of a vicious circle and of building up a virtuous one in its place.

The time has now come when we must ask ourselves in what precisely a good education consists. In the first years and months of infancy education is mainly physiological; the child, to use the language of the kennel, is house-trained. In the past this seemed a trivial and unsavoury matter which it was at once unnecessary and indelicate to discuss. In the words of Uncle Toby

Shandy, one wiped it up and said no more about it. Modern psychologists have discovered that the subject is by no means a trivial one and that, for the infant at least, excretion and the process of house-training · are matters of the deepest concern. In this context I need mention only the work of the late Dr. Suttie, whose book, "The Origins of Love and Hatred," contains an interesting chapter on the effects of early house-training upon the emotional life of human beings. These effects, it would seem, are generally bad; and he gives reasons for supposing that our emotional life would be much more serene if our training in cleanliness had not started so early. Messy children are a nuisance; but if, by allowing them to make their messes, we can guarantee that they shall grow up into gentle, unquarrelsome adults, free from what Suttie calls our "taboo on tenderness," the nuisance will be very bearable.

So much for the physiological education of infancy. We now come to the moral and intellectual education of later childhood. The two are, of course, inseparable; but it will be convenient to consider them one at a time. Let us begin by asking in what a desirable moral education consists. Our aim, let us recall, is to train up human beings for freedom, for justice, for peace. How shall it be done? In his recent book, "Which Way to Peace?" Bertrand Russell has written a significant paragraph on this subject. "Schools," he says, "have very greatly improved during the present century, at any rate in the countries which have remained democratic. In the countries which have military dictatorships, including Russia, there has been a great retrogression during the last ten years, involving a revival of strict discipline, implicit obedience, a ridiculously subservient behaviour towards teachers and passive rather than active methods of acquiring knowledge. All this is rightly held by the governments concerned to be a method of producing a militaristic mentality, at once obedient and domineering, cowardly and brutal. . . . From the practice of the despots, we can see that they agree with the advocates of 'modern' education as regards the connection between discipline in schools and the love of war in later life."

Dr. Maria Montessori has developed the same theme in a recent pamphlet: "The child who has never learned to act alone, to direct his own actions, to govern his own will, grows into an adult who is easily led and must always lean upon others. The school child, being continually discouraged and scolded, ends by acquiring that mixture of distrust of his own powers and of fear, which is called shyness and which later, in the grown man, takes the form of discouragement and submissiveness, of incapacity to put up the slightest moral resistance. The obedience which is expected of a child both in the home and in the school—an obedience admitting neither of reason nor of justice—prepares the man to be docile to blind forces. The punishment, so common in schools, which consists in subjecting the culprit to public reprimand and is almost tantamount to the torture of the pillory, fills the soul with a crazy, unreasoning fear of public opinion, even an opinion manifestly unjust and false. In the midst of these adaptations and many others which set up a permanent inferiority complex,

is born the spirit of devotion—not to say of idolatry—
to the *condottieri*, the leaders." Dr. Montessori might
have added that the inferiority complex often finds expression in compensatory brutality and cruelty. The
traditional education is a training for life in a hierarchical, militaristic society, in which people are abjectly obedient to their superiors and inhuman to their
inferiors. Each slave "takes it out of" the slave below.

In the light of these two citations, we are able to
understand more clearly why history should have taken
the course it actually has taken in recent years. The intensification of militarism and nationalism, the rise of
dictatorships, the spread of authoritarian rule at the expense of democratic government—these are phenomena
which, like all other events in human history, have a
variety of interacting causes. Most conspicuous among
these, of course, are the economic and political causes.
But these do not stand alone. There are also educational
and psychological causes. Among these must be reckoned
the fact that, for the last sixty years, all children have
been subjected to the strict, authoritarian discipline of
state schools. In recent European history, such a thing
has never happened before. At certain periods, it is true,
and in certain classes of society, the discipline imposed
within the family was exceedingly strict. For example,
the seventeenth-century Puritan family was governed
almost as arbitrarily and as harshly as the family of the
Roman farmer or the Japanese Samurai. Samurai and
Roman had the same end in view—to train up children
in the military virtues, so that they should become good
soldiers. The Puritan had a religious end in view; he

was imitating Jehovah; he was breaking his children's will because St. Augustine and Calvin had taught him that that will was essentially evil. And yet, though the ends were different, the results of the Puritan's educational system were the same as those attained by the essentially similar system devised by the Roman and the Samurai for quite another end. His children became first-rate soldiers; and when they were not called upon to go to war, they exhibited their militaristic qualities in the field of commerce and industry, becoming (as Tawney and Weber have shown) the first and almost the most ruthless of the capitalists. The Puritans, I repeat, were strict disciplinarians within the family. But not all the population was composed of Puritans. When most children were brought up within the family, a great many experienced only kindness and consideration. In other cases spasmodic brutality alternated with spasmodic affection. In yet others, no doubt, parents would have liked to impose a strict Roman or Hebrew discipline, but were too lazy to do so systematically, so that the child came through almost unscathed. It is a highly significant fact that the members of the upper classes, who, as children had been under tutors or sent to school, were always the actively militaristic element in mediaeval and early modern society. The common people were seldom spontaneously bellicose. War and imperialistic brigandage were the preoccupation of their masters—men who had enjoyed the privilege, during boyhood, of being bullied by some sharp-tongued, hard-hitting pedagogue.

In the first half of the nineteenth century, secondary

education for the middle classes was enormously extended; in the second half, primary education was made universally compulsory. For the first time, *all* children were subjected to strict, systematic, unremitting discipline—the kind of discipline that "produces a militaristic mentality, at once obedient and domineering." The members of the middle and upper classes still undergo, in most countries, a longer period of education than do the poor. This is why the members of the middle and upper classes are still, on the whole, more bellicose than the members of the working class. (Such organizations as the Peace Pledge Union have more adherents among the poor than among the rich.) Even the poor, however, are now given several years of authoritarian discipline. The decline of democracy has coincided exactly with the rise to manhood and political power of the second generation of the compulsorily educated proletariat. This is no fortuitous coincidence. By 1920 all the Europeans who had escaped compulsory primary education were either dead or impotently old. The masses had gone through, first, six or seven years of drilling in school, then, in most countries, anything from one to three years of conscription, and finally the four years of the war. Enough military discipline to make them "at once obedient and domineering." The most actively domineering ones climbed to the top, the rest obeyed and were given, as a reward, the privilege of bullying those beneath them in the new political hierarchies.

The early educational reformers believed that universal primary and, if possible, secondary education would free the world from its chains and make it "safe for democracy." If it has not done so—if, on the contrary, it has merely prepared the world for dictatorship and universal war—the reason is extremely simple. You cannot reach a given historical objective by walking in the opposite direction. If your goal is liberty and democracy, then you must teach people the arts of being free and of governing themselves. If you teach them instead the arts of bullying and passive obedience, then you will not achieve the liberty and democracy at which you are aiming. Good ends cannot be achieved by inappropriate means. The truth is infinitely obvious. Nevertheless we refuse to act upon it. That is why we find ourselves in our present predicament.

The two types of education—education for freedom and responsibility, education for bullying and subordination—coexist in the democracies of the West, where nursery schools belong to the first and most other schools to the second type. In Fascist countries, not even nursery schools may belong to the first type. Significantly enough, the Montessori Society of Germany was dissolved by the political police in 1935; and, in July 1936 Mussolini's Minister of Education decreed the cessation of all official Montessori activities in Italy. In the days of Lenin, Russian education was based, at every stage, upon principles essentially similar to those enunciated by Dr. Montessori. In the manifestos and decrees published shortly after Lenin's seizure of power one may read such phrases as these. "Utilization of a system of marks for estimating the knowledge and conduct of the pupil is abolished. . . . Distribution of medals and insignia is abolished. . . . The old form of discipline which corrupts the entire life of the school and the untrammeled development of the personality of the child, cannot be maintained in the schools of labour. The progress of labour itself develops this internal discipline without which collective and rational work is unimaginable. . . . All punishment in school is forbidden. . . . All examinations are abolished. . . . The wearing of school uniform is abolished."

On September 4, 1935, a Decree on Academic Reform was issued by the Stalin Government.' This decree contained, among others, the following orders. "Instruct a commission . . . to elaborate a draft of a ruling for every type of school. The ruling must have a categoric and absolutely obligatory character for pupils as well as for teachers. This ruling must be the fundamental document . . . which strictly establishes the regime of studies and the basis for order in the school. . . . Underlying the ruling on the conduct of pupils is to be placed a strict and conscientious application of discipline. . . . In the personal record there will be entered for the entire duration of his studies the marks of the pupil for every quarter, his prizes and his punishments. . . . A special apparatus of Communist Youth organizers is to be installed for the surveillance of the pupil inside and outside of school. They are to watch over the morality and the state of mind of the pupils. . . . Establish a single form of dress for the pupils of the primary, semi-secondary and secondary schools, this uniform to be introduced, to begin with, in 1936 in the schools of Moscow."

This decree was followed by another, issued in February 1937, ordering that the existing organizations for giving military training to young children (from eight years old upwards) should be strengthened and extended. Such systems of infantile conscription already exist in the Fascist countries and, if the threat of war persists, will doubtless soon be imposed upon the democracies of the West.

Any change for the worse in educational methods means a change for the worse in the mentality of millions of human beings during their whole lifetime. Early conditioning, as I have pointed out, does not irrevocably and completely determine adult behaviour; but it does unquestionably make it difficult for individuals to think, feel and act otherwise than as they have been taught to do in childhood. Where social conditions are in harmony with the prevailing system of education, the task of getting outside the circle of early conditioning may be almost insuperably difficult. Stalin has made it practically certain that, for the next thirty or forty years, the prevailing Russian philosophy of life shall be essentially militaristic.

Discipline is not the only instrument of character training. One of the major psychological discoveries of modern times was the discovery that the play, not only of small children, but (even more significantly) of adolescents and adults could be turned to educational purposes. Partly by accident, partly by subtle and profound design, English educators of the second half of the nineteenth century evolved the idea of organizing sport for the purpose of training the character of their pupils. At Rugby, during Tom Brown's schooldays, there were no organized games. Dr. Arnold was too whole-heartedly a low-church social reformer, too serious-minded a student of Old Testament history, to pay much attention to a matter seemingly so trivial as his boys' amusements. A generation later, cricket and football was compulsory in every English Public School, and organized sport was being used more and more consciously as a means of shaping the character of the English gentleman.

Like every other instrument that man has invented, sport can be used either for good or for evil purposes. Used well, it can teach endurance and courage, a sense of fair play and a respect for rules, co-ordinated effort and the subordination of personal interests to those of the group. Used badly, it can encourage personal vanity and group vanity, greedy desire for victory and hatred for rivals, an intolerant *esprit de corps* and contempt for people who are beyond a certain arbitrarily selected pale. In either case sport inculcates responsible co-operation; but when it is used badly the co-operation is for undesirable ends and the result upon the individual character is an increase of attachment; when it is used well, the character is modified in the direction of non-attachment. Sport can be either a preparation for war or, in some measure, a substitute for war; a trainer either of potential war-mongers or of potential peace-lovers; an educative influence forming either militarists or men who will be ready and able to apply the principles of pacifism in every activity of life. It is for us to choose which part the organized amusements of children and adults shall play. In the dictatorial countries the choice has been made, consciously and without compromise.

Sport there is definitely a preparation for war—doubly a preparation. It is used, first of all, to prepare children for the term of military slavery which they will have to serve when they come of age—to train them in habits of endurance, courage and co-ordinated effort, and to cultivate that *esprit de corps*, that group-vanity and group-pride which are the very foundations of the character of a good soldier. In the second place, it is used as an instrument of nationalistic propaganda. Football matches with teams belonging to foreign countries are treated as matters of national prestige, victory is hailed as a triumph over an enemy, a sign of racial or national superiority; a defeat is put down to foul play and treated almost as a *casus belli*. Optimistic theorists count sport as a bond between nations. In the present state of nationalistic feeling it is only another cause of international misunderstanding. The battles waged on the football field and the race-track are merely preliminaries to, and even contributory causes of, more serious contests. In a world that has no common religion or philosophy of life, but where every national group practises its own private idolatry, international football matches and athletic contests can do almost nothing but harm.

The choice of the dictators has been, as I have said, definite and uncompromising. They have decided that sport shall be used above all as a preparation for war. In the democratic countries we are, as usual, of two minds. The idea of using sport solely as a preparation for war seems to us shocking; at the same time we cannot bring ourselves to use it, consciously or consistently, as an instrument for training active peace-lovers. To some extent we still use sport as a training for militarists. "The battle of Waterloo was won on the playing fields of Eton"; and it was on these and a score or two other school playgrounds that the Indian Empire was conquered and held down. The Amritsar massacre is a genuine, hall-marked product of the prefectorial system and compulsory cricket. "His captain's hand on his shoulder smote: 'Play up, and play the game.'" The game was played in that high-walled Jalianwallabagh to the tune of I forget how many hundreds of dead and wounded. But if India was conquered and is now held down on the playing fields of the English Public Schools, it is also administered there, and administered with a considerable degree of justice and incorruptibility. It is even in process (very gradually and reluctantly, it is true) of being liberated on those same fields. In the half-democracy of modern England, sport is not used solely as a preparation for war and the fostering of group-vanity and group-pride; it is also used for teaching boys to behave with genuine decency—in other words, as a training in non-attachment. In the world as it is at present we cannot afford to be of two minds. Either we must make use of sport (and in general the whole educational system) as a device for training up non-attached, non-militaristic men and women; or else, under the urgent threat of war, we must make up our minds to out-Prussianize the Nazis and, on the playing fields of Eton and the other schools, prepare for the winning of future Waterloos. The first alternative involves great risk, but may lead, not only the English, but the whole world beside, out of the valley of destruction in which the human race is now precariously living. The second alternative can lead only to the worsening of international relations and ultimately to general catastrophe. Unhappily, it is towards the second alternative that the rulers of England now seem to be inclining.

I have spoken hitherto as though there were only one type of sound education. But we have seen, in the chapter on Inequality, that human beings are of several different types. This being so, is it not a mistake to prescribe one system of character-training? Should there not be several systems? The answer to these questions is at once yes and no. It is not a mistake to prescribe only one system of character-training, because (to repeat the words used in an earlier chapter) it is always in men's power to move away from the territories in which psychological divisions exist, because it is always possible for them, if they so desire, to find in the common world of action the site for a broad, substantial bridge connecting even the most completely incommensurable of psychological universes. Character-training through self-government, through responsible co-operation, through the voluntarily accepted discipline of games, is something which goes on in that common world of action, in which alone it is possible for individuals of different psychological types to come together. To prescribe one fundamental technique of character-training is therefore no mistake. On the other hand it would obviously be foolish not to adapt the one fundamental technique to the different types of individual. To discuss the nature of these variations would take a long time and, since the matter is not one of fundamental importance,

I will proceed at once to a consideration of my next topic, which is education as instruction.

In most of the civilized countries of the West primary education has been universal and compulsory for sixty years and more. Secondary and higher education have also been made available—less freely in England than in America, in France and Italy than in Germany, but everywhere to very considerable numbers of young people and adults. When we compare the high hopes entertained by the early advocates of universal education with the results actually achieved after two generations of intensive and extensive teaching, we cannot fail to be somewhat discouraged. Millions of children have passed thousands of millions of hours under schoolroom discipline, reading the Bible, listening to pi-jaws—and the peoples of the world are preparing for mutual slaughter more busily and more scientifically than ever before; humanitarianism is visibly declining; the idolatrous worship of strong men is on the increase; international politics are conducted with a degree of brutal cynicism unknown since the days of Pope Alexander VI and Cesare Borgia. From moral we pass to intellectual education. The best that has been thought and said has been bawled by millions of pedagogues, millions of times, into millions of little ears—and the yellow press, the tabloids, the *grands journaux d'information* circulate by scores of millions every morning and evening of the year; each month the pulp magazines offer to millions of readers their quota of true confessions, film fun, spicy detective stories, hot mysteries; all day long in the movie palaces millions of feet of imbecile and morally squalid films are unrolled before a succession of audiences; from a thousand transmitting stations streams of music (mostly bad) and political propaganda (mostly false and malevolent) are poured out, for eighteen hours out of the twenty-four, into the contaminated ether. Instruments of marvellous ingenuity and power on the one hand; and, on the other, ways of using those instruments which are either idiotic, or criminal, or both together. Such are the moral and intellectual fruits of our system of education. It is time that something was done to change the nature of the tree that bears these fruits.

In earlier paragraphs I have indicated what must be done if we wish to breed up a race of non-attached, actively peace-loving men and women. We now have to consider the best methods for fostering intelligence and imparting knowledge.

At the present time education-as-instruction assumes one of two forms—academic (or liberal) education and technical education. Academic education is supposed to do two things for those who are subjected to it; it is supposed, first of all, to be a gymnastic, by means of which they will be able to develop all the faculties of their minds, from the power of logical analysis to that of aesthetic appreciation; and, in the second place, it is supposed to provide young people with a framework of historical, logical and physico-chemico-biological relationships, within which any particular piece of information acquired in later life may find its proper and significant place. Technical education, on the other hand, aims merely at practical results and is supposed to give young people proficiency in some particular trade or profession.

Recent investigations (for example, that which was carried out a few years ago by the Scottish education authorities) have given statistical form and content to the conclusions which personal experience had long since forced upon the practising teacher: namely, that academic education (although grudgingly dispensed, at any rate in its secondary and higher forms) is given to large numbers of boys and girls who are unable to derive much profit from it. To some extent, no doubt, this failure to profit by academic education is due to the defects of our teaching system or to the shortcomings of individual teachers. (Teaching is an art, not a science; bad artists have always greatly outnumbered the good.) However, when all allowances have been made, it seems perfectly clear that very many young people—probably an absolute majority of them—are congenitally incapable of receiving what academic education has to offer. At the same time it is no less clear that many of those who are able to stay the course of an academic education emerge from the ordeal either as parrots, gabbling remembered formulas which they do not really understand; or, if they *do* understand, as specialists, knowing everything about one subject and taking no interest in anything else; or, finally, as intellectuals, theoretically knowledgeable about everything, but hopelessly inept in the affairs of ordinary life. Something analogous happens to the pupils of technical schools. They come out into the world, highly expert in their particular job, but knowing very little about anything else and having no

[222]

integrating principle in terms of which they can arrange and give significance to such knowledge as they may subsequently acquire.

Can these defects in our educational system be remedied? I think they can. We must begin by the frankest, the most objectively scientific acceptance of the fact that human beings belong to different types. Congenitally, the cerebrotonic is not such a "good mixer" as the viscerotonic, who may be so deeply absorbed in his rich emotional life as to be unwilling to concern himself with the intellectual pursuits at which the cerebrotonic excels. Again, the somatotonic is predestined by his psychophysical make-up to be more interested in, and more proficient at, muscular than intellectual or emotional activity. Or take particular talents; these, it would seem, are often given and can be developed only at the expense of other talents. (For example, good mathematicians are often musical, but very rarely have any appreciation of the visual arts.) Then there is the problem—still to some extent the subject of controversy— of the degrees of intelligence. Intelligence tests have been improved in recent years; but they will become fully significant only when the results of the tests are given in their proper context. The affirmation that A's intelligence quotient is higher than B's tells us, as it stands, very little; if it is to be really significant, we must know a number of other facts—whether, for example, A and B belong to the same psycho-physical type or to different types, whether they approximate to the pure type or are greatly mixed. And so on. The intelligence test, then, is an imperfect instrument; but, imperfect as it is, it has done something to give statistical form and content to the universally held conviction that some people are stupider than others. Having accepted the fact that human beings belong to different types, are gifted with different talents and have different degrees of intelligence, we must attempt to give each the education best calculated to develop his or her capacities to their utmost. In a rather crude and inefficient way, this is what we are attempting to do even now. Clever boys pass examinations and are given scholarships that take them from primary to secondary schools and from secondary schools to universities. Handy boys are apprenticed or sent to technical schools to learn some skilled trade. And so on. A rough and ready system—a good deal rougher than readier. Its defects are twofold. First, the methods employed for choosing the candidates for the different kinds of education are far from satisfactory. And, second, the kinds of education to which successful candidates are subjected are even less satisfactory than the methods of choice.

About the examination system it is unnecessary for me to speak at length. Most educators agree in theory that a single crucial examination does not provide the best test of a person's ability. Many of them have even passed from theory to practice and are giving up the single, crucial examination in favour of a series of periodical tests of knowledge and intellience and the reports, over a span of years, of teachers and inspectors. Supplemented by an expert grading in terms of psychophysical type, the second method of choosing candidates for the various kinds of education should prove quite satisfactory.

We must now consider the various kinds of education to which (according to their type) young people should be subjected.

We have seen that both the existing kinds of education, technical as well as academic or liberal, are unsatisfactory. The problem before us is this: to amend them in such a way that technical education shall become more liberal, and academic education, a more adequate preparation for everyday life in a society which is to be changed for the better.

A liberal education is supposed to provide, first, a gymnastic, second, a frame of reference. In other words, it is supposed to be simultaneously a device for fostering intelligence and the source of a principle of integration.

In academic education as we know it today, the principle of integration is mainly scientific and historical. We can put the matter in another way and say that the frame of reference is logical and factual, and that the facts with which the logical intellect is trained to deal are mainly facts about the material universe and about humanity as a part of the material universe. (History, as taught in schools and colleges, is of two kinds: non-scientific history, which is merely a branch of nationalistic propaganda, and scientific history, which is almost a branch of physics. Scientific historians treat facts about human beings as though they were facts about the material universe; they write about men as though men were gas molecules that could be dealt with most effectively in terms of the law of averages.)

The man who goes through a course of our academic education may come out a parrot. In this case we say that the education has failed of its purpose. Or he may come out as an efficient specialist. In this case we say that the education has been only partially successful. Or else (and when this happens we think that education has worked very successfully) he may emerge as an intellectual—that is to say, a person who has learned to establish relations between the different elements of his sum of knowledge, one who possesses a coherent system of relationships into which he can fit all such new items of information as he may pick up in the course of his life. We can define this system of relationships in terms of what is known and say (what has been said above) that it is predominantly scientific and historical, logical and factual. We can also define it in terms of the knower and say that it is predominantly cognitive, not affective or conative.

The parrot repeats, but does not understand; the narrow specialist understands, but understands only his speciality; the accomplished intellectual understands the relations subsiding between many sectors of apprehended reality, but does so only theoretically. He knows, but is fired by no positive desire to act upon his knowledge and has received no training in such action. We see, then, that even the man whom we are accustomed to regard as the successful product of our academic education is an unsatisfactory person.

To the pupils of our technical schools, no principle of

integration is given. Their teachers provide them with no frame of reference, no coherent system of relationships. They are taught a job and no more—equipped with a technique and just so much of the theory lying behind that particular technique as will make them efficient workers. They emerge into the world wholly unprepared to deal in an intelligent way with the facts of experience. The web of understanding which, in the mind of the accomplished intellectual, connects the atom with the spiral nebula and both with this morning's breakfast, the music of Bach, the pottery of neolithic China, what you will—this network of cognitive relationships is all but completely lacking. Bits of information exist for the technically educated man, not as parts of one vast continuum, but in isolation, like so many stars dotted about in a gulf of black incomprehension. Or if there is a continuum, the chances are that it will be composed of ideas borrowed from a bronze-age theology, from anecdotal history, from philosophy as taught in the newspaper and the films. The successful product of technical education is as unsatisfactory as the successful product of academic education.

What is the remedy for this state of things? Some people have suggested that technical education should be liberalized, like academic education, in terms of general knowledge—above all, knowledge of scientific facts and theories. They have suggested that technicians should be given a principle of integration fundamentally similar to that employed by the intellectual—a principle of integration which the knower feels to be mainly cognitive and which, defined in terms of the known, is mainly scientific.

There are two good reasons for thinking that this suggestion is unsound. First of all, the great majority of those who undergo technical education are incapable of using this principle of integration and, being incapable of using it, are therefore uninterested in it. Even among those who go through a course of our academic education, only a few emerge as accomplished intellectuals. Most of them emerge as parrots or specialists. (A good proportion of these return to the schools as teachers and proceed to train up other parrots and specialists.) Minds that delight in what may be called large-scale knowledge—knowledge, that is to say, of the relations subsisting between things and events widely separated in space or time and seemingly irrelevant one to another—are rare. Academic education is supposed to impart such knowledge and to infect men and women with the desire to possess it; but in actual fact few are so infected and few go out into the world possessing it. To provide people with a principle of integration which it is almost certain that they will not wish or be able to use is mere foolishness.

Nor is this all. We have seen that even the accomplished intellectual is a far from satisfactory person. His involvement with the world is only cognitive, not affective nor conative. Moreover, the framework into which he fits his experience is the framework of the natural sciences and of history treated as though it too were one of the natural sciences. He is concerned mainly with the material universe and with humanity as a part of the material universe. He is not concerned with humanity as human, as potentially more than human. One of the results of this preoccupation with the material universe is that, on the rare occasions when the intellectual does become affectively and conatively involved with the world of human reality, he tends to exhibit a curious impatience which easily degenerates into ruthlessness. Thinking of human beings "scientifically," as parts of the material universe, he doesn't see why they shouldn't be handled as other parts of the material universe are handled—dumped here, like coal or sand, made to flow there, like water, "liquidated" (the Russians preserve the vocabulary of the intellectuals who prepared and made their revolution), like so much ice over a fire.

Technical education is without a principle of integration; academic education makes use of a principle that integrates only on the cognitive plane, only in terms of a natural science preoccupied with the laws of the material universe. What is needed is another principle of integration—a principle which the technicians and the unsuccessful academics will be congenitally capable of using; a principle that will co-ordinate the scattered fragments, the island universes of specialized or merely professional knowledge; a principle that will supplement the scientifico-historical frame of reference at present used by intellectuals, that will help, perhaps, to transform them from mere spectators of the human scene into intelligent participants.

What should be the nature of this new principle of integration? The answer seems clear enough, at any rate

[229]

in its main outlines: it should be psychological and ethical. Within the new frame of reference, co-ordination of knowledge and experience would be made in human terms; the network of significant relations would be, not material, but psychological, not indifferent to values, but moral, not merely cognitive, but also affective and conative.

A concrete example will make my meaning clear. Here is a young man in process of being trained in engineering and practical mechanics. Under the existing dispensation, the chances are that he will come out into the world profoundly ignorant of everything but his specialty. His education will have failed to equip him with any principle by means of which he can integrate his future experiences and accessions of knowledge. Educationists trained up in the existing academic schools believe that it will be possible to liberalize his education by somehow leading him from the practical and the particular to general scientific theory. Give him, they say, a mastery of general scientific theory, and he will have a principle by means of which he will be able to integrate all his knowledge and experience. In the abstract this scheme seems good enough; but in practice it just doesn't work. For the probability is that the young man will not be interested in general scientific theory, that he will have neither the wish nor the ability to integrate his experience and his knowledge in terms of the laws of the material universe. As a matter of brute historical fact, the great advances in scientific theory have very seldom been made by skilled artisans. The practical man who knows his job is interested in

the job and perhaps in just as much of the theory underlying his practice as will enable him to do the job better. Very rarely does he develop into the scientist, and
few indeed are the fruitful generalizations which we
owe to such men. In general, the advances in scientific
theory have been made by men of another type—men
who did not concern themselves professionally with
technical problems, but who merely looked at them as
outsiders and then proceeded to generalize and rationalize what was merely particular and empirical. Between
the practical man and the man who is interested in
scientific theories of the universe at large a gulf is fixed.
They belong to different types. The attempt to liberalize
technical education by means of the principle which
intellectuals use to integrate their experience is foredoomed to failure.

Man is the only subject in which, whatever their
type or the degree of their ability, all men are interested. The future engineer may be unable and unwilling to go far in the study of the laws of the material
universe. There will be no difficulty, however, in getting him to take an interest in human affairs. It is,
therefore, in terms of human affairs that his technical
education can best be liberalized. There would be no
difficulty in integrating any technical subject into a
comprehensive scheme of relations within our human,
ethico-psychological framework. The technical course
would be accompanied by a course explaining the effects, as measured in terms of good and evil, well-being
and suffering, of the technique in question. Our hypothetical young man would learn, not only to be a mecha-

nician, but also to understand the ways in which machinery affects, has affected and is likely to affect, the lives of men and women. He could begin with the effects of machinery upon the individual—such effects as are discussed, for example, in Stuart Chase's essay in contemporary history, "Men and Machines," or in the Hammonds' account of the industrial revolution. Next, the broader social effects could be studied —the transformation of technically backward countries, the destruction of old-established trades, the creation of new industries. In these and similar ways a complete network of relationships could be created in the student's mind, a network binding together things seemingly as irrelevant to one another as down-draught carburetters and the education of children in New Mexico, aluminum alloys and the slaughter of Abyssinians and Spaniards, viscose fibres and the ruin of peasants in Japan and the Rhone Valley. A similar frame of psychological, sociological and ethical reference could be used, not indeed to replace, but to supplement the frame of scientific reference used in academic education. The technician would integrate his experience and special knowledge in human terms only; the intellectual would integrate in terms of the non-human, material universe as well as of the human world. Both educations would thus be made genuinely liberal—liberal in the academic sense, because even the technical student would be given a wide range of knowledge and a principle of integration; liberal also in the political sense, because it would be hard indeed to receive such an education and not emerge with a wider range of sympathy, a keener desire to act.

It would be impossible, in the space at my disposal, to give an account of all the hopeful experiments in education undertaken in recent years. The most I can do is to mention a few of the more outstanding essays in the liberalization of our existing system. Of Dr. Montessori's work for young children and of the reasons why we have hesitated to apply her methods to the teaching of adolescents, I have already spoken. It is true, as Mr. Russell points out in the passage I have quoted above, that, in the democratic countries, our hesitation has not amounted to a complete refusal to apply the Montessori principles. But the applications have been partial and have almost always been made in an intrinsically un-Montessorian context. Consider, by way of example, the English Public Schools. Within a fixed framework, their pupils are in a measure self-governing. Unhappily the rules, customs and loyalties which constitute the supporting framework are the rules, customs and loyalties of a hierarchical, competitive, imperialistic society. Such training in self-government and self-teaching as the young people receive serves merely to make them more efficient and enterprising members of this intrinsically undesirable society. Something similar takes place in an army preparing for war in modern conditions. The old-fashioned drill, by means of which soldiers were conditioned to overcome fear, cultivate rage and blindly obey their superiors, is an inadequate training for men who are to fight with modern weapons. The mechanization of war has made necessary a new kind of training. The soldier has to be educated to co-operate with small groups of his fellows, to make quick decisions, to use his judgment. Tennyson's advice to soldiers was good enough in the eighteen-fifties. But for the crew of a tank or a motorized machine-gun unit, doing and dying is not sufficient; they are also required to reason why. Within the framework of the rules, customs, and loyalties of militarism, soldiers are taught to use their intelligence and act upon their own initiative. To this extent Montessori principles have been adopted even in the army. But under the present dispensation, the partially self-governing and self-teaching soldier is not being trained for freedom and justice any more than is his younger brother, the partially self-governing and self-teaching schoolboy.

A particularly hopeful attempt to enlarge the scope and humanize the character of academic education was made, in the years immediately following the War, by Dr. A. E. Morgan (subsequently director of the Tennessee Valley Authority) at Antioch College. Under the educational dispensation developed by Dr. Morgan, periods of study, as has been noted earlier, are alternated with periods of labour in the factory, the office, the farm—even the prison and the asylum. Three months of theory are supplemented and illustrated by three months of practice. The intellectual is taught to make use of a frame of human reference as well as a frame of natural-scientific and historical reference—and taught, what is more, in the most effective of all possible ways, in terms of physical contact with actual samples of human reality. His principle of integration is not merely cognitive; thanks to an educational system which compels him to take part in many different kinds of practical work, it is also conative and effective.*

A system of education somewhat similar to that developed at Antioch is used in the schools attached to factories in Soviet Russia. All such systems are but the modern extensions and systematization of the traditional Hebrew system of education. "He who does not teach his son a trade," so it is written in the Talmud, "virtually teaches him to steal." St. Paul was not only a scholar; he was also a tent-maker. The ideal of the scholar and the gentleman originated among the slave-owning philosophers of Athens and Ionia. It is one of the ironies of history that the modern world should have taken over from the Hebrews all that was worst in their cultural heritage—their ferocious bronze-age literature; their paeans in praise of war; their tales of divinely inspired slaughter and sanctified treachery; their primitive belief in a personal, despotic and passionately unscrupulous God; their low, Samuel-Smilesian notion that virtue deserves a reward in cash and social position. It is, I repeat, one of the ironies of history that we should have taken over all this and have rejected the admirably sensible rabbinical tradition of an all-round education, at once academic and technical, in favour of the narrow and immoral ideal of the Hellenic slavers.

To perfect the Antioch system, it would probably be

---

* Note in this context the use of "occupational therapy" in mental disease. There are certain forms of mental disease for which hand-work is the best cure.

necessary to extend its provisions from the student to the teaching body. The fossil professor is a familiar object to those who have rambled through university towns. The onset of petrifaction might be delayed, if teachers were given periodically, not merely sabbatical, but also non-sabbatical years—years during which they would have to work at some job entirely unconnected with the academic world.

A good deal of attention has been paid in recent years to the education of the emotions through the arts. In many schools and colleges, music, "dramatics," poetry and the visual arts are used more or less systematically as a device for widening consciousness and imparting to the flow of emotion a desirable direction.

Music, for example, may be used to teach a number of valuable lessons. When they listen to a piece of good music, people of limited ability are given the opportunity of actually experiencing the thought-and-feeling processes of a man of outstanding intellectual power and exceptional insight. (This applies, of course, to all the arts; but there is reason to believe that more people are able to participate, and participate more intensely, in the experience of the music-maker than in that of the painter, say, or the architect, or perhaps even the imaginative writer.) The finest works of art are precious, among other reasons, because they make it possible for us to know, if only imperfectly and for a little while, what it actually feels like to think subtly and feel nobly.

Music also serves to teach a very valuable kind of emotional co-operation. Singing and playing instruments together, people learn, not only to perform complicated actions requiring great muscular skill and the mind's entire attention, but also to feel in harmony, to be united in a shared emotion.

Coming next to literature, we see that the acting of plays can also be used for the purposes of emotional training. By playing the part of a character who is either very like or very unlike himself, a person can be made aware of his own nature and of his relations with others. To some extent, it may be, the watching of plays can serve the same purpose. We must, however, be on our guard against attributing to drama educative virtues which, at any rate in its present form, it certainly does not possess. In relation to the modern play or film it is sheer nonsense to talk about the Aristotelian catharsis. A Greek tragedy was much more than a play; it was also a cathedral service, it was also one of the ceremonies of the national religion. The performance was an illustration of the scriptures, an exposition of theology. Modern dramas, even the best of them, are none of these things. They are, essentially, secular. People go to them, not in order to be reminded of their philosophy of life, not to establish some kind of communion with their gods, but merely to "get a kick," merely to titillate their feelings. The habit of self-titillation grows with what it feeds upon. For the Greeks, dramatic festivals were "solemn and rare." For us they are an almost daily stimulant. Abused as we abuse it at present, dramatic art is in no sense cathartic; it is merely a form of emotional masturbation. All arts can be used as a form of self-abuse; but masturbation through the drama is probably the worst form of artistic debauchery, and for this reason: acting is one of the most dangerous of trades. It is the rarest thing to find a player who has not had his character affected for the worse by the practice of his profession. Nobody can make a habit of self-exhibition, nobody can exploit his personality for the sake of exercising a kind of hypnotic power over others, and remain untouched by the process. (In the Oneida community it was found that "prima donna fever," as John Noyes called it, could produce disruptive effects of extraordinary magnitude. Noyes, who was a psychologist of genius and the shrewdest of practical moralists, took the greatest pains to prevent a recrudescence of this disease, which has been the ruin of so many actors and virtuosi.) * Acting inflames the ego in a way which few other professions do. For the sake of enjoying regular emotional self-abuse, our societies condemn a considerable class of men and women to a perpetual inability to achieve non-attachment. It seems a high price to pay for our amusement.

The chief educative virtue of literature consists in its power to provide its readers with examples which they can follow. To some extent, all human beings are, in Jules de Gaultier's phrase "bovaristic"—that is to say they have a capacity for seeing themselves as they are not, for playing a part other than that which heredity and circumstances seem to have assigned to them. The heroine of Flaubert's novel came to a tragic end; but there is no reason why all bovaristic behaviour should

* See "A Yankee Saint" (the latest and best biography of Noyes) by Robert Allerton Parker. New York, 1935.

turn out so disastrously as it did in the case of the original Mme. Bovary. There is good bovarism as well as bad
bovarism. Educationists have always known this fact and,
from time immemorial, have tried to mould the character of their pupils by providing them with literary
models to be imitated in real life. Such models may be
mythical, historical or fictional. Hercules and Thor are
instances of the first kind of heroic model; Plutarch's
statesmen and soldiers and the saints of the Christian
calendar are instances of the historical model; Hamlet
and Werther, Julien Sorel and Alyosha Karamazov,
Juliet and Lady Chatterley are instances of fictional
heroes and heroines upon whom, at one time or another,
great numbers of human beings have patterned themselves. In all cases, whether mythical, historical or
fictional, some measure of literary art is necessary; if
the story is told inadequately, the pupil will remain
unimpressed, will feel no desire to imitate the model
set before him. Hence the importance, even in ethical
instruction, of good art. Moreover, every generation
must produce its stock of imitable models, described
in terms of an art which is not merely good, but also
up-to-date. Old good art can never have the same
appeal as new good art; for most people, indeed, it
cannot rival with new bad art. More people bovarize
themselves upon the models provided by the pulp magazines than upon those provided by Shakespeare. There
are two reasons for this. The first is that, though crude
and incompetent, the pulp magazines deal with contemporary characters, while Shakespeare, though incomparable in his power to "put things across," is more than

three hundred years out of date; the second must be sought in the fact that the moral effort required to imitate Shakespeare's heroes, and even his villains, is far greater than that which is needed to imitate the personages of pulp-magazine fiction. Pulp-magazine stories are transcriptions of the commonest and easiest daydreams—dreams of sexual titillation, of financial success, of luxury, of social recognition. Shakespeare's personages are on a larger scale. They embody the hardly realizable, extravagant day-dreams of paranoiacs—of men who dream of being kings and heroes, lovers uniquely faithful, proud saviours of their country uniquely disinterested and uniquely adored, villains uniquely vengeful and malignant. In this context it is worth remarking that except for the Duke in *Measure for Measure*—and he is scarcely a human being, only a symbol—Shakespeare gives no picture of a non-attached human being. Indeed good pictures of non-attached men and women are singularly rare in the world's literature. The good people in plays and novels are rarely complete, fully adult personages. They are either a bit deficient, like Dostoievsky's epileptic Prince Mishkin, like Gorki's virtuous but imbecile hermit, or Dickens's charitable but utterly infantile Cheerybles, or else, like Pickwick, they are made lovable by being represented as eccentric to the point of absurdity; we can tolerate their superiority in virtue because we feel superior in common sense. Finally and most frequently they are shown as being good without being intelligent, like Colonel Newcome, or the peasant who talks to Tolstoy's Pierre in prison. These individuals are personally good within an abominably bad system which they do not even question. Men who are profoundly good without being intelligent have often attained to sainthood. The Curé d'Ars and St. Peter Claver are cases in point. One must admire such men for the, by ordinary standards, superhuman qualities of character which they display. At the same time, it is, I think, necessary to admit that they are not complete, not fully adult. Perfect non-attachment demands of those who aspire to it, not only compassion and charity, but also the intelligence that perceives the general implications of particular acts, that sees the individual being within the system of social and cosmic relations of which he is but a part. In this respect, it seems to me, Buddhism shows itself decidedly superior to Christianity. In the Buddhist ethic stupidity, or un-awareness, ranks as one of the principal sins. At the same time people are warned that they must take their share of responsibility for the social order in which they find themselves. One of the branches of the Eightfold Path is said to be "right means of livelihood." The Buddhist is expected to refrain from engaging in such socially harmful occupations as soldiering, or the manu-facture of arms and intoxicating drugs. Christian moral-ists made and still make the enormous mistake of not insisting upon right means of livelihood. The church allows people to believe that they can be good Christians and yet draw dividends from armament factories, can be good Christians and yet imperil the well-being of their fellows by speculating in stocks and shares, can be good Christians and yet be imperialists, yet partici-pate in war. All that is required of the good Christian is chastity and a modicum of charity in immediate personal relations. An intelligent understanding and appraisal of the long-range consequences of acts is not insisted upon by Christian moralists.* One of the results of this doctrinal inadequacy is that there is a singular lack, as well in imaginative as in biographical literature, of intelligently virtuous, adultly non-attached personages, upon whom young people may model their behaviour. This is a deplorable state of things. Literary example is a powerful instrument for the moulding of character. But most of our literary examples, as we have seen, are mere idealizations of the average sensual man. Of the more heroic characters the majority are just grandiosely paranoiac; the others are good, but good incompletely and without intelligence; are virtuous within a bad system which they fail to see the need of changing; combine a measure of non-attachment in personal matters with loyalty to some creed, such as fascism or communism or nationalism, that entails, if acted upon, the commission of every kind of crime. There is a great need for literary artists as the educators of a new type of human being. Unfortunately most literary artists are human beings of the old type. They have been educated in such a way that, even when they are revolutionaries, they think in terms of the values accepted by the essentially militaristic society of which they are members. *Quis custodiet custodes?* Who will educate the educators? The answer, of course, is painfully sim-

* In the Middle Ages the Church made a serious effort to moralize economic activity—the attempt, as Tawney has shown in "Religion and the Rise of Capitalism," was abandoned after the Reformation.

ple: nobody but the educators themselves. Our human world is composed of an endless series of vicious circles, from which it is possible to escape only by an act, or rather a succession of acts, of intelligently directed will.

Dictatorial governments regard free intelligence as their worst enemy. In this they are probably perfectly right. Tyranny cannot exist unless there is passive obedience on the part of the tyrannized. But passive obedience to authority is not compatible with the free exercise of intelligence. It is for this reason that all tyrants try so hard either to suppress intelligence altogether or to compel it to exercise itself only within certain prescribed limits and along certain channels carved out for it in advance. Hence the systematic use which all dictators make of the instruments of propaganda.

In societies more primitive than our own, societies in which a traditional religion and a traditional code of morality are unquestioningly accepted, there is no need of deliberate propaganda. People behave in the traditional way "by instinct," and never stop dispassionately to consider what they are doing, feeling, thinking. Even in societies like ours there is an astonishing amount of unquestioning acceptance of customary behaviour patterns, thought patterns, feeling patterns. A very large number even of intelligent men and women use their intelligence only for the purpose of making a good job of what is traditionally regarded as their duty; they seldom or never use it to pass judgment upon the duty itself. Hence the dismal spectacle of scientists and technicians using all their powers to help their country's rulers to commit mass murder with increased efficiency and indiscriminateness; of scholars and men of letters prostituting their talents for the purpose of bolstering national prestige with learned lies and fascinating rhetoric. Even in the democratic countries, intelligence is generally used only to create (in Thoreau's words) improved means to unimproved ends—to ends that are dictated by socially sanctioned prejudice and the lowest passions. Such, I repeat, is generally the case; but fortunately not always. Where intelligence is permitted to exercise itself freely, there will always be a few people prepared to use their wits for the purpose of judging traditional ends as well as for devising effective means to those ends. It is thanks to such individuals that the very idea of desirable change is able to come into existence.

For the dictator such questioning free intelligences are exceedingly dangerous; for it is essential, if he is to preserve his position, that the socially sanctioned prejudices should not be questioned and that men should use their wits solely for the purpose of finding more effective means to achieve those ends which are compatible with dictatorship. Hence the persecution of daring individuals, the muzzling of the press, and the systematic attempt by means of propaganda to create a public opinion favourable to tyranny. In the dictatorial countries the individual is subjected to propaganda, as to military training, almost from infancy. All his education is propagandist and, when he leaves school, he is exposed to the influence of a controlled press, a controlled cinema, a controlled literature, a controlled radio. Within a few years controlled television and possibly a controlled teletype service functioning in every home will have to be added to this list of weapons in the dictator's armoury. Nor is this all; it is likely enough that pharmacology will be called in as an ally of applied psychology. There are drugs, such as a mixture of scopolamine and chloral, that enormously increase the individual's suggestibility. It is more than likely that dictators will soon be making use of such substances in order to heighten their subjects' loyalty and blind faith.

In the democratic countries, intelligence is still free to ask whatever questions it chooses. This freedom, it is almost certain, will not survive another war. Education-ists should therefore do all they can, while there is yet time, to build up in the minds of their charges a habit of resistance to suggestion. If such resistance is not built up, the men and women of the next generation will be at the mercy of any skilful propagandist who contrives to seize the instruments of information and persuasion. Resistance to suggestion can be built up in two ways. First, children can be taught to rely on their own in-ternal resources and not to depend on incessant stimula-tion from without. This is doubly important. Reliance on external stimulation is bad for the character. More-over such stimulation is the stuff with which propa-gandists bait their hooks, the jam in which dictators conceal their ideological pills. An individual who relies on external stimulations thereby exposes himself to the full force of whatever propaganda is being made in his neighbourhood. For a majority of people in the West, purposeless reading, purposeless listening-in, purpose-less looking at films have become addictions, psychological equivalents of alcoholism and morphinism. Things have come to such a pitch that there are many millions of men and women who suffer real distress if they are cut off for a few days or even a few hours from newspapers, radio music, moving pictures. Like the addict to a drug, they have to indulge their vice, not because the indulgence gives them any active pleasure, but because, unless they indulge, they feel painfully sub-normal and incomplete. Without papers, films and wireless they live a diminished existence; they are fully themselves only when bathing in sports news and murder trials, in radio music and talk, in the vicarious terrors, triumphs and eroticisms of the films. Even by intelligent people, it is now taken for granted that such psychological addictions are inevitable and even desirable, that there is nothing to be alarmed at in the fact that the majority of civilized men and women are now incapable of living on their own spiritual resources, but have become abjectly dependent on incessant stimulation from without. Recently, for example, I read a little book in which an eminent American biologist gives his view about the Future. Science, he prophesies, will enormously increase human happiness and intelligence—will do so, among other ways, by providing people with micro-cinematographs which they can slip on like spectacles whenever they are bored. Science will also, no doubt, be able very soon to supply us with micro-pocket-flasks and micro-hypodermic-syringes, micro-alcohol, micro-cigarettes and micro-cocaine. Long live science!

How can children be taught to rely upon their own

spiritual resources and resist the temptation to become reading-addicts, hearing-addicts, seeing-addicts? First of all, they can be taught how to entertain themselves—by making things by playing musical instruments, by purposeful study, by scientific observation, by the practice of some art, and so on. But such education of the hand and the intellect is not enough. Psychology has its Gresham's Law; its bad money drives out the good. Most people tend to perform the actions that require least effort, to think the thoughts that are easiest, to feel the emotions that are most vulgarly commonplace, to give rein to the desires that are most nearly animal. And they will tend to do this even if they possess the knowledge and skill to do otherwise. Along with the necessary knowledge and skill must be given the will to use them, even under the pressure of incessant temptation to take the line of least resistance and become an addict to psychological drugs. Most people will not wish to resist these temptations unless they have a coherent philosophy of life, which makes it reasonable and right for them to do so, and unless they know some technique by means of which they can be sure of giving practical effect to their good intentions.

> *Video meliora proboque;*
> *Deteriora sequor.*

To see and approve the better is useless, if one then regularly proceeds to pursue the worse. What is the philosophy of life that should be taught? And what are the proper techniques by means of which people can per-

[247]

suade themselves to act upon their convictions? These are questions which will be dealt with in a later chapter.

So much for the first method of heightening resistance to suggestion. It will be seen that this consists essentially in teaching young people to dispense with the agreeable stimulations offered by the newspapers, wireless and films—stimulations which serve, as I have said, to bait the propagandist's hooks. A boycott of sports-news and murder stories, of jazz and variety, of film love, film thrills and film luxury, is simultaneously a boycott of political, economic and ethical propaganda. Hence the vital importance of teaching as many young people as possible how to amuse themselves and at the same time inducing them to wish to amuse themselves.

The other method of heightening resistance to suggestion is purely intellectual and consists in training young people to subject the devices of the propagandists to critical analysis. The first thing that educators must do is to analyse the words currently used in newspapers, on platforms, by preachers and broadcasters. What, for example, does the word "nation" mean? To what extent are speakers and writers justified in talking of a nation as a person? Who precisely is the "she," of whom people speak when discussing a nation's foreign politics? ("Britain is an imperial power. She must defend her Empire.") In what sense can a nation be described as having a will or national interests? Are these interests and will the interests and will of the entire population? or of a majority? or of a ruling caste and a few professional politicians? In what way, if any, does "the state" differ from Messrs. Smith, Brown, Jones and the other gentle-

men who happen for the moment to have secured political power? Given the character of Brown, Jones, etc.,
why should "the state" be regarded as an institution
worthy of almost religious respect? Where does national
honour reside? Why would the loss of Hong-Kong, for
example, be a mortal blow to Britain's honour, while
its seizure after a war in which Britain attempted to
force the Chinese to buy opium was in no way a stain
upon the same honour? And so on. "Nation" is only
one of several dozens of rich and resonant words which
are ordinarily accepted without a thought, but which it
is essential, if we would think clearly, that we should
subject to the most searching analysis.

It is no less important that children should be taught
to examine all personifications, all metaphors and all
abstractions occurring in the articles they read, the
speeches they listen to. They must learn to translate
these empty words into terms of concrete contemporary
reality. When an Asquith says, "we shall not sheathe the
sword which we have not lightly drawn," when an
Archbishop of Canterbury affirms "that force, the sword,
is the instrument of God for the protection of the people," they must learn to translate this noble verbiage
into the language of the present. Swords have played
no appreciable part in war for the last two hundred
years. In 1914 Asquith's sword was high explosives and
shrapnel, machine guns, battleships, submarines. In
1936 the "instrument of God for the protection of the
people" was all the armaments existing in 1914 plus
tanks, plus aeroplanes, plus thermite, plus phosgene,
plus arsenic smokes, plus Lewisite and many other in-

struments of murder, more efficient and more indiscriminate than anything known in the past. It is frequently in the interest of the rulers of a country to disguise the true facts of contemporary reality under thick veils of misleading verbiage. It is the business of educators to teach their pupils to translate these picturesque or empty phrases into the language of contemporary reality.

Verbal propaganda is not the only nor even, perhaps, the most effective form of organized suggestion. There is another kind, specially favoured by modern commercial propagandists and used from time immemorial by such non-commercial advertisers as kings, priests and soldiers. This consists in arbitrarily associating the idea which is to be suggested with some object, some image, some sound, some literary description, that is either intrinsically delightful or in some way suggestive of pleasantness. For example, the advertiser of soap will show a picture of a young, voluptuous female, about to take a bath among plumbing fixtures of pink marble and chromium. The advertiser of cigarettes will show people dining in what the lady novelists describe as "faultless evening dress," or reproduce the photograph of some well-known film star, millionairess, or titled lady. The advertiser of whisky will illustrate a group of handsome men lounging in luscious upholstery and being waited upon by the most obsequious of family retainers. The aim in all such cases is the same—to associate the idea of the goods offered for sale with ideas which the public already regards as delightful, such as the idea of erotic pleasure, the idea of personal charm, the idea of wealth and social superiority. In other cases the idea of the merchandise is associated with intrinsically delightful landscapes, with funny or pathetic children, with flowers or pet animals, with scenes of family life. In countries where radio advertising is permitted, commercial propagandists find it worth their while to associate the idea of their cars, their cigarettes, their breakfast cereal or what not with performances by comedians or concerts of vocal or orchestral music. This last is the type of association favoured by kings, soldiers and priests. From the beginning of history, rulers have "put themselves across" by associating the idea of their government with magnificent pageantry, with impressive architecture, with every kind of rare, splendid and beautiful thing. It is the same with the soldier. Military music intoxicates like wine and a military review is, in its own way, no less inebriating. (The author of the Song of Songs goes so far as to establish an emotional equivalence between a sexually desirable person and an army with banners.) Priests make use of an essentially similar type of propaganda. Systematically, they have always associated the idea of their god and of themselves as the god's representatives with intrinsically delightful works of art of every kind, from music and architecture to dressmaking, with symbols of wealth and power, with organized joy and organized terror and mystery, even, in many religions, with organized cruelty and lust.

Propaganda of this kind generally proves irresistible. Cigarettes are bought in ever increasing quantities; ever vaster and more loyal crowds flock to military reviews, to royal and dictatorial pageants, to the splendid ceremonials of nationalistic idolatry. Once again resistance to suggestion can be heightened only by sharpening the critical faculty of those concerned. The art of dissociating ideas should have a place in every curriculum. Young people must be trained to consider the problems of government, international politics, religion and the like in isolation from the pleasant images, with which a particular solution of these problems has been associated, more or less deliberately, by those whose interest it is to make the public think, feel and judge in a certain way. The training might begin with a consideration of popular advertising. Children could be shown that there is no necessity and organic connection between the pretty girl in her expensive dressing-gown and the merits of the tooth paste she is intended to advertise. This lesson might be brought home by practical demonstrations. Chocolates could be wrapped in a paper adorned with realistic pictures of scorpions, and castor oil and quinine distributed from containers in the form of Sealyham terriers or Shirley Temple. Having mastered the art of dissociation in the field of commercial advertising, our young people could be trained to apply the same critical methods to the equally arbitrary and even more dangerously misleading associations which exist in the fields of politics and religion. They would be shown that it is possible for a man to get the fullest aesthetic enjoyment out of a military or religious pageant without allowing that enjoyment in any way to influence his judgment regarding the value of war as a political instrument or the truth and moral usefulness of the religion in question. They would be taught to

[252]

consider monarchy and dictatorship on their own political and ethical merits, not on the choreographical merits of processions and court ceremonials, not on the architectural merits of palaces, not on the rhetorical merits of speeches, not on the organizational merits of a certain kind of technical efficiency. And so on.

That the art of dissociation will ever be taught in schools under direct state control is, of course, almost infinitely improbable. Those who use the power of the state always desire to preserve a certain given order of things. They therefore always try to persuade or compel their subjects to accept, as right and reasonable, certain solutions (hardly ever the best) of the outstanding problems of politics and economics. Hence the insistence, on the part of governments, that the ideas embodying these solutions shall always be associated with intrinsically pleasing images. The art of dissociation can be taught only by individuals who are not under direct government control. This is one of the reasons why it is so important that state-aided education shall, wherever possible, be supplemented by education in the hands of private persons. Some of this privately organized education will certainly be bad; some will probably exist solely for reasons of snobbery. But a few of the private educators will be genuinely experimental and intelligent; a few will use their blessed independence to make the desirable change which state-controlled teachers are not allowed to initiate. *"Les enfants n'appartiennent qu'à la République."* So wrote the Marquis de Sade. That such a man should have been so ardent a supporter of exclusive state education is a fact that, in the light of the history of contemporary dictatorships, is highly significant.

Using an arbitrary, but unavoidable, system of classification, I have spoken in turn of education as character-training, education as instruction, education as training of the emotions. It is now necessary to speak of another form of education, a form which must underlie and accompany all the other forms, namely the education of the body.

In the world as we know it mind and body form a single organic whole. What happens in the mind affects the body; what happens in the body affects the mind. Education must therefore be a process of physical as well as mental training.

Of what nature should this physical training be? The question cannot be properly answered except in terms of our first principles. We are agreed that the ideal human being is one who is non-attached. Accordingly all education, including physical education, must ultimately aim at producing non-attachment. If we would discover which is the best form of physical training, we must begin by setting forth the physical conditions of non-attachment.

First of all, it is pretty clear that non-attachment is very hardly realizable by any one whose body is seriously maladjusted. A maladjusted body affects the mind in several ways. When the maladjustment is very great, the body is subject to pain and discomfort. Pain and discomfort invade the field of consciousness, with the result that the owner of the body finds great difficulty in not identifying himself with his faulty physical processes. From a being who is potentially more than what is conventionally styled a "person," he is reduced by pain and discomfort to a being who is less than a person. He comes to be equated with one of his body's badly functioning organs.

In other cases pain and discomfort may not be present; but the maladjusted body may be subject, without its owner being aware of the fact, to chronic strains and stresses. What happens in the body affects the mind. Physical strains set up psychological strains. The body is the instrument used by the mind to establish contact with the outside world. Any modification of this instrument must correspondingly modify the mind's relations with external reality. Where the body is maladjusted and under strain, the mind's relations, sensory, emotional, intellectual, conative, with external reality are likely to be unsatisfactory. And the same would seem to be true of the mind's relations with what may be called internal reality—with that more-than-self which, if we choose, we can discover within us and which the mystics have identified with God, the Law, the Light, the integrating principle of the world. All the Eastern mystics are insistent on the necessity of bodily health. A sick man cannot attain enlightenment. They further point out that it is very difficult for a man to acquire the art of contemplation, unless he observes certain rules of diet and adopts certain bodily postures. Similar observations have been made by Christian mystics in the West. For example, the author of *The Cloud of Unknowing* insists, in a very striking and curious passage which I shall quote in a later chapter, that enlightenment, or mystical union with God, is unattainable by those who are physically uncontrolled to the extent of fidgeting, nervously laughing, making .odd gestures and grimaces. Such tics and compulsions (it is a matter of observation) are almost invariably associated with physical maladjustment and strain. Where they exist, the highest forms of non-attachment are unachievable. It follows therefore that the ideal system of physical education must be one which relieves people of maladjustment and strain.

Another condition of non-attachment is awareness. Unawareness is one of the main sources of attachment or evil. "Forgive them, for they know not what they do." Those who know not what they do are indeed in need of forgiveness; for they are responsible for an immense amount of suffering. Yet more urgent than their need to be forgiven is their need to know. For if they knew, it may be that they would not perform those stupid and criminal acts whose ineluctable consequences no amount of human or divine forgiveness can prevent. A good physical education should teach awareness on the physical plane—not the obsessive and unwished-for awareness that pain imposes upon the mind, but voluntary and intentional awareness. The body must be trained to think. True, this happens every time we learn a manual skill; our bodies think when we draw, or play golf, or take a piano lesson. But all such thinking is specialist thinking. What we need is an education for our bodies that shall be, on the bodily plane, liberal and not merely technical and narrowly specific. The awareness that our bodies need is the knowledge of some general principle of right integration and along with it, a knowledge of the proper way to apply that principle in every phase of physical activity.

There can be no non-attachment without inhibition. When the state of non-attachment has become "a second nature," inhibition will doubtless no longer be necessary; for impulses requiring inhibition will not arise. Those in whom non-attachment is a permanent state are few. For everyone else, such impulses requiring inhibition arise with a distressing frequency. The technique of inhibition needs to be learned on all the planes of our being. On the intellectual plane—for we cannot hope to think intelligently or to practise the simplest form of "recollection" unless we learn to inhibit irrelevant thoughts. On the emotional plane—for we shall never reach even the lowest degree of non-attachment unless we can check as they arise the constant movements of malice and vanity, of lust and sloth, of avarice, anger and fear. On the physical plane—for if we are maladjusted (as most of us are in the circumstances of modern urban life), we cannot expect to achieve integration unless we inhibit our tendency to perform actions in the, to us, familiar, maladjusted way. Mind and body are organically one; and it is therefore inherently likely that, if we can learn the art of conscious inhibition on the physical level, it will help us to acquire and practise the same art on the emotional and intellectual levels. What is needed is a practical morality working at every level from the bodily to the intellectual. A good physical education will be one which supplies the body with just such a practical morality. It will be a curative morality, a morality of inhibitions and conscious control, and at the same time, by promoting health and proper physical integration it will be a system of what I have called preventive ethics, forestalling many kinds of trouble by never giving them the opportunity to arise.

So far as I am aware, the only system of physical education which fulfils all these conditions is the system developed by F. M. Alexander. Mr. Alexander has given a full account of his system in three books, each of which is prefaced by Professor John Dewey.* It is therefore unnecessary for me to describe it here—all the more so as no verbal description can do justice to a technique which involves the changing, by a long process of instruction on the part of the teacher and of active co-operation on that of the pupil's, of an individual's sensory experiences. One cannot describe the experience of seeing the colour, red. Similarly one cannot describe the much more complex experience of improved physical co-ordination. A verbal description would mean something only to a person who had actually had the experience described; to the mal-co-ordinated person, the same words would mean something quite different. Inevitably, he would interpret them in terms of his own sensory experiences, which are those of a mal-co-ordinated person. Complete understanding of the system can come only with the practice of it. All I need say in this place is that I am sure, as a matter of personal experience and observation, that it gives us all the things we have been looking for in a system of physical education:

* "Man's Supreme Inheritance," "Creative Conscious Control" and "The Use of the Self."

—relief from strain due to mal-adjustment, and consequent improvement in physical and mental health; increased consciousness of the physical means employed to
gain the ends proposed by the will and, along with this,
a general heightening of consciousness on all levels; a
technique of inhibition, working on the physical level
to prevent the body from slipping back, under the influence of greedy "end-gaining," into its old habits of mal-
co-ordination, and working (by a kind of organic anal-
ogy) to inhibit undesirable impulses and irrelevance on
the emotional and intellectual levels respectively. We
cannot ask more from any system of physical education;
nor, if we seriously desire to alter human beings in a
desirable direction, can we ask any less.

XIII

Religious Practices

RELIGION is, among many other things, a system of education, by means of which human beings may train themselves, first, to make desirable changes in their own personalities and, at one remove, in society and, in the second place, to heighten consciousness and so establish more adequate relations between themselves and the universe of which they are parts.

Religion is this, I repeat, among many other things. For, alas, by no means all the doctrines and practices of the existing religions are calculated to ameliorate character or heighten consciousness. On the contrary, a great deal of what is taught and done in the name of even the most highly evolved religions is definitely pernicious, and a great deal more is ethically neutral—not particularly bad, but, on the other hand, not particularly good. Towards the kind of religion whose fruits are moral evil and a darkening of the mind the rational idealist can only show an uncompromising hostility. Such things as persecution and the suppression or distortion of truth are intrinsically wrong, and he can have nothing to do with religious organizations which countenance such iniquities.

His attitude towards the ethically neutral customs, rites and ceremonies of organized religion will be determined exclusively by the nature of their effects. If such things help to maintain a satisfactory social pat-

[260]

tern, if they serve to facilitate and enrich the relations between man and man, between group and group, then he will accord them a certain qualified favour. True, he may recognize very clearly that such practices do not help men to attain to the highest forms of human development, but are actually impediments in the path. The Buddha put down ritualism as one of the Ten Fetters which bind men to illusion and prevent them from attaining enlightenment. Nevertheless, in view of the fact that most individuals will certainly not wish to attain enlightment—in other words, develop themselves to the limits of human capacity—there may be something to be said in favour of ritualism. Attachment to traditional ceremonials and belief in the magical efficacy of ritual may prevent men from attaining to enlightenment; but on the other hand they may help such individuals as have neither the desire nor the capacity for enlightenment to behave a little better than they otherwise would have done.

It is impossible to discuss the value of rites and symbolic ceremonials without reopening a question already touched upon in the chapters on Inequality and Education: the question of psychological types and degrees of mental development. Significantly enough, most of the historical founders of religions and a majority of religious philosophers have been in agreement upon this matter. They have divided human beings into a minority of individuals capable of making the efforts required to "attain enlightenment" and, a great majority incapable of making such efforts. This conception is fundamental in Hinduism, Buddhism and, in general, all Indian philosophy. It is implicit in the teaching of Lao Tsu, and again in that of the Stoics. Jesus of Nazareth taught that "many are called, but few are chosen" and that there were certain people who constituted "the salt of the earth" and who were therefore able to preserve the world, to prevent it from decaying. The Gnostic sects believed in the existence of esoteric and exoteric teachings, the latter reserved for the many, the former for the few who were capable of profiting by them. The Catholic Church exterminated the Gnostics, but proceeded to organize itself as though the Gnostic belief in esoteric and exoteric teachings were true* For the vulgar it provided ceremonial, magically compulsive formulas, the worship of images, a calendar of holy days. To the few it taught, through the mouth of the mystics, that such external "aids to devotion" were (as Buddha had pointed out many centuries before) strong fetters holding men back from enlightenment or, in Christian phraseology, from communion with God. In practice, Christianity, like Hinduism or Buddhism, is not one religion, but several religions, adapted to the needs of different types of human beings. A Christian church in Southern Spain, or Mexico, or Sicily is singularly like a Hindu temple. The eye is delighted by the same gaudy colours, the same tripe-like decorations, the same gesticulating statues; the nose inhales the same intoxicating smells; the ear and, along with it, the understanding, are lulled by the drone of the same incomprehensible incantations, roused by the same loud, im-

* One of the charges levelled by the Inquisition against Eckhart was that he had spoken openly to the people of holy mysteries.

pressive music. At the other end of the scale, consider the chapel of a Cistercian monastery and the meditation hall of a community of Zen Buddhists. They are equally bare; aids to devotion (in other words fetters holding back the soul from enlightenment) are conspicuously absent from either building. Here are two distinct reli gions for two distinct kinds of human beings.

The history of ideas is to a great extent the history of the misinterpretation of ideas. An outstanding individual makes a record of his life or formulates, in the light of his personal experience, a theory about the nature of the world. Other individuals, not possessing his natural endowments, read what he has written and, because their psychological make-up is different from that of the author, fail to understand what he means. They reinterpret his words in the light of their own experience, their own knowledge, their own prejudices. Consequently they learn from their teacher, not to be like him, but to be more themselves. Misunderstood, his words serve to justify *their* desires, rationalize *their* beliefs. Not all of the magic, the liturgy, the ritual existing in the historical religions is a survival from a more primitive age. A good part of it, it is probable, is relatively new—the product of misunderstanding. Mystical writers recording psychological experiences in symbolic language were often supposed by the non-mystics to be talking about alchemy or magic rites. Episodes in the inner life were projected, in a strangely distorted form, into the outer world, where they helped to swell the majestic stream of primitive superstition. There is a danger that the present widespread interest in oriental psychology and philosophy may lead, through misunderstanding, to a recrudescence of the grossest forms of superstition.

To what extent can rites and formularies, symbolic acts and objects be made use of in modern times? The question has been asked at frequent intervals ever since organized Christianity began to lose its hold upon the West. Attempts have been made to fabricate synthetic rituals. Without much success. The French Revolutionary cult of Reason and the Supreme Being died with the Thermidorean reaction. Comte's religion of Humanity—"Catholicism without Christianity," as T. H. Huxley called it—never took root. Even the rituals and ceremonies devised from time to time by successful Christian revivalists seldom outlive their authors or spread beyond the buildings in which they were originally practised.

On the other hand, new rituals and ceremonials have sprung up in connection with the cults of nationalism and socialism—have sprung up and continued to flourish over a long period of years.

Considering these instances, let us risk a few generalizations. Ritual and ceremonial will arise almost spontaneously wherever masses of people are gathered together for the purpose of taking part in any activity in which they are emotionally concerned. Such rites and ceremonials will survive and develop for just so long as the emotional concern is felt. It is impossible to persuade people who are not emotionally concerned in any given idea, or person, to make a habit of performing rites and ceremonies in connexion with that idea or person. To create a ritual, as Comte did, in the hope that it will create a religious emotion, is to put the cart before the horse. Where the emotional concern exists, ritual will serve to strengthen it, even to revive it when enthusiasm grows weary; but it cannot create emotion. (To be more accurate, it cannot create a lasting sentiment. A ceremony well performed is a work of art from which even the sceptical spectator may "get a kick." But one can be deeply moved by *Macbeth* without being converted to a permanent belief in witchcraft—can be stirred by a Papal Mass or a review of Brownshirts without feeling impelled to become a Catholic or a Nazi.)

At the present time and in the industrialized West, there is not very much to be said in favour of the rites, customs and ceremonies of traditional Christianity. There is not much to be said for them, for the simple reason that they are demonstrably very ineffective. They do absolutely nothing to hold together the social pattern of Christendom, and they have proved themselves incapable of standing up to the competition of the new rites and ceremonies of nationalistic idolatry. Men are much more German or imperialistically British than Protestant, much more French or Fascist than Catholic. In the past, the fetters of Christian ritualism may have held people back from enlightenment; but these fetters did at least serve as strong ties binding individuals to the body of Christian society. Today they have, to a great extent, outlived this social function. Indeed, it would be almost true to say that preoccupation with traditional religious rites and ceremonies is something which actually separates people from the society in the midst of which they live. There are only too many men and women who think that, if they have scrupulously repeated the prescribed phrases, made the proper gestures and observed the traditional taboos, they are excused from bothering about anything else. For these people, the performance of traditional custom has become a substitute for moral effort and intelligence. They fly from the problems of real life into symbolical ceremonial; they neglect their duties towards themselves, their neighbours and their God in order to give idolatrous worship to some traditionally hallowed object, to play liturgical charades or go through some piece of ancient mummery. Let me cite a recent example of this. In the early autumn of 1936 the London *Times* recorded the fact that, in deference to religious sentiment, flying boats were henceforward not to be allowed to come down on the Sea of Galilee. This is a characteristic instance of the way in which preoccupation with sacred objects acts as a fetter holding men back, not only from personal enlightenment, but even from a rational consideration of the facts of contemporary reality. Here is a "religious sentiment" which feels itself deeply offended if flying machines settle on a certain hallowed sheet of water, but which (to judge by the published utterances of Anglican deans and bishops) does not find anything specially shocking in the thought that these same flying machines may be used to drop fire, poison and high-explosives upon the inhabitants of unfortified towns. If this is religion, then God deliver us from such criminal imbecility.

For the rational idealist, what is the moral of the preceding paragraphs, what the practical lesson to be drawn from a consideration of the nature of religious rites and ceremonies? He will conclude, first of all, that, ritualism being a fetter to which a great many human beings are firmly attached, it is useless to try to get rid of it. Next, observing that rites and ceremonies may be used, like any other instrument, for evil purposes no less effectively than for good, he will do all in his power to encourage their use for good purposes and, whether by argument, persuasion or satire, to prevent them from being used to further causes that are evil. Finally, taking warning from the failures of the past, he will not waste his time in fabricating new ceremonials for any movement in which its participants are not already emotionally concerned.

So much for the positively mischievous and the ethically neutral aspects of religion. Let us now consider those elements in religious practice and belief which have a positive value.

All systems of classification tend in some measure to distort reality; but it is impossible to think clearly about reality unless we make use of some classificatory system. At the risk, then, of over-simplifying the facts, I shall classify the varieties of religious practice and religious belief under a number of separate heads.

The present chapter treats solely of existing religious practices, (not of beliefs), and treats them predominantly from a humanistic point of view. From the humanistic point of view, religious practices are valuable in so far as they provide methods of self-education, methods which men can use to transform their characters and enlarge their consciousness.

The methods of which we know the least in the contemporary West are those which I will call the physiological methods. These physiological methods may be classified under a few main headings, as follows.

Most savage peoples and even certain devotees of the higher religions make use of repeated rhythmical movement as a method of inducing unusual states of mind. This rhythmic movement may take almost any form, from the solitary back-and-forward pacing of the Catholic priest reading his breviary, to the elaborate ritual dances of primitives all over the world. The repetition of rhythmical movement seems to have much the same effects as the repetition of verbal formulas or phrases of music: It lulls to rest the superficial part of the consciousness and leaves the deeper mind free either to concentrate on ultimate reality (as in the case of the solitary priest, pacing up and down with his breviary) or to experience a profound sense of solidarity with other human beings and with the presiding divinity (as happens in the case of ritual dancers). Christianity, it would seem, made a great mistake when it allowed the dance to become completely secularized. For men and women of somatotonic type, ritual dances provide a religious experience that seems more satisfying and convincing than any other.

Another physiological method is that of asceticism. Fasting, sleeplessness, discomfort and self-inflicted pain have been used by devotees of every religion as methods, not only of atoning for sin, but also of schooling the will and modifying the ordinary, everyday consciousness.

This last is also the aim of those Indian ascetics who train their bodies systematically, until they are able to exercise conscious control over physiological processes that are normally carried out unconsciously. In many cases they go on to produce unusual mental states by the systematic and profound modification of certain bodily functions, such as respiration and the sexual act.

There is good evidence to show that such practices may produce very valuable results. It is possible for a man who employs the methods of mortification or of Yoga to achieve a high degree of non-attachment to "the things of this world" and at the same time so to heighten his consciousness that he can attach himself more completely than the normal man to that which is greater than himself, to the integrating principle of all being. It is possible, I repeat; but it is not easy. All those who know anything about the methods of mortification and of Yoga, whether as observers or by personal experience, agree that they are dangerous methods. To begin with, they are physiologically dangerous; many bodies break down under the strain imposed upon them. But this is not all; there is also a moral danger. Of those who undertake such methods, only a few are ready to do so for the right reason. Ascetics easily degenerate into record-breakers. There is little to choose between Simeon the Stylite and modern American pole-sitters, or between a fakir on his bed of nails and the self-tormenting competitors in a dancing Marathon. Vanity and the craving for pre-eminence, for distinction, for public recognition figure only too frequently among the motives of the ascetics. Moreover, in all but the most highly trained individuals, physical pain tends to heighten, rather than allay, the normal preoccupation with the body. A man in pain has the greatest difficulty in not identifying himself with the afflicted organ. (The same, of course, is equally true of a man experiencing intense pleasure.) A few ascetics may be able so to school their minds that they can ignore their pain and identify themselves with that which is more than the pain and more than the totality of their personal being. Many, on the contrary, will end up as diminished beings, identified with their pain and with their pride in being able to stand so much of it.

The danger inherent in the practice of methods of conscious physiological control is of a somewhat different kind. The methods of Hatha Yoga, as they are called in India, are said to result in heightened mental and physical powers. (Arthur Avalon gives much interesting information on this subject in his "Kundalini.") *
It is for the sake solely of enjoying these powers and not in order to use them as a means to "enlightenment," that many adepts of Hatha Yoga undertake their training. Pride and sensuality are their motives and the heightened ability to dominate and to enjoy are their rewards. Such people emerge from their training, possessed, indeed, of heightened powers, but of heightened powers that are the instruments of a character that has grown worse instead of better.

Acting, as he must, on the principle that the tree is

* See also Dr. K. Behanan's "Yoga" (New York, 1937).

known by its fruits, the rational idealist will avoid all methods of religious self-education involving extreme asceticism or the profound modification of physiological functions—will go on avoiding them until such time as increased scientific knowledge permits of their being used more safely than is possible at present. Meanwhile, of course, he will not neglect any system of training which promises to increase, without danger, the individual's conscious control of his organism. (This matter has been discussed in some detail at the end of the chapter on Education.)

The second method of self-education taught by the various religions consists essentially in the cultivation of an intimate emotional relationship between the worshipper and a personal God or other divine being. This emotional method is the one of which the West knows most; for it is the method used by the majority of Christians. In India it is known as *bhakti-marga*, the path of devotional faith, as opposed to *karma-marga*, the path of duty or works, and *jñana-marga*, the path of knowledge. *Bhakti-marga* played a relatively small part in Indian religion—at any rate in the religion of the educated classes—until the coming of the Bhagavata reformation of the Middle Ages. Revolting against the pantheism of the Vedanta and the atheism of the Sankhya philosophy and of Buddhism, the leaders of the Bhagavata reformation insisted on the personal nature of God and the eternally personal existence of individual souls. (There is reason to believe that Christian influences were at work on the reformers.) A kind of *bhakti-marga* crept into Buddhism with the rise of the Greater

Vehicle. In this case, however, theologians were careful to insist that the objects of Bhakti, the Buddhas, were not eternal gods and that the ultimate reality substantial to the world, was impersonal.

I have said that, for people of predominantly somatotonic type, rituals involving rhythmical movement provide a particularly satisfying form of religious experience. It is with their muscles that they most easily obtain knowledge of the divine. Similarly, in people of viscerotonic habit religious experience tends naturally to take an emotional form. But it is difficult to have an emotional relation except with a person; the viscerotonic tend, therefore, to rationalize their temperament preferences in terms of a personalistic theology. Their direct intuition, they might say, is of a personal God. But here a very significant fact comes to light (it is discussed at length in the next chapter and need only be mentioned here). Those who take the trouble to train themselves in the arduous technique of mysticism always end, if they go far enough in their work of recollection and meditation, by losing their intuitions of a personal God and having direct experience of an ultimate reality that is impersonal. The experience of the great mystics of every age and country is there to prove that the theology associated with *bhakti-marga* is inadequate, that it misrepresents the nature of ultimate reality. Those who persist in having emotional relationships with a God whom they believe to be personal are people who have never troubled to undertake the arduous training which alone makes possible the mystical union of the soul with the integrating principle of all being. To viscerotonics, with

[272]

a craving for emotional experience, as also to somato-tonics, with a craving for muscular experience, such training must seem particularly arduous. Indeed, the genuine mystical intuition may be an experience which it is all but impossible for many people belonging to these psycho-physiological types ever to have. Be that as it may, the fact remains that such people generally choose the types of religious experience they find most agreeable and easiest to have.

The theology of *bhakti-marga* may be untrue; but it often produces very considerable results with great rapidity. In other words, the emotional method of religious self-education is demonstrably effective. It should be remarked, however, that the emotional method of secular self-education is no less effective. In his volume, *God or Man,* Professor Leuba has pointed out that startling conversions can take place without the question of religion ever arising; that the imitation of admired human models can produce desirable changes of character no less effectively than the imitation of divine models. The trouble with *bhakti-marga* is that it is really too effective by half. Devotion to any object of worship, however intrinsically grotesque or even evil, is capable of producing great changes in the character of the devotees—changes that, up to a point, are genuine ameliorations. Those who have followed the contemporary American cult of the negro man-god, Father Divine, must have been struck by the fact that many, probably most, of Father's worshippers have undergone a striking "change of heart" and are in many respects better men and women than they were before their conversion to

Divinism.* But this improvement of character has very definite limitations. Divinists are committed by their theology to a belief in the perfection of Father. The commands of a perfect being should be obeyed. And, in fact, they are obeyed, even when—and this would seem to be the case in certain of the new church's financial transactions—they are not in accord with the highest principles of morality. The abnormal is worthy of study because of the light it throws upon the normal. Divinism is a kind of fantastic parody of a religion of personal devotion; but just because it is a parody, it exhibits very clearly the dangers and defects, as well as the virtues, of *bhakti-marga*. *Bhakti* towards Father produced excellent results for just so long as Father himself behaved with perfect virtue, or as his followers attributed perfect virtue to him. The moment he ceased to be virtuous, or the moment non-virtuous actions were attributed to him under the mistaken belief that they were virtuous, the devotion of his followers ceased to be an influence for good in their lives and became an influence for evil. It is obvious that the obedient devotees or imitators of a person who either is or is believed to be in some way evil, cannot themselves be wholly good.

What applies to the worship of Father Divine, applies, *mutatis mutandis*, to all other forms of *bhakti-marga*. Devotion to, and imitation of, a personal divinity provide worshippers with more energy to change themselves and the world around them than any other form of religious self-education. This is an empirical fact. Now,

* See "The Incredible Messiah" by Robert Allerton Parker (New York, 1937).

energy is a good thing provided it be well directed. Devotion to a personal deity produces a great deal of energy; does it also give a satisfactory direction to the energy produced? A study of history shows that the results of worshipping a personality are by no means necessarily good. Indeed, the energy developed by devotion to a person has been directed to undesirable ends almost as often as to desirable ones. That this should be so is, in the very nature of the case, only to be expected. Devotion to a human person who is still alive, but who has been deified by general acclaim, can hardly fail to be disastrous in the long run. *Bhakti-marga* in regard to an Alexander the Great, a Napoleon, a Hitler may begin by producing certain desirable changes in the worshippers; but it cannot fail to produce degenerative changes in the person worshipped. "Power always corrupts," wrote Lord Acton. "Absolute power absolutely corrupts. All great men are bad." A deified man is morally ruined by the process of being worshipped. Those who adoringly obey and imitate him are making it inevitable, by their very adoration, that they shall obey and imitate a thoroughly bad, corrupted person.

In cases where the adored man is no longer alive, adoration cannot corrupt its object. But even the best human persons have their defects and limitations; and to these, if they happen to be dead, must be added the defects and limitations of their biographers. Thus, according to his very inadequate biographers, Jesus of Nazareth was never preoccupied with philosophy, art, music, or science and ignored almost completely the problems of politics, economics and sexual relations. It is also recorded of him that he blasted a fig tree for not bearing fruit out of season, that he scourged the shop-keepers in the temple precincts and caused a herd of swine to drown. Scrupulous devotion to and imitation of the person of Jesus have resulted only too frequently in a fatal tendency, on the part of earnest Christians, to despise artistic creation and philosophic thought; to disparage the inquiring intelligence, to evade all long-range, large-scale problems of politics and economics, and to believe themselves justified in displaying anger, or as they would doubtless prefer to call it, "righteous indignation."

In many cases devotion is directed, not to a living human person, nor to a human person who lived in the past, but to an eternal, omniscient, all-powerful God, who is regarded as being in some way a person. Even in this case *bhakti-marga* is apt to lead to unsatisfactory results. The theologians are at great pains to insist that the personal God is an absolutely perfect person; but, in spite of all their precautions, the deity tends to be thought of by his adorers as being like the only kind of person of whom they have direct knowledge—that is to say, the human individual. This natural tendency to con-ceive of a personal God as a being similar to a human person is especially prevalent among Christians, brought up on the Old Testament. In this remarkable compen-dium of Bronze-Age literature, God is personal to the point of being almost sub-human. Too often the believer has felt justified in giving way to his worst passions by the reflection that, in doing so, he is basing his conduct on that of a God who feels jealousy and hatred, cannot

[276]

control his rage and behaves in general like a particularly ferocious oriental tyrant. The frequency with which men have identified the prompting of their own passions with the voice of an all too personal God is really appalling. The history of those sects which have believed that individuals could base their conduct upon the moment-to-moment guidance of a personal deity makes most depressing reading. From Thomas Schucker, the Swiss Anabaptist, who was divinely guided to cut off his brother's head, and who actually did so in the sight of a large audience, including his own father and mother, down to Smyth-Piggott who believed that he was God and who fathered upon the parlour-maid two illegitimate children called respectively Power and Glory— the long succession of divinely justified cranks and lunatics and criminals comes marching down through history into the present time. Belief in a personal God has released an enormous amount of energy directed towards good ends; but it has probably released an equal amount of energy directed towards ends that were silly, or mad, or downright evil. It has also led to that enormous overvaluation of the individual ego, which is so characteristic of Western popular philosophy. All the great religions have taught the necessity of transcending personality; but the Christians have made it particularly difficult for themselves to act upon this teaching. They have accompanied the injunction that men should lose their lives in order to save them by the assertion that God himself is a person and that personal values are the highest that we can know.

A personal deity tends to be regarded as completely

[277]

transcendent, as somebody *out there*, apart from the percipient and different from him. At various times in the history of Christendom, thinkers have insisted with particular emphasis upon the incommensurable otherness of God. Augustine, Calvin, Kierkegaard and, in our own day, Barth have dwelt emphatically and at length upon this theme. The doctrine of the complete transcendence and otherness of God is probably untrue and its results in the lives of those who believed it have always been extremely undesirable. God being completely other is regarded as being capable of anything—even (in Kierkegaard's phrase) of the most monstrous "teleological suspensions of morality." Again, belief in the otherness of God entails belief that grace alone is effective in procuring salvation and that works and a systematic cultivation of the inner life are useless. There is nothing fortuitous in the fact that the first and most ruthless capitalists were men brought up in the tradition of Calvinism. Believing that good works and the inner life were without any eternal significance, they gave up charity and self-education and turned all their attention to getting on in the world. Borrowing from the Old Testament the sordid doctrine that virtue deserves a material reward, they were able to amass wealth and oppress the poor with a thoroughly good conscience; their wealth, they were convinced, was a sign of God's favour, the other fellow's poverty, of moral turpitude.

It would be possible to multiply such instances of the disastrous practical effects of wrong metaphysical beliefs. "All that we are," writes the author of the Dhammapada, "is the result of what we have thought." If we think wrongly, our being and our actions will be unsatisfactory. Thus, the Aztecs believed that the sun was a living person who required for his food the blood of human victims. If the blood were not provided in sufficient quantities, the sun would die and all life on the earth would come to an end. Therefore the Aztecs had to devote a great part of their energy to making war in order that they might have enough prisoners to satisfy the sun's appetite.

Another case. In the basement of the London Museum there hangs a broadsheet describing the trial in the late eighteen-thirties of two men who had been accused of homosexual practices. Condemning them, the judge pointed out that, by their crime, these two men were gravely endangering their country. Sodom had been destroyed because of Sodomy. There was every reason to suppose that, if homosexuality were allowed to flourish there, London would suffer the same fate. It followed therefore that the two delinquents richly deserved their death. Accordingly it was ordered that they should be hanged—on a different scaffold from that on which the other criminals were executed, lest by their presence they should somehow contaminate the relatively innocent murderers, coiners and housebreakers condemned at the same assize.

Yet another instance. Hitlerian theology affirms that there is a Nordic race, inherently superior to all others. Hence it is right that Nordics should organize themselves for conquest and should do their best to exterminate people like the Jews, who are members of inferior races.

It is worth remarking that, in all these cases, the presiding deity was personal. For the Aztecs the sun was a person, capable of feeling hunger for blood. The God, who, it was feared, would destroy London because of the sexual eccentricities of its male inhabitants, was the all too personal God of the Old Testament. Hitler's God is a rejuvenated version of the Kaiser's "old German God" —a divine person deeply concerned in the fate of Bismarck's empire and ready to fight on the side of its armies, as Athena fought on the side of the Greeks.

Theological beliefs leading to undesirable conduct need not necessarily be associated with the dogma of the personality of God. But as a matter of historical fact, the more eccentric theological errors have very often been associated with a belief in God's personality. This is only natural. A person has passions and caprices; and it is therefore natural that he should do odd things— clamour for the hearts of sacrificial victims, demand the persecution of the Jews, threaten destruction to whole cities because a few of their inhabitants happen to be homosexuals.

The dangers of *bhakti-marga* are manifest; but unfortunately the fact that its results are often pernicious does nothing to lessen its attractiveness to human beings of a certain psychological type. Many people enjoy the actual process of *bhakti-marga* too much to be able to pay any attention to its effects on themselves and on society at large. History shows that, where the emotional method has once taken root, it tends to remain in possession of the field. I have already mentioned the Bhagavata reformation which so profoundly changed the nature of Indian religion during the Middle Ages. To this day *bhakti-marga* retains the popularity it won between the twelfth and the fifteenth centuries. Japanese Buddhism, as readers of "The Tale of Genji" will recall, had become in Lady Murasaki's day (at the beginning of the eleventh century) predominantly a religion of personal devotion. "The Indian founder of Buddhism," to quote Professor Geden, "was hardly more than a figure and a name." Sakyamuni's religion, a combination of *karma-marga* with *jñana-marga*, had been replaced by *bhakti-marga* directed towards Amida Buddha. "A reform movement was initiated in Japan in the thirteenth century, the object of which was to reinstate Sakyamuni in the supreme place. It proved, however, an entire failure." The way of devotion seemed more agreeable to the Japanese than the ways of knowledge and duty.

In Christianity *bhakti* towards a personal being has always been the most popular form of religious practice. Up to the time of the Counter-Reformation, however, the way of knowledge ("mystical theology" as it is called in Christian language) was accorded an honourable place beside the way of devotion. From the middle of the sixteenth century onwards the way of knowledge came to be neglected and even condemned. We are told by Dom John Chapman that "Mercurian, who was general of the society (of Jesus) from 1573 to 1580, forbade the use of the works of Tauler, Ruysbroek, Suso, Harphius, St. Gertrude, and St. Mechtilde." Every effort was made by the Counter-Reformers to heighten the worshipper's devotion to a personal divinity. The literary content of Baroque art is hysterical, almost epileptic, in the violence of its emotionality. It even becomes necessary to call in physiology as an aid to feeling. The ecstasies of the saints are represented by seventeenth-century artists as being frankly sexual. Seventeenth-century drapery writhes like so much tripe. In the equivocal personage of Margaret Mary Alacocque, seventeenth-century piety pores over a bleeding and palpitating heart. From this orgy of emotionalism and sensationalism Catholic Christianity seems never completely to have recovered.

The significance of *bhakti* in its relation to cosmological belief is discussed in the next chapter. Our business here is only with its psychological and social aspects. Its results, as we have already seen, are generally good up to a certain point, but bad beyond that point. Nevertheless, *bhakti* is so enjoyable, especially to people of viscerotonic habit, that it is bound to survive. In our own day a majority of Europeans find it intellectually impossible to pay devotion to the supernatural persons who were the objects of worship during the Counter-Reformation period. But the desire to worship persists, the process of worshipping still retains its attraction. The masses continue to tread the path of devotion; but the objects of this *bhakti* are no longer saints and a personal God; they are the personified nation or class, and the deified Leader. The change is wholly for the worse.

It is clear that, given the existence of viscerotonic and somatotonic types, religious practices of the emotional and physiological kind will always be popular. Physiological practices can adapt themselves to almost any sort

[282]

of belief. The emotional method, on the other hand, inevitably imposes upon those who practise it a personalistic theology. Those who enjoy *bhakti* can never be persuaded to give up their pleasurable practices and the belief correlated with them. In these circumstances, what is the rational idealist to do? So far as I can see, he has two main tasks. He must do his best to advertise the fact that the physiological and the emotional are not the only methods of religious self-education, and especially that there is an alternative to *bhakti* and the almost certainly false beliefs with which *bhakti* is always associated. Owing to the disparagement during recent centuries of mystical theology, or the way of knowledge, many religiously minded Europeans are not even aware that an alternative to *bhakti* exists. The existence of that alternative must be proclaimed and its practical uses and cosmological implications set forth. The second task before the rational idealist is the harder of the two. Accepting as inevitable the continued existence of a large residuum of practisers of *bhakti-marga*, he will have to do all in his power to turn this irrepressible stream of *bhakti* into the channels in which it will do the least mischief. For example, it is manifest that *bhakti* directed towards deified leaders and personified nations, classes or parties must result in evil, not only for society, but ultimately (whatever the immediate good effects in regard to the minor virtues) for the individual as well. To repeat this obvious fact in and out of season is perhaps the most wearisome but also the most necessary of the tasks which the rational idealist must undertake. Towards the transcendental religions his attitude should be discriminatingly critical. The point that he must always remember and of which he must remind the world is that, whenever God is thought of, in Aristotle's phrase, as the commander-in-chief rather than as the order of the army—as a transcendent person rather than as an immanent-and-also-transcendent principle of integration—persecution always tends to arise. It is an extremely significant fact that, before the coming of the Mohammedans, there was virtually no persecution in India. The Chinese pilgrim Hiuen Tsiang, who visited India in the first half of the seventh century and has left a circumstantial account of his fourteen-year stay in the country, makes it clear that Hindus and Buddhists lived side by side without any show of violence. Each party attempted the conversion of the other; but the methods used were those of persuasion and argument, not those of force. Neither Hinduism nor Buddhism is disgraced by anything corresponding to the Inquisition; neither was ever guilty of such iniquities as the Albigensian crusade or such criminal lunacies as the religious wars of the sixteenth and seventeenth centuries. The Moslems who invaded India brought with them the idea of a God who was not the order of the army of being, but its general. *Bhakti* towards this despotic person was associated with wholesale slaughter of Buddhists and Hindus. Similarly *bhakti* towards the personal God of Christianity has been associated, throughout the history of that religion, with the wholesale slaughter of pagans and the retail torture and murder of heretics. It is the business of the rational idealist to harp continually upon this all-important fact. In this way, perhaps, he may be able to mitigate the evil

[284]

tendencies which history shows to be inherent in the way of devotion and the correlated belief in a personal deity.

It has been necessary to dwell at considerable length on the subject of the emotional method of religious self-education, for the good reason that this method possessed, and still possesses, very great historical importance. To the third method of religious self-education, the method of meditation, I must also devote a good deal of space. It is important not only historically, because of its influence on the affairs of men, but also metaphysically, because of the light it throws on the nature of ultimate reality. With its metaphysical significance I shall deal in the next chapter. In this place I am concerned mainly with the social and psychological results of the methods.*

The method of meditation has often been used in conjunction with the emotional and physiological methods. In its purest form, however, it would seem to be quite independent of either. It is possible for meditation to be practised by those who are neither extreme ascetics, nor Hatha Yogis, and also by those who do not believe in a personal God. Indeed, it might even be argued that it is impossible for those who do believe in a personal God ever adequately to practise meditation or to have a genuine mystical experience. Of this I shall have more to say later. Meanwhile, we must concern ourselves with the practical aspects of the subject. From a humanistic point of view, what precisely is the point and purpose of

* For further information on the subject consult A. Tillyard, "Religious Exercises"; Bede Frost, "The Art of Mental Prayer"; and the anonymous "Concentration and Meditation" published by the Buddhist Lodge, London. All these contain bibliographies.

[285]

meditation? The following words from Professor Irving Babbitt's very valuable essay on "Buddha and the Occident" supply the answer. "We come here," writes Professor Babbitt, "to what is for Buddha fundamental in religion. To many things that have been regarded as indispensable by other faiths—for example, prayer and belief in a personal deity—he grants a secondary place or even no place at all; but without the act of recollection or spiritual concentration he holds that the religious life cannot subsist at all." What is the purpose of meditation and what, for the rational idealist, is its value? Here again Babbitt is enlightening. He says of Buddhist love and compassion that they can, like Nirvana, "be understood only in connection with the special form of activity that is put forth in meditation. Buddhist love does not well forth spontaneously from the natural man, but is, like Christian charity, the supernatural virtue *par excellence*. The current confusion on this point is perhaps the most striking outcome of the sentimentalism of the eighteenth century, and of the emotional romanticism of the nineteenth century that prolonged it. This confusion may be defined psychologically as a tendency to substitute for a superrational concentration of will a subrational expansion of feeling." The function, then, of meditation is to help a man to put forth a special quality of will. ("Meditation," says San Pedro de Alcantara, "is nothing but a discourse addressed by the intellect to the will.") This special quality of will, which is peculiar to a man, must be regarded as a fact of observation and experience. How shall this fact be explained? The Christian, as Babbitt points out, explains it in terms of divine grace, as something imparted from some supernatural source existing outside the individual. The Buddhist affirms that "self is the lord of self" and sees the super-rational will as something latent in the individual psyche, a potentiality that any man, if he so desires and knows how, can actualize either in his present existence or (more probably, since the road to enlightenment is long and steep) in some future life. We see then, that, from a humanistic point of view, meditation is a particularly effective method of self-education.

Rites and ceremonials are essentially social activities. (The person who wishes to perform rites in private is generally the victim of a compulsion neurosis, which forces him, as Dr. Johnson was forced, to live his life to the accompaniment of elaborate gesticulations and formulas.) They provide, among other things, a mechanism by means of which people having a common emotional concern may have their sense of solidarity revived. Ritual is a kind of emotional cement which can give cohesion to great masses of people.

Physiological religion may be either solitary or social. Thus, considerable numbers of individuals can take part in a religious dance; but where the training is by means of ascetic practices or the acquisition of conscious control over hitherto unconscious physical processes, it must in the nature of things be solitary.

In the same way emotional religion may be either solitary or social. The attempt to establish an emotional relationship with a divine person may be made either alone or in the company of others. In the latter case some form of ritual is frequently made to serve, as it were, as

a channel along which the shared emotion of the worshippers may flow towards its object.

Meditation is generally practised in solitude; but there
is also such a thing as group meditation. The conditions
for successful group meditation are as follows. First, the
group must not exceed a certain size, otherwise it is extremely unlikely that its members will attain to that
intuition of solidarity with one another and with something greater than themselves, which it is the purpose of
group meditation to achieve. Second, the individuals
composing the group must be exercised in the art of
recollection and have some experience of its good re-
·sults. A group into which children are admitted, or
which contains adults who, however well intentioned,
do not know how to practise recollection, nor what is
its value when practised, is practically certain to achieve
nothing. Neglecting to study the psychology of their
religion, the Quakers have often made the mistake of
attempting group-meditation in meetings of unwieldy
size, disturbed by the presence of fidgeting children and
untrained adults. Such meetings are almost always a failure. Not all Quaker meetings, however, are failures.
Where conditions are favourable, the purpose of group
meditation is still achieved, just as it was in the early
days of Quakerism. Group meditation is known among
the Hinayana Buddhists of Ceylon and the Mahayana
Buddhists in Tibet. In Japan the Zen monks practise
recollection all together, each in his appointed place in
the meditation hall of the monastery. Group meditation
is also practised by certain Moslem dervishes in Asia

Minor—or at least was practised by them, until Kemal Ataturk saw fit, a few years ago, to hang them all.

It is worth while in this context to expand a statement made in an earlier chapter to the effect that all dictators and, in general, all politically minded reformers are profoundly distrustful of the mystic. The reason for this is not far to seek. "Religion," in Professor Whitehead's words, "is world loyalty." There is a "connection between universality and solitariness," inasmuch as "universality is a disconnection from immediate surroundings." But disconnexion from immediate surroundings is precisely what the politician, especially the dictatorial politician who thinks in terms of class and nation, cannot tolerate. All the dictators, whatever their colour, have attacked religion. Where the dictatorship is revolutionary, this hostility to religion is due in part to the fact that, as a political institution, the Church is generally on the side of the vested interests. But even where, as in Germany, the dictatorship supports and is supported by the vested interests, hostility to religion is hardly less intense than in countries where the dictatorship is revolutionary. In Italy, it is true, Mussolini has made his peace with the Church—but has made it on his own terms. The Church has received a few square miles of independent territory; but Mussolini has taken in exchange the Church's influence over the Italian mind. Italy, then, is only an apparent exception to the rule. Any religion—whether theistic, pantheistic or, like Buddhism, atheistic—which trains men to be non-attached to the "things of this world" and which teaches them loyalty to the integrating principle of the universe is anathema to the dictator, who demands of his subjects intense attachment, in the form of a frenzied nationalism, and a loyalty addressed exclusively to himself and the State of which he is the head. The dictator and, in general, the politician cannot admit an individual's right to universality and solitariness. He demands that all men shall be passionately gregarious and parochial. Hence Hitler's persecution of Christians, Protestant and Catholic alike; hence Russia's anti-God campaigns; hence the liquidation of the mystical sects of dervishes, not only by Kemal, but also by Ibn Saud; hence Mussolini's machiavellian use of religion as an instrument of government, hence his policy of making God play second fiddle to Caesar, hence the care he takes that the young shall not be taught monotheistic world loyalty, but only loyalty to the local idols, the nation, the Party and himself. In Japan the ruling classes have used the technique of meditation to train the will in the service of militarism. Naval cadets were, perhaps still are, put through a course of Zen mind-training. Like all other instruments, this method can be misused by those who wish to do so.

XIV

Beliefs

IN THE preceding chapters I have posed and attempted to answer three questions. First: what do we want to become? Second: what are we now? Third: how do we propose to pass from our present condition to the condition we desire to reach? Of these three questions, the third has been answered methodically, in a series of more or less elaborate discussions of ways and means. The second has been answered incidentally at different stages of these discussions. The first, it will be remembered, was asked in the opening chapter and received only the briefest and most categorical answer. In what follows I propose to examine those answers—to consider the social ideals of the prophets and the personal ideals of the founders of religion in the light of what we know about the world. "All that we are, is the result of what we have thought." Men live in accordance with their philosophy of life, their conception of the world. This is true even of the most thoughtless. It is impossible to live without a metaphysics. The choice that is given us is not between some kind of metaphysic and no metaphysic; it is always between a good metaphysic and a bad metaphysic, a metaphysic that corresponds reasonably closely with observed and inferred reality and one that doesn't. Logically, this discussion of the nature of the world should have preceded the discussion of the practical ways and means for modifying ourselves and the society in which we live. But the arrangement that is logically most correct is not always the most convenient. For various reasons it has seemed to be expedient to reserve this discussion of first principles to the last chapters.

Let us begin by a summary, in the most general terms, of what we know about the world we live in. Science, in Meyerson's phrase, is the reduction of diversity to identity.* The diverse, the brute irrational fact, is given by our senses. But we are not content to accept diversity as so given. We have a hunger and thirst for explanation and, for the human mind, explanation consists in the discovery of identity behind diversity. Any theory which postulates the existence of identities behind diversities strikes us as being intrinsically plausible.

Nature seems to satisfy the mind's craving; for, upon investigation, it turns out that identities do in fact underlie apparent diversity. But explanation in these terms is never quite complete. The facts of sensation and of irreversible change in time are irrationals which cannot be completely rationalized by reduction to identity. Science recognizes the specificity of things as well as their underlying sameness. Hegel's mistake was to imagine that nature was wholly rational and therefore deducible *a priori*. It would be convenient if this were the case; but unfortunately it isn't.

The diversity of the material world has been reduced, so far as such reduction is possible, to an ultimate identity. All matter, according to the physicist, is built up, in a limited number of patterns, out of units of energy which, in isolation, seem to possess none of the qualities

* See chapter II.

ordinarily associated with matter in the mass. Between a billion sub-atomic units and one sub-atomic unit there is a difference, not only of quantity, but also of quality. The natural sciences, such as physics, chemistry, biology, are concerned with matter as built up into varying degrees of patterned complexity. The specificity of things, immediately perceived by our senses, is found to be correlated with the number and the arrangement of ultimate units of energy.

The material universe is pictured by science as composed of a diversity of patterns of a single substance. Common-sense arbitrarily selects certain packets of patterned energy-units and regards them as separate, individual existents. This proceeding would seem to be entirely unjustifiable. So-called separate, individual existents are dependent upon one another for their very being. They are inter-connected by a network of relationships—electro-magnetic, gravitational, chemical and, in the case of sentient beings, mental. That network gives them their being and reality. An individual existent is nothing except in so far as it is a part of a larger whole. In other words, it is not an individual existent. The things we ordinarily call objects or individuals—a tree, a man, a table—are not "concrete realities," as the romantic anti-intellectuals would have us believe. They are abstractions from a reality that consists, as systematic investigation reveals, of a network of relations between the interdependent parts of an incalculably greater whole. A man, for example, is what he is only in virtue of his relationship with the surrounding universe. His entire existence is conditioned by his neighbourhood to the earth, with its powerful gravitational field; radiations of many kinds make him dependent on distant heavenly bodies; he is the *locus* of a continuous process of chemical exchange; mentally, he is related to and conditioned by the minds of his contemporaries and predecessors. The common-sense claim that we live among, and ourselves are, independent existents is based upon ignorance. In present circumstances, however, those who insist on talking of men and women as though they were "concrete" independent existents can excuse themselves on the ground that such a description, though incorrect, is less misleading than that of the political theorists who consider that human beings should be sacrificed to such entities as "the nation," "the state," "the party," "the destiny of the race" and so on. The truth is that there are many different levels of abstraction from reality. The entities with which political theory deals belong to a higher order of abstraction than do the separate, individual existents of common sense— are more remote, that is to say, from concrete reality, which consists of the interdependent parts of a totality. The monstrous evils which arise when remote abstractions, like "nation" and "state" are regarded as realities more concrete and of greater significance than human beings may be remedied, in some measure, by the insistence on the relative concreteness of individual men and women. But this last doctrine is itself the source of very great evils, which cannot be remedied until we recognize, and choose to act upon, the truth that the "individual" is also an abstraction from reality. Separate, individual existents are illusions of common sense. Scientific investigation reveals (and these findings, as we shall see later on, are confirmed by the direct intuition of the trained mystic and contemplative) that concrete reality consists of the interdependent parts of a totality and that independent existents are merely abstractions from that reality.

Recent scientific investigations have made it clear that the world of sense experience and of common sense is only a small part of the world as a whole. It is small for two reasons: first, because we are confined to a particular point in space and have scarcely any knowledge by direct acquaintance and little knowledge even by inference of the conditions prevailing in distant parts of the universe; second, because the organs by means of which we establish direct communication with the outside world are incapable of apprehending the whole of reality. This second limitation is of more significance than the first. Even if we were able to make voyages of exploration through inter-stellar space, we should still be incapable of seeing electro-magnetic vibrations shorter than those we now perceive as violet or longer than those of which we are conscious as red. We should still be unable actually to see or feel even so large an object as a molecule. The shortest instant of time perceptible to us would still be a large fraction of a second. We should still be stone deaf to all sounds above a certain pitch. We should still be without the faculties that enable migrating birds to find their way. And so on. Every animal species inhabits a home-made universe, hollowed out of the real world by means of its organs of perception and its intellectual faculties. In man's case the intellectual faculties are so highly developed that he is able, unlike the other animals, to infer the existence of the larger world enclosing his private universe. He cannot see beyond the violet; but he knows by inference that ultra-violet radiations exist and he is even able to make practical use of these radiations, which sense and common sense assure him do not exist. The universe in which we do our daily living is the product of our limitations. We ourselves have made it, selecting it (because we wished to or were incapable of doing otherwise) from a total reality much larger than, and qualitatively different from, the universe of common-sense. To this most important of fundamental scientific discoveries I shall have occasion to return, in another context, later on.

So much for the scientific picture of the material world. The scientific picture of mind is unfortunately much less clearly outlined. Indeed, there is no single scientific picture of mind; there are several irreconcilably different pictures. Some scientific investigators insist that mind is merely an epiphenomenon of matter; that the brain secretes thought as the liver secretes bile; that the very notion of consciousness can be discarded altogether and that all mental activity can be explained in terms of conditioned reflexes; that the mind is nothing but an instrument, forged during the course of evolution, for securing food, sexual satisfaction and the conditions of physical survival. Others, on the contrary, argue that the phenomena investigated by science are to a considerable extent constructs of the investigating consciousness; that mind cannot be determined by a "matter" which is itself in part a creation of mind; that mind

is a fundamental reality in the universe and is consequently able to pass valid judgments about the nature
of the world; that the laws of thought are also laws of
things. Which of these two parties is in the right? In
this context one fact emerges as highly significant. All
men of science, whatever their views, consistently act *as
though* they believed in the ability of the human intellect, using the method of logic, to make true judgments
about the nature of the world. Such is the behaviour even
of the Behaviourist. But, according to his own theory,
the Behaviourist (like the other disparagers of mind)
has no right to behave in this way. If mind is merely an
epiphenomenon of matter, if consciousness is completely determined by physical motions, if the intellect
is only a machine for securing food and sexual pleasure,
then there is absolutely no reason for supposing that any
theory produced by this instrument can have universal
validity. If Behaviourism, for example, is correct, there
is no reason for supposing that the mind can make any
kind of valid judgment about the world. But among
judgments about the world figures the theory of Behaviourism. Therefore, if Behaviourism is correct, there
is no reason for attaching the slightest importance to the
opinions, among others, of Behaviourists. In other
words, if Behaviourism is correct, it is probable that Behaviourism is incorrect.

All who advance theories of mind containing the
words "nothing but," tend to involve themselves in this
kind of contradiction. The very fact that they formulate
theories which they believe to have general validity, the
very fact that, having studied a few phenomena (which

[297]

are anyhow not phenomena but "epiphenomena," facts of consciousness), they should feel themselves justified in making inductions about all phenomena past, present and future, constitutes in itself a sufficient denial of the validity of "nothing-but" judgments concerning the nature of the mind. All science is based upon an act of faith—faith in the validity of the mind's logical processes, faith in the ultimate explicability of the world, faith that the laws of thought are laws of things. In practice, I repeat, if not always in theory, such conceptions are fundamental to all scientific activity. For the rest, scientists are opportunists. They will pass from a common-sense view of the world to advanced idealist theories, making use of one or the other according to the field of study in which they are at work. Unfortunately, few scientists in these days of specialization are ever called upon to work in more than one small field of study. Hence there is a tendency on the part of individual specialists to accept as true particular theories which are in fact only temporarily convenient. It is highly unfortunate that so few scientists are ever taught anything about the metaphysical foundations of science.

Recent research in medicine, in experimental psychology and in what is still called parapsychology has thrown some light on the nature of mind and its position in the world. During the last forty years the conviction has steadily grown among medical men that very many cases of disease, organic as well as functional, are directly caused by mental states. The body becomes ill because the mind controlling it either secretly wants to make it ill, or else because it is in such a state of agitation that it cannot prevent the body from sickening. Whatever its physical nature, resistance to disease is unquestionably correlated with the psychological condition of the patient.* That even so grossly "physical" a complaint as dental caries may be due to mental causes was maintained in a paper read before the American Dental Congress in 1937. The author pointed out that children living on a perfectly satisfactory diet may still suffer from dental decay. In such cases, investigation generally shows that the child's life at home or at school is in some way unsatisfactory. The teeth decay because their owner is under mental strain.

Mind not only makes sick, it also cures. An optimistic patient has more chance of getting well than a patient who is worried and unhappy. The recorded instances of faith healing include cases in which even organic diseases were cured almost instantaneously.

Experimenters in hypnotism have shown that it is possible to raise a blister by merely telling a deeply hypnotized subject that he is being burnt. The metal which touches the skin is cold; but the subject feels pain and displays all the physical symptoms of a burn. Conversely, hypnotism can be used to produce anesthesia, even in major operations. Thus, in the late 'forties of last century, James Esdaile performed over two hundred operations upon patients anesthetized by means of hypnosis. Esdaile's surgical technique was pre-Listerian; nevertheless, the mortality among his hypnotized patients was extremely low.

* For the physical basis of resistance see "The Nature of Disease" by J. E. R. MacDonagh, F.R.C.S.

[299]

Systematic researches designed to demonstrate the existence of telepathy have been conducted at intervals during the last fifty years. Of these the most recent and the most considerable are those which Professor Rhine has been carrying out at Duke University in North Carolina. Rhine's work, which has been successfully repeated by several other investigators, leaves no doubt as to the existence of telepathy and clairvoyance and very little doubt as to the existence of pre-vision. In his presidential address delivered before the Society for Psychical Research in 1936 Professor C. D. Broad discusses the problems raised by telepathy. How does telepathy work? That it is not a physical process akin to radio transmission is obvious; for the strength of the messages does not diminish with distance. After discussing various other alternatives Professor Broad concludes that it is probably necessary to postulate the existence of some kind of purely mental medium, in which individual minds are bathed, as in a kind of non-physical ether. If there is such a thing as pre-vision, we must presume that this mental medium has its existence outside time. It would seem, then, that mind, or at any rate something of a mental nature—a "psychic factor," within a psychic medium—exists independently of the body and of the spatial and temporal conditions of bodily life.

I have considered the scientific picture of the material world and the scientific pictures of mind. It is now time to consider the scientific picture of the history of this mental-material conglomerate. The only part of the universe with which we have direct acquaintance is this planet. It is also the only part of the universe in which we can study life and consciousness. How far are we justified in drawing inferences about the general nature of things from the inferences previously drawn from the rather scanty evidence about the history of life on this planet? It is hard indeed to say. We have seen that matter on the earth seems to be built up from the same energy-units as constitute matter in remote parts of the universe and that the laws of thought are laws of things, not only here, but, to all appearances, also there. This being so, to generalize from our inferences regarding the nature of our planetary history would seem to be a process that is at any rate not completely illegitimate. Meanwhile, however, we have to discover what the nature of that history is.

I am not qualified to discuss the methods of evolution, nor, in the present context, does there seem to be any good reason for embarking upon such a discussion. For our particular purposes, the results of evolution are more significant than the mechanism by which those results were achieved. In regard to this mechanism, the evidence available seems to point to the conclusion that mutation, hybridism, retardation of growth and foetalization (which are themselves the products of mutation), and natural selection are sufficient to account for evolutionary change and that it is unnecessary to invoke such concepts as orthogenesis or the inheritance of acquired characters. Lamarckism has often been supported by those who are anxious to vindicate the pre-eminence of mind in the world. But, as Haldane has pointed out, these crusaders are really doing a disservice to their cause. If characters acquired as the result of more or less intelligently directed effort are inherited, then we should expect evolution to be a rapid process. But in fact it is extremely slow. If evolution is due to "cunning" rather than "luck," then the cunning must be of a pretty feeble kind; for it has brought life a relatively short way in a very long time. In fact, the evidence for Lamarckism is extremely inadequate. (Neither Lamarckism nor the orthogenetics theory seems to be compatible with the fact that most mutations are demonstrably deleterious.) Mind, as we know, can affect the body profoundly and in a great variety of ways. But, as a matter of empirical fact, this power of affecting the body is limited. To modify the arrangement of the genes must be numbered, it would seem, among the things it cannot do.

There is only one other point in regard to the mechanism of selection about which I need speak in the present context. Competition, when it exists, is of two kinds: between members of different species (inter-specific) and between members of the same species (intra-specific). Intra-specific selection is commoner among abundant species than among species with a small membership and plays a more important part in their evolution. Many of the results of natural selection are demonstrably deleterious and this is found to be the case above all where the selection has been brought about by intra-specific competition. For example, intra-specific competition leads to an excessively precise adaptation to a given set of circumstances—in other words to excessive specialization which, as we shall see later on, is always inimical to genuine biological progress. Haldane regards all intra-specific competition as being, on the whole, biologically evil. Competition between adults of the same species tends to "render the species as a whole less successful in coping with its environment. . . . The special adaptation favoured by intra-specific competitions divert a certain amount of energy from other functions." Man has now little to fear from competition with other species. His worst enemies outside his own species are insects and bacteria; and even with these he has been, and doubtless will continue to be, able to deal successfully. For man, competition is now predominantly intra-specific. A dispassionate analysis of the circumstances in which the human race now lives makes it clear that most of this intra-specific competition is not imposed by any kind of biological necessity, but is entirely gratuitous and voluntary. In other words, we are wantonly and deliberately pursuing a policy which we need not pursue and which we have the best scientific reasons for supposing to be disastrous to the species as a whole. We are using our intelligence to adapt ourselves more and more effectively to the modern conditions of intra-specific competition. We are doing our best to develop a militaristic "hypertely," to become, in other words, dangerously specialized in the art of killing our fellows.

Evolution has resulted in the world as we know it today. Is there any reason for regarding this world as superior to the world of earlier geological epochs? In other words, can evolution be regarded as a genuine progress? These questions can be answered, with perfect justification, in the affirmative. Certain properties, which it is impossible not to regard as valuable, have been developed in the course of evolution. The lower forms of life persist more or less unchanged; but among the higher forms there has been a definite trend towards greater control and greater independence of the physical environment. Beings belonging to the highest forms of life have increased their capacity for self-regulation, have created an internal environment capable of remaining stable throughout very great changes in the outer world, have equipped themselves with elaborate machinery for picking up knowledge of the outer world, as well as of the inner, and have developed a wonderfully effective instrument for dealing with that knowledge. Evolutionary progress is of two kinds: general, all-round progress and one-sided progress in a particular direction. This last leads to specialization. From the evidence provided by the study of fossils and living forms, we are justified in inferring that any living form which has gone in for one-sided progress thereby makes it impossible for itself to achieve generalized progress. Nothing fails like success; and creatures which have proved eminently successful in specializing themselves to perform one sort of task and to live in one sort of environment are by that very fact foredoomed to ultimate failure.

Failure may take the form of extinction or alternatively of survival and adaptive radiation into forms that reach a relatively stable position and become incapable of further development, since such development would imperil the equilibrium existing between the living creature and its environment. Only one species, of all the millions that exist and have existed has hitherto resisted the temptation to specialize. Sooner or later all the rest have succumbed and have thus put themselves out of the running in the evolutionary race. This is true even of the mammals. After achieving a stable inner environment, placental and, in some cases, monotocous birth, highly developed sense organs, and a well co-ordinated nervous system, all but one proceeded to specialize in killing or browsing, in climbing, or running, or swimming—in teeth or claws, or hoofs, in a fine nose, or a prehensile tail—and so shut themselves off from the possibility of further progress. Man alone kept himself free from specialization and was therefore able to go on progressing in the direction of greater awareness, greater intelligence, greater control over environment. Moreover, alone of all living beings upon this planet he is in a position to advance from his present position. If man were to become extinct, it seems certain that no other existing animal would be able to develop into a being comparable to man for control over or independence of environment, for capacity to know the world and its own mind.

What are the general conclusions to be drawn from the scientific picture of life's history on this planet? There is no need, in this context, to consider any of the lower forms of life. It is enough to point out, for example, that cold-bloodedness limits the power of any animal to become independent of its environment; that effective control over the environment is impossible for animals of less than a certain size; that some animals are not only too small but are predestined, as the arthropods are predestined by their system of tracheal breathing, to remain small to the end of the chapter; that absolute smallness limits the size of the nervous system and so, apparently, of the amount of mental power which any animal can dispose of. And so forth. We can sum the matter up by saying that progress can be achieved only by the highest types of animal life. Even among these highest types, evolution can continue to be a genuine progress only when certain conditions are fulfilled. Let us enumerate the most important of these conditions.

First of all the organism must advance, so to speak, along the whole biological front and not with one part of itself or in one particular direction only. One-sided specialized advance is incompatible with genuine progress. But one-sided specialist advance is encouraged, as we have seen, by intra-specific competition. This brings us to the second of our conditions which is that intra-specific competition shall be reduced to a minimum. Progress is dependent on the preponderance of intra-specific co-operation over intra-specific competition. Other things being equal, that species will make most progress whose members are least combative, most inclined to work together instead of against one another. The third condition of biological progress is intelligence. There can be no effective co-operation on any level above the instinctive except among creatures which are aware of one another's needs and are able to communicate with one another. (It is worth noting that intelligence cannot be developed except on the fulfilment of certain physiological and mechanical conditions.

These conditions have been set forth by Elliot Smith and other authorities. For example, among the conditions of human intelligence must be numbered man's erect carriage and the consequent development of the hand.)

Intelligence is essential; but intelligence cannot function properly where it is too often or too violently interfered with by the emotions, impulses and emotionally charged sensations. The sensations most heavily charged with emotional content are sensations of smell. Man's sense of smell is relatively poor and this apparent handicap has proved to be an actual advantage to him.* Instead of running round like a dog, sniffing at lampposts and becoming deeply agitated by what he smells on them, man is able to stand away from the world and use his eyes and his wits, relatively unmoved. Nor is this all. His power of inhibiting emotion once aroused is evidently much greater than that of most other animals. When a human baby was brought up with a baby chimpanzee (see "The Ape and the Child" by Professor and Mrs. Kellogg), it was found that the chimpanzee's intelligence, at least during the first eighteen months of life, was more or less equal to the human's. On the contrary, its power of inhibiting emotion was far lower and it was consequently unable very often to make use of its intelligence. (For example, when its parents went away, the baby would cry for a few minutes, then settle down cheerfully to play; the ape would be inconsolable for

* Elliot Smith has shown that the parts of the human brain correlated with the higher intellectual functions have developed at the expense of the olfactory centre.

ENDS AND MEANS

several hours, during which it was incapable of doing anything else but grieve.) Animals are almost as heavily handicapped by excess of emotionality as by a lack of intelligence. It is this excess of emotionality which has made it impossible for all animals except man to pass from emotional to conceptual speech. Beasts can make noises expressive of their feelings; but they cannot make noises which stand for objects and ideas as such, objects and ideas considered apart from the desires and emotions they arouse. Conceptual speech made possible the development of disinterested thinking, and the capacity to think disinterestedly was responsible for the development of conceptual speech.

No account of the scientific picture of the world and its history would be complete unless it contained a reminder of the fact, frequently forgotten by scientists themselves, that this picture does not even claim to be comprehensive. From the world we actually live in, the world that is given by our senses, our intuitions of beauty and goodness, our emotions and impulses, our moods and sentiments, the man of science abstracts a simplified private universe of things possessing only those qualities which used to be called "primary." Arbitrarily, because it happens to be convenient, because his methods do not allow him to deal with the immense complexity of reality, he selects from the whole of experience only those elements which can be weighed, measured, numbered, or which lend themselves in any other way to mathematical treatment. By using this technique of simplification and abstraction, the scientist has succeeded to an astonishing degree in understanding and dominating the physical environment. The success was intoxicating and, with an illogicality which, in the circumstances, was doubtless pardonable, many scientists and philosophers came to imagine that this useful abstraction from reality was reality itself. Reality as actually experienced contains intuitions of value and significance, contains love, beauty, mystical ecstasy, intimations of godhead. Science did not and still does not possess intellectual instruments with which to deal with these aspects of reality. Consequently it ignored them and concentrated its attention upon such aspects of the world as it could deal with by means of arithmetic, geometry and the various branches of higher mathematics. Our conviction that the world is meaningless is due in part to the fact (discussed in a later paragraph) that the philosophy of meaninglessness lends itself very effectively to furthering the ends of erotic or political passion; in part to a genuine intellectual error—the error of identifying the world of science, a world from which all meaning and value has been deliberately excluded, with ultimate reality. It is worth while to quote in this context the words with which Hume closes his *Enquiry*. "If we take in our hand any volume; of divinity or school metaphysics, for instance; let us ask, Does it contain any abstract reasoning concerning quantity or number? No. Does it contain any experimental reasoning concerning matter of fact or evidence? No. Commit it then to the flames; for it can contain nothing but sophistry and illusion." Hume mentions only divinity and school metaphysics; but his argument would apply just as cogently to poetry, music, painting, sculpture and all ethical and religious teaching. Hamlet contains no abstract reasoning concerning quantity or number and no experimental reason concerning evidence; nor does the Hammerklavier Sonata, nor Donatello's David, nor the *Tao Te Ching*, nor the *Following of Christ*. Commit them therefore to the flames: for they can contain nothing but sophistry and illusion.

We are living now, not in the delicious intoxication induced by the early successes of science, but in a rather grisly morning-after, when it has become apparent that what triumphant science has done hitherto is to improve the means for achieving unimproved or actually deteriorated ends. In this condition of apprehensive sobriety we are able to see that the contents of literature, art, music—even in some measure of divinity and school metaphysics—are not sophistry and illusion, but simply those elements of experience which scientists chose to leave out of account, for the good reason that they had no intellectual methods for dealing with them. In the arts, in philosophy, in religion men are trying—doubtless, without complete success—to describe and explain the non-measurable, purely qualitative aspects of reality. Since the time of Galileo, scientists have admitted, sometimes explicitly but much more often by implication, that they are incompetent to discuss such matters. The scientific picture of the world is what it is because men of science combine this incompetence with certain special competences. They have no right to claim that this product of incompetence and specialization is a complete picture of reality. As a matter of historical fact, however, this claim has constantly been made. The successive

steps in the process of identifying an arbitrary abstraction from reality with reality itself have been described, very fully and lucidly, in Burtt's excellent
"Metaphysical Foundations of Modern Science"; and it
is therefore unnecessary for me to develop the theme
any further. All that I need add is the fact that, in recent
years, many men of science have come to realize that the
scientific picture of the world is a partial one—the product of their special competence in mathematics and
their special incompetence to deal systematically with
aesthetic and moral values, religious experiences and intuitions of significance. Unhappily, novel ideas become
acceptable to the less intelligent members of society only
with a very considerable time-lag. Sixty or seventy years
ago the majority of scientists believed—and the belief
often caused them considerable distress—that the product of their special incompetence was identical with
reality as a whole. Today this belief has begun to give
way, in scientific circles, to a different and obviously
truer conception of the relation between science and
total experience. The masses, on the contrary, have just
reached the point where the ancestors of today's scientists were standing two generations back. They are convinced that the scientific picture of an arbitrary abstraction from reality is a picture of reality as a whole and
that therefore the world is without meaning or value.
But nobody likes living in such a world. To satisfy
their hunger for meaning and value, they turn to such
doctrines as nationalism, fascism and revolutionary
communism. Philosophically and scientifically, these
doctrines are absurd; but for the masses in every com-

munity, they have this great merit: they attribute the meaning and value that have been taken away from the world as a whole to the particular part of the world in which the believers happen to be living.

These last considerations raise an important question, which must now be considered in some detail. Does the world as a whole possess the value and meaning that we constantly attribute to certain parts of it (such as human beings and their works) ; and, if so, what is the nature of that value and meaning? This is a question which, a few years ago, I should not even have posed. For, like so many of my contemporaries, I took it for granted that there was no meaning. This was partly due to the fact that I shared the common belief that the scientific picture of an abstraction from reality was a true picture of reality as a whole; partly also to other, non-intellectual reasons. I had motives for not wanting the world to have a meaning; consequently assumed that it had none, and was able without any difficulty to find satisfying reasons for this assumption.

Most ignorance is vincible ignorance. We don't know because we don't want to know. It is our will that decides how and upon what subjects we shall use our intelligence. Those who detect no meaning in the world generally do so because, for one reason or another, it suits their books that the world should be meaningless.

The behaviour of the insane is merely sane behaviour, a bit exaggerated and distorted. The abnormal casts a revealing light upon the normal. Hence the interest attaching, among other madmen, to the extravagant figure of the Marquis de Sade. The marquis prided himself upon being a thinker. His books, indeed, contain more philosophy than pornography. The hungry smut-hound must plough through long chapters of abstract speculation in order to find the cruelties and obscenities for which he hungers. De Sade's philosophy was the philosophy of meaninglessness carried to its logical conclusion. Life was without significance. Values were illusory and ideals merely the inventions of cunning priests and kings. Sensations and animal pleasures alone possessed reality and were alone worth living for. There was no reason why any one should have the slightest consideration for any one else. For those who found rape and murder amusing, rape and murder were fully legitimate activities. And so on.

Why was the Marquis unable to find any value or significance in the world? Was his intellect more piercing than that of other men? Was he forced by the acuity of his vision to look through the veils of prejudice and superstition to the hideous reality behind them? We may doubt it. The real reason why the Marquis could see no meaning or value in the world is to be found in those descriptions of fornications, sodomies and tortures which alternate with the philosophizings of *Justine* and *Juliette*. In the ordinary circumstances of life, the Marquis was not particularly cruel; indeed, he is said to have got into serious trouble during the Terror for his leniency towards those suspected of anti-revolutionary sentiments. His was a strictly sexual perversion. It was for flogging actresses, sticking pen-knives into shop girls, feeding prostitutes on sugar-plums impregnated with cantharides, that he got into trouble with the police.

His philosophical disquisitions, which, like the porno-
graphic day-dreams, were mostly written in prisons and
asylums, were the theoretical justification of his erotic
practices. Similarly his politics were dictated by the desire to avenge himself on those members of his family
and his class who had, as he thought, unjustly persecuted
him. He was enthusiastically a revolutionary—at any
rate in theory; for, as we have seen, he was too gentle in
practice to satisfy his fellow Jacobins. His books are of
permanent interest and value because they contain a
kind of *reductio ad absurdum* of revolutionary theory.
Sade is not afraid to be a revolutionary to the bitter end.
Not content with denying the particular system of values embodied in the *ancien regime*, he proceeds to deny
the existence of any values, any idealism, any binding
moral imperatives whatsoever. He preaches violent revolution not only in the field of politics and economics,
but (logical with the appalling logicality of the maniac)
also on that of personal relations, including the most
intimate of all, the relations between lovers. And, after
all, why not? If it is legitimate to torment and kill in
one set of circumstances, it must be equally legitimate
to torment and kill in all other circumstances. De Sade
is the one completely consistent and thorough-going
revolutionary of history.

If I have lingered so long over a maniac, it is because
his madness illuminates the dark places of normal behaviour. No philosophy is completely disinterested. The
pure love of truth is always mingled to some extent with
the need, consciously or unconsciously felt by even the
noblest and the most intelligent philosophers, to justify

a given form of personal or social behaviour, to rationalize the traditional prejudices of a given class or community. The philosopher who finds meaning in the
world is concerned, not only to elucidate that meaning,
but also to prove that it is most clearly expressed in
some established religion, some accepted code of morals.
The philosopher who finds no meaning in the world is
not concerned exclusively with a problem in pure metaphysics. He is also concerned to prove that there is no
valid reason why he personally should not do as he wants
to do, or why his friends should not seize political power
and govern in the way that they find most advantageous
to themselves. The voluntary, as opposed to the intellectual, reasons for holding the doctrines of materialism,
for example, may be predominantly erotic, as they were
in the case of Lamettrie (see his lyrical account of
the pleasures of the bed in *La Volupté* and at the end of
L'Homme Machine), or predominantly political, as they
were in the case of Karl Marx. The desire to justify a
particular form of political organization and, in some
cases, of a personal will to power has played an equally
large part in the formulation of philosophies postulating the existence of a meaning in the world. Christian
philosophers have found no difficulty in justifying imperialism, war, the capitalistic system, the use of torture,
the censorship of the press, and ecclesiastical tyrannies
of every sort from the tyranny of Rome to the tyrannies
of Geneva and New England. In all these cases they have
shown that the meaning of the world was such as to be
compatible with, or actually most completely expressed
by, the iniquities I have mentioned above—iniquities

which happened, of course, to serve the personal or sectarian interests of the philosophers concerned. In due course, there arose philosophers who denied not only the right of these Christian special pleaders to justify iniquity by an appeal to the meaning of the world, but even their right to find any such meaning whatsoever. In the circumstances, the fact was not surprising. One unscrupulous distortion of the truth tends to beget other and opposite distortions. Passions may be satisfied in the process; but the disinterested love of knowledge suffers eclipse.

For myself as, no doubt, for most of my contemporaries, the philosophy of meaninglessness was essentially an instrument of liberation. The liberation we desired was simultaneously liberation from a certain political and economic system and liberation from a certain system of morality. We objected to the morality because it interfered with our sexual freedom; we objected to the political and economic system because it was unjust. The supporters of these systems claimed that in some way they embodied the meaning (a Christian meaning, they insisted) of the world. There was one admirably simple method of confuting these people and at the same time justifying ourselves in our political and erotic revolt: we could deny that the world had any meaning whatsoever. Similar tactics had been adopted during the eighteenth century and for the same reasons. From the popular novelists of the period, such as Crébillon and Andréa de Nerciat, we learn that the chief reason for being "philosophical" was that one might be free from prejudices—above all prejudices of a sexual nature.

More serious writers associated political with sexual prejudice and recommended philosophy (in practice, the philosophy of meaninglessness) as a preparation for social reform or revolùtion. The early nineteenth century witnessed a reaction towards meaningful philosophy of a kind that could, unhappily, be used to justify political reaction. The men of the new Enlightenment, which occurred in the middle years of the nineteenth century, once again used meaninglessness as a weapon against the reactionaries. The Victorian passion for respectability was, however, so great that, during the period when they were formulated, neither Positivism nor Darwinism was used as a justification for sexual indulgence. After the War the philosophy of meaninglessness came once more triumphantly into fashion. As in the days of Lamettrie and his successors the desire to justify a certain sexual looseness played a part in the popularization of meaninglessness at least as important as that played by the desire for liberation from an unjust and inefficient form of social organization. By the end of the twenties a reaction had begun to set in—away from the easy-going philosophy of general meaninglessness towards the hard, ferocious theologies of nationalistic and revolutionary idolatry. Meaning was reintroduced into the world, but only in patches. The universe as a whole still remained meaningless, but certain of its parts, such as the nation, the state, the class, the party, were endowed with significance and the highest value. The general acceptance of a doctrine that denies meaning and value to the world as a whole, while assigning them in a supreme degree to certain arbitrarily selected parts of the totality, can have only evil and disastrous results. "All that we are (and consequently all that we do) is the result of what we have thought." We have thought of ourselves as members of supremely meaningful and valuable communities—deified nations, divine classes and what not—existing within a meaningless universe. And because we have thought like this, rearmament is in full swing, economic nationalism becomes ever more intense, the battle of rival propagandas grows ever fiercer, and general war becomes increasingly more probable.

It was the manifestly poisonous nature of the fruits that forced me to reconsider the philosophical tree on which they had grown. It is certainly hard, perhaps impossible, to demonstrate any necessary connexion between truth and practical goodness. Indeed it was fashionable during the Enlightenment of the middle nineteenth century to speak of the need for supplying the masses with "vital lies" calculated to make those who accepted them not only happy, but well behaved. The truth—which was that there was no meaning or value in the world—should be revealed only to the few who were strong enough to stomach it. Now, it may be, of course, that the nature of things has fixed a great gulf between truth about the world on the one hand and practical goodness on the other. Meanwhile, however, the nature of things seems to have so constituted the human mind that it is extremely reluctant to accept such a conclusion, except under the pressure of desire or self-interest. Furthermore those who, to be liberated from political or sexual restraint, accept the doctrine of absolute meaninglessness tend in a short time to become so much dissatisfied with their philosophy (in spite of the services it renders) that they will exchange it for any dogma, however manifestly nonsensical, which restores meaning if only to a part of the universe. Some people, it is true, can live contentedly with a philosophy of meaninglessness for a very long time. But in most cases it will be found that these people possess some talent or accomplishment that permits them to live a life which, to a limited extent, is profoundly meaningful and valuable. Thus an artist, or a man of science can profess a philosophy of general meaninglessness and yet lead a perfectly contented life. The reason for this must be sought in the fact that artistic creation and scientific research are absorbingly delightful occupations, possessing, moreover, a certain special significance in virtue of their relation to truth and beauty. Nevertheless, artistic creation and scientific research may be, and constantly are, used as devices for escaping from the responsibilities of life. They are proclaimed to be ends absolutely good in themselves—ends so admirable that those who pursue them are excused from bothering about anything else. This is particularly true of contemporary science. The mass of accumulated knowledge is so great that it is now impossible for any individual to have a thorough grasp of more than one small field of study. Meanwhile, no attempt is made to produce a comprehensive synthesis of the general results of scientific research. Our universities possess no chair of synthesis. All endowments, moreover, go to special subjects—and almost always to subjects which have no need of further endowment, such as physics, chemistry and mechanics. In our institutions of higher learning about ten times as much is spent on the natural sciences as on the sciences of man. All our efforts are directed, as usual, to producing improved means to unimproved ends. Meanwhile intensive specialization tends to reduce each branch of science to a condition almost approaching meaninglessness. There are many men of science who are actually proud of this state of things. Specialized meaninglessness has come to be regarded, in certain circles, as a kind of hall mark of true science. Those who attempt to relate the small particular results of specialization with human life as a whole and its relation to the universe at large are accused of being bad scientists, charlatans, self-advertisers. The people who make such accusations do so, of course, because they do not wish to take any responsibility for anything, but merely to retire to their cloistered laboratories, and there amuse themselves by performing delightfully interesting researches. Science and art are only too often a superior kind of dope, possessing this advantage over booze and morphia: that they can be indulged in with a good conscience and with the conviction that, in the process of indulging, one is leading the "higher life." Up to a point, of course, this is true. The life of the scientist or the artist is a higher life. Unfortunately, when led in an irresponsible, one-sided way, the higher life is probably more harmful for the individual than the lower life of the average sensual man and certainly, in the case of the scientist, much worse for society at large.

We see, then, that the mind is so constituted that a

philosophy of meaninglessness is accepted only at the suggestion of the passions and is persisted in only by those whose heredity and upbringing make it possible for them to live as though the world were at least partially meaningful. The fact that the mind has a certain difficulty in accepting the philosophy of meaninglessness is significant, if only to the extent that it raises the question whether truth and goodness may not be somehow correlated in the nature of things. Nor is the old Stoic appeal to the *consensus gentium* by any means entirely negligible. That so many philosophers and mystics, belonging to so many different cultures, should have been convinced, by inference or by direct intuition, that the world possesses meaning and value is a fact sufficiently striking to make it worth while at least to investigate the belief in question.

Let us begin the investigation by considering the stock arguments used in support of theism. Of these the argument from design was at one time the most popular. Today it no longer carries conviction. To begin with we are no longer certain that the design, upon which Paley and the earlier thinkers based their arguments, is more than the appearance of design. What looks as though it had been planned in advance may be in fact merely the result of long-drawn process of adaptation. The relationship existing between X and Y may be the kind of relationship that an intelligent being would have planned. But that is no reason for supposing that an intelligent being did in fact plan it. Such a relationship may equally well be the result of natural selection working blindly to produce a state of equilibrium between two originally discordant and mutually unadapted entities. Moreover, even if the. evidence for design is taken at its face value (as it was taken by Kant), there is still no reason for supposing that the designer was a single supreme being. Upon this point the arguments adduced by Hume and Kant are decisive.

The ontological argument is even less convincing than the argument from design. Anselm was decisively refuted by Aquinas and Descartes by Kant. In recent years, the verbal foundations of logic have been subjected to the most searching analysis, as the result of which the ontological argument seems still less satisfactory than it did even in Kant's day.

The cosmological proof of the existence of God is based upon the argument that if contingent beings exist there must exist a necessary being; and that if there is an *ens necessarium* it must be at the same time an *ens realissimum*. In his earlier writings Kant produced a very elaborate speculative proof of God's existence, based upon the argument that the possible presupposes the actual. Later, when he had developed his Critical Philosophy, he rejected this proof and sought to show that all the arguments for natural theology, including the cosmological, were unsound. In the course of his later refutation of the cosmological proof, Kant has to dispose of the natural theologian's argument that the existence of causally related events implies the existence of a First Cause. He does this by arguing that causality is merely a principle for ordering appearances in the sensible world, therefore cannot legitimately be used for transcending the world of sense. This argument has been revived in a less pedantic form, by Brunschvicg in his *"Progrès de la Conscience"* (II, 778). *"En toute évidence, ceux-là même qui invoquent le principe de la causalité comme une loi fondamentale de la raison humaine, ne peuvent y obéir strictement que s'ils en font usage pour relier de l'unité d'un jugement deux objets dont l'existence leur est préalablement certifiée. C'est la loi elle-même qui s'oppose à ce qu'ils aillent forger de leur autorité privée le terme qui manque pour la mise en oeuvre effective du principe: l'application transcendentale de la causalité revient à la pétition d'un objet imaginaire."* The question arises: what are the objects which can be legitimately connected by the principle of causality? Kant involved himself in extraordinary difficulties by limiting causality to events in the world of sense. But the only form of causality with which we have direct acquaintance is our own voluntary activity. We know directly that our will is the cause of our performing a given action in the world of sense. It is no doubt true, as Brunschvicg says, that we have no right to apply the principle of causality except to objects of which we already know, either by direct acquaintance or by inference, that they exist. Acting on this principle, we may legitimately postulate a causal connexion between one sense object and another sense object and also between a sense object and a mental state which is not a sense object. Whether in fact there can be mental states which do not belong to individual human beings or animals is another question. All that we can say in this particular context is that, if such mental states exist, there seems to be no reason why (supposing them to be analogous to our own mental states) they should not be causally related to events in the world of sense.

The moral argument for theism may be very briefly summed up as follows. Moral action aims at the realization of the highest good. The highest good cannot be realized except where there is a virtuous rational will in persons and a world in which this virtuous rational will is not thwarted—a world where virtue is united with happiness. But it is a matter of brute empirical fact that, in the world of phenomena, the most virtuous are not necessarily the happiest and that the rational will is not always that which gets itself done. It follows therefore that the union of virtue and happiness, without which the highest good cannot be realized, must be effected by some power external to ourselves, a power which so arranges things that, whatever partial and temporary appearance may be, the total world order is moral and demonstrates the union of virtue with happiness.

Those who oppose this argument do so, first, on the ground that it is merely a piece of "wishful thinking," and, second, that words like "virtue," "the good" and all the rest have no definite meaning, but change from one community to another.

We discredit thoughts which have wishes as their fathers; and in very many circumstances, we are certainly right in doing so. But there are certain circumstances in which wishes are a reliable source of information, not only about ourselves, but also about the outside world. From the premiss, for example, of thirst we are justified in arguing the existence of something which can satisfy thirst. Nor is it only in the phenomenal world that such wishful arguments have validity. We have, as I have pointed out in an earlier paragraph, a craving for explanation. This craving is satisfied by the reduction of diversity to identity, so much so that any theory which postulates the existence of identity behind diversity seems to us intrinsically plausible. Like philosophy and religion, science is an attempt systematically to satisfy the craving for explanation in terms of theories which seem plausible because they postulate the existence of identity behind diversity. But here an interesting and highly significant fact emerges: observation and experiment seem to demonstrate that what the human mind regards as intrinsically plausible is in fact true and that the craving for explanation, which is a craving for identity behind diversity, is actually satisfied by the real world; for the real world reveals itself as being in effect a unity in diversity. The craving for explanation was felt by men thousands of years before the instruments, by means of which that craving could be scientifically satisfied had been invented. The old philosophers of nature assuaged that craving by postulating the existence of some single substance, material or mental, underlying the apparent diversity of independent existents, or by proclaiming that all matter must be built of identically similar atoms, variously arranged. Within the last half-century investigation by means of instruments of precision has actually demonstrated that these cosmological theories which, up till then, could only be described as pieces of wishful thinking designed to satisfy the inborn craving for explanation, were in fact remarkably consonant with the facts of the empirical world. The craving for righteousness seems to be a human characteristic just as fundamental as the craving for explanation. The moral argument in favour of theism is certainly a piece of wishful thinking; but it is no more wishful than the arguments in favour of the atomic theory propounded by Democritus and Epicurus, or even by Boyle and Newton. The theory by means of which these natural philosophers tried to satisfy their craving for explanation was found to be in toierably close accord with the facts discovered by the later investigators, equipped with more effective instruments for exploring physical reality. Whether it will ever be possible to verify the theories of the moral philosophers by direct observation and experiment seems doubtful. But that is no reason for denying the truth of such theories. Nor, as we have seen, is the fact that they originate in wishes, *"Tu ne me chercherais pas si tu ne me possédais,"* wrote Pascal. *"Ne t'inquiète donc pas."* The theories devised to satisfy the craving for explanation have proved to be remarkably accurate in their account of the nature of the world; we have no right to reject as mere subjective illusions the analogous thesis devised to satisfy the cravings for righteousness, for meaning, for value.

At this point we are confronted by the argument that such words as "good," "virtue" and the like have no definite meaning, but signify now this, now that, according to the degree of latitude, the colour of the skin, the local mythology. This is, of course, perfectly true.

The content of judgments of value is demonstrably variable. Two important points should, however, be noted in this context. The first is that such judgments are passed by all human beings, that the category of value is universally employed. The second is that, as knowledge, sensibility and non-attachment increase, the contents of the judgments of value passed even by men belonging to dissimilar cultures, tend to approximate. The ethical doctrines taught in the Tao Te Ching, by Gotama Buddha and his followers of the Lesser and above all the Greater Vehicle, in the Sermon on the Mount and by the best of the Christian saints, are not dissimilar. Among human beings who have reached a certain level of civilization and of personal freedom from passion and social prejudice there exists a real *consensus gentium* in regard to ethical first principles. These first principles are, of course, in constant danger from the passions and from ignorance, itself in many cases the fruit of passion. Passion and ignorance work, not only on individuals, but sometimes also on entire communities. In the latter case a systematic attempt is made to replace the ethical first principles of civilized humanity by other first principles more in accord with the prevailing mass-emotions and national interests. This process is taking place at the present time all over the world. Nationalistic and revolutionary passions find themselves in conflict with the standards of civilized morality. Consequently the standards of civilized morality are everywhere denounced as false and wicked, and new standards are set up in their place. The nature of these new standards varies with the political ideals of

the countries in which they are set up—but varies only
very slightly. Essentially all the new moralities, Communist, Fascist, Nazi or merely nationalist, are singularly alike. All affirm that the end justifies the means; and
in all the end is the triumph of a section of the human
species over the rest. All justify the unlimited use of
violence and cunning. All preach the subordination of
the individual to a ruling oligarchy, deified as "the
State." All inculcate the minor virtues, such as temperance, prudence, courage and the like; but all disparage
the higher virtues, charity, and intelligence, without
which the minor virtues are merely instruments for
doing evil with increased efficiency.

Examples of reversion to barbarism through mere
ignorance are unhappily abundant in the history of
Christianity. The early Christians made the enormous
mistake of burdening themselves with the Old Testament, which contains, along with much fine poetry and
sound morality the history of the cruelties and treach-
eries of a Bronze-Age people, fighting for a place in the
sun under the protection of its anthropomorphic tribal
deity. Christian theologians did their best to civilize and
moralize this tribal deity; but, inspired in every line,
dictated by God himself, the Old Testament was always
there to refute them. Ancient ignorance had been sanctified as revelation. Those whom it suited to be ignorant
and, along with them, the innocent and uneducated
could find in this treasure-house of barbarous stupidity
justifications for every crime and folly. Texts to justify
such abominations as religious wars, the persecution of
heretics, breaking of faith with unbelievers, could be

found in the sacred books and were in fact used again
and again throughout the whole history of the Christian
Church, to mitigate the inconvenient decency of civilized morality. In the last analysis, all this folly and
wickedness can be traced back to a mistaken view of the
world. The Hebrews of the Bronze Age thought that the
integrating principle of the universe was a kind of
magnified human person, with all the feelings and passions of a human person. He was wrathful, for example,
he was jealous, he was vindictive. This being so, there
was no reason why his devotees should not be wrathful,
jealous and vindictive. Among the Christians this primitive cosmology led to the burning of heretics and
witches, the wholesale massacre of Albigensians, Cath-
arists, Protestants, Catholics and a hundred other sects.
In the modern world ignorance about the nature of
the universe takes the form of a refusal to speculate
about that nature and an insistence that there is no
meaning or value except in such small and arbitrarily
selected parts of the whole as the nation, the state, the
class and the party. To believe that the nation is god is
a mistake just as grotesque as was the mistake of supposing that the sun would die if it did not get victims or
that God is a kind of large invisible man, with all the
most disgraceful human passions.

We are back again at the point reached on an earlier
page—the point at which we discover that an obviously
untrue philosophy of life leads in practice to disastrous
results; the point where we realize the necessity of seeking an alternative philosophy that shall be true and
therefore fruitful of good. In the interval, we have con-

sidered the classical arguments in favour of theism and have found that some carry no conviction whatever, while the rest can only raise a presumption in favour of the theory that the world possesses some integrating principle that gives it significance and value. There is probably no argument by which the case for theism, or for deism, or for pantheism in either its pancosmic or acosmic form, can be convincingly proved. The most that "abstract reasoning" (to use Hume's phrase) can do is to create a presumption in favour of one or other hypothesis; and this presumption can be increased by means of "experimental reasoning concerning matter of fact or evidence." Final conviction can only come to those who make an act of faith. The idea is one which most of us find very distressing. But it may be doubted whether this particular act of faith is intrinsically more difficult than those which we have to make, for example, every time we frame a scientific hypothesis, every time that, from the consideration of a few phenomena, we draw inference concerning all phenomena, past, present and future. On very little evidence, but with no qualms of intellectual conscience, we assume that our craving for explanation has a real object in an explicable universe, that the aesthetic satisfaction we derive from certain arguments is a sign that they are true, that the laws of thought are also laws of things. There seems to be no reason why, having swallowed this camel, we should not swallow another, no larger really than the first. The reasons why we strain at the second camel have been given above. Once recognized, they cease to exist and we become free to consider on their merits the evidence and arguments that would reasonably justify us in making the final act of faith and assuming the truth of a hypothesis that we are unable fully to demonstrate.

"Abstract reasoning" must now give place to "experimental reasoning concerning matter of fact or evidence." Natural science, as we have seen, deals only with those aspects of reality that are amenable to mathematical treatment. The rest it merely ignores. But some of the experiences thus ignored by natural science—aesthetic experiences, for example, and religious experiences— throw much light upon the present problem. It is with the fact of such experiences and the evidence they furnish concerning the nature of the world that we have now to concern ourselves.

To discuss the nature and significance of aesthetic experience would take too long. It is enough, in this place, merely to suggest that the best works of literary, plastic and musical art give us more than mere pleasure; they furnish us with information about the nature of the world. The *Sanctus* in Beethoven's Mass in D, Seurat's *Grande Jatte, Macbeth*—works such as these tell us, by strange but certain implication, something significant about the ultimate reality behind appearances. Even from the perfection of minor masterpieces—certain sonnets of Mallarmé, for instance, certain Chinese ceramics —we can derive illuminating hints about the "something far more deeply interfused," about "the peace of God that passeth all understanding." But the subject of art is enormous and obscure, and my space is limited, I shall therefore confine myself to a discussion of certain religious experiences which bear more directly upon the present problem than do our experiences as creators and appreciators of art.

I have spoken in the preceding chapter of meditation as a device, in Babbitt's words, for producing a "super-rational concentration of the will." But meditation is more than a method of self-education; it has also been used, in every part of the world and from the remotest periods, as a method for acquiring knowledge about the essential nature of things, a method for establishing communion between the soul and the integrating principle of the universe. Meditation, in other words, is the technique of mysticism. Properly practised, with due preparation, physical, mental and moral, meditation may result in a state of what has been called "transcendental consciousness"—the direct intuition of, and union with, an ultimate spiritual reality that is perceived as simultaneously beyond the self and in some way within it. ("God in the depths of us," says Ruysbroeck, "receives God who comes to us; it is God contemplating God.") Non-mystics have denied the validity of the mystical experience, describing it as merely subjective and illusory. But it should be remembered that to those who have never actually had it, any direct intuition must seem subjective and illusory. It is impossible for the deaf to form any idea of the nature or significance of music. Nor is physical disability the only obstacle in the way of musical understanding. An Indian, for example, finds European orchestral music intolerably noisy, complicated, over-intellectual, inhuman. It seems incredible to him that any one should be able to perceive beauty and meaning, to recognize an expression of the deepest and subtlest emotions in this elaborate cacophony. And yet, if he has patience and listens to enough of it, he will come at last to realize, not only theoretically but also by direct, immediate intuition, that this music possesses all the qualities which Europeans claim for it. Of the significant and pleasurable experiences of life only the simplest are open indiscriminately to all. The rest cannot be had except by those who have undergone a suitable training. One must be trained even to enjoy the pleasures of alcohol and tobacco; first whiskies seem revolting, first pipes turn even the strongest of boyish stomachs. Similarly first Shakespeare sonnets seem meaningless; first Bach fugues, a bore; first differential equations, sheer torture. But training changes the nature of our spiritual experiences. In due course, contact with an obscurely beautiful poem, an elaborate piece of counterpoint or of mathematical reasoning, causes us to feel direct intuitions of beauty and significance. It is the same in the moral world. A man who has trained himself in goodness comes to have certain direct intuitions about character, about the relations between human beings, about his own position in the world—intuitions that are quite different from the intuitions of the average sensual man. Knowledge is always a function of being. What we perceive and understand depends upon what we are; and what we are depends partly on circumstances, partly, and more profoundly, on the nature of the efforts we have made to realize our ideal and the nature of the ideal we have tried to realize. The fact that knowing depends upon being leads, of course, to an immense amount of misunderstanding. The meaning of words, for example, changes profoundly according to the character and experiences of the user. Thus, to the saint, words like "love," "charity," "compassion" mean something quite different from what they mean to the ordinary man. Again, to the ordinary man, Spinoza's statement that "blessedness is not the reward of virtue, but is virtue itself" seems simply untrue. Being virtuous is, for him, a most tedious and distressing process. But it is clear that to some one who has trained himself in goodness, virtue really is blessedness, while the life of the ordinary man, with its petty vices and its long spells of animal thoughtlessness and insentience, seems a real torture. In view of the fact that knowing is conditioned by being and that being can be profoundly modified by training, we are justified in ignoring most of the arguments by which non-mystics have sought to discredit the experience of mystics. The being of a colour-blind man is such that he is not competent to pass judgment on a painting. The colour-blind man cannot be educated into seeing colours, and in this respect he is different from the Indian musician, who begins by finding European symphonies merely deafening and bewildering, but can be trained, if he so desires, to perceive the beauties of this kind of music. Similarly, the being of a non-mystical person is such that he cannot understand the nature of the mystic's intuitions. Like the Indian musician, however, he is at liberty, if he so chooses, to have some kind of direct experience of what at present he does not understand. This training is one which he will certainly find extremely tedious; for it involves, at first,

the leading of a life of constant awareness and unremitting moral effort; second, steady practice in the technique of meditation, which is probably about as difficult
as the technique of violin playing. But, however tedious,
the training can be undertaken by any one who wishes
to do so. Those who have not undertaken the training
can have no knowledge of the kind of experiences open
to those who have undertaken it and are as little justified
in denying the validity of those direct intuitions of an
ultimate spiritual reality, at once transcendent and immanent, as were the Pisan professors who denied, on *a
priori* grounds, the validity of Galileo's direct intuition
(made possible by the telescope) of the fact that Jupiter
has several moons.

The validity of the mystical experience is often questioned on the ground that the mystics of each religion
have direct intuition only of the particular deities they
are accustomed to worship. This is only partially true.
There are good mystics and bad mystics, just as there
are good and bad artists. The great majority of artists
are, and always have been, bad or indifferent; and the
same is probably true of the majority of mystics. Significantly enough it is always among those mystics, whom
qualified critics regard as second-rate, that the intuitions
of ultimate reality take a particularized form. To the
mystics who are generally regarded as the best of their
kind, ultimate reality does not appear under the aspect
of the local divinities. It appears as a spiritual reality so
far beyond particular form or personality that nothing
can be predicated of it.

"The *atman* is silence"; is what the Hindus say of

ultimate spiritual reality. The only language that can convey any idea about the nature of this reality is the language of negation, of paradox, of extravagant exaggeration. The pseudo-Dionysius speaks of the "ray of the divine darkness," of "the super-lucent darkness of silence" and of the necessity to "leave behind the senses and the intellectual operations and all things known by sense and intellect." "If anyone," he writes, "seeing God, understands what he has seen, he has not seen God." *"Nescio, nescio,"* was what St. Bernard wrote of the ultimate reality; *"neti, neti,"* was Yajnavalkya's verdict at the other side of the world. "I know not, I know not: not so, not so." We are a long way from particularized Hindu or Christian divinities.

The biography of most of the first-class Christian mystics is curiously similar. Brought up to believe in the personality of the triune God and in the existence and ubiquitous presence of other divine persons, such as the Virgin and the saints, they begin their mystical career by entering, as they suppose, into relations with supernatural personalities. Then, as they advance further along the path—and all the mystics are agreed that this process is genuinely an advance—they find that their visions disappear, that their awareness of a personality fades, that the emotional outpourings which were appropriate when they seemed to be in the presence of a person, become utterly inappropriate and finally give place to a state in which there is no emotion at all. For many Christian mystics this process has been extremely distressing. The anguish of losing contact with personality, of having to abandon the traditional beliefs, constitutes what St. John of the Cross calls the Night of the Senses, and it would seem that the same anguish is an element of that still more frightful desolation, the Night of the Spirit. St. John of the Cross considers that all true mystics must necessarily pass through this terrible dark night. So far as strictly orthodox Christians are concerned, he is probably right. In this context, a most valuable document is the life of Marie Lataste.* Marie Lataste was an uneducated peasant girl, completely ignorant of the history of mysticism. She begins by having visions of the Virgin and of Christ. Her mystical experience at this period consists essentially of emotional relationships with divine persons. In the course of time the sense of a personal presence leaves her. She feels lonely and abandoned. It is the dark night of the soul. In the end, however, she comes to understand that this new form of experience—the imageless and emotionless cognition of some great impersonal force—is superior to the old and represents a closer approach to ultimate reality. Marie Lataste's case is particularly interesting, because her ignorance of mystical literature precludes the possibility that she deliberately or unconsciously imitated any other mystic. Her experience was wholly her own. Brought up in the traditional belief that God is a person, she gradually discovers by direct intuition that he is not a person; and for a time, at least, the discovery causes her considerable distress. For orthodox Christians, I repeat, the dark night of the soul would seem to be an unescapable horror.

Significantly enough this particular form of spiritual

* Summarized in Miss Tillyard's "Spiritual Exercises," p. 202.

anguish is not experienced by unorthodox Christians nor by those non-Christian mystics who profess a religion that regards God as impersonal. For example, that most remarkable of the later mediaeval mystics, the author of "The Cloud of Unknowing," makes no mention of any phase of spiritual distress. The fact is that he has no reason to be distressed. From the first his preoccupation is with God the Father rather than with God the Son; and from the first he assumes that God is impersonal. He is therefore never called upon to make any excruciating abandonment of cherished beliefs. The doctrine with which he starts out is actually confirmed by the direct intuition of ultimate reality which comes to him in his moments of mystical experience. Similarly, we never, so far as I know, hear anything about the dark Night of the Senses in the literature of Buddhist or Hindu mysticism. Here again the belief with which the oriental mystic sets out is in accord with the testimony of his own experience. He has no treasured belief to give up; therefore enlightenment entails for him no spiritual anguish.

All the writers in the great tradition of Christian "mystical theology" have insisted on the necessity of purging the mind, during meditation on the ultimate reality, of all images. From Clement of Alexandria who died at the beginning of the third century and who was the first Christian writer on mystical theology, down to St. John of the Cross in the sixteenth, the tradition is unbroken. It is agreed that the attempt to think of God in terms of images, to conceive ultimate reality as having form or a nature describable in words, is foredoomed to failure. In the latter part of the sixteenth century there was a complete reversal of tradition. The subject has been treated with a wealth of learned detail by Dom John Chapman in the admirable essay on Roman Catholic Mysticism, which is printed in Hasting's *Encyclopaedia of Religion and Ethics*, and it is unnecessary for me to do more than briefly summarize his conclusions. "At this very time (the end of the sixteenth century), the dogmatic theologians were rising up against mystical theology. The great Dominicans, following the example of St. Thomas in his *Summa* ignored it; the great Jesuits denied its very existence." (The Jesuits, of course, had been brought up on Ignatius's spiritual exercises in which every effort is made, not to suppress the image-forming phantasy—that worst obstacle, according to St. John of the Cross and all the earlier mystics, in the way of a genuine intuition of ultimate reality—but to develop it, if possible, to the pitch of hallucination.) By the middle of the seventeenth century Cardinal Bona could state that "pure prayer exercised without phantasmata is universally denied by the scholastics." At the same time, "art began no longer to represent the saints as kneeling calmly in adoration, but as waving their arms and stretching their necks and rolling their eyes, in ecstasies of sensuous longing, while they tear aside their clothes to relieve their burning bosoms." Contemplation, meanwhile, has come to be regarded, as "mainly the sensible tasting of mysteries, especially of the Passion." (It is worth remarking that "the tendency to substitute for a super-rational concentration of will a subrational expansion of feeling" began, at any rate in the sphere of religion, not in the eighteenth century, as Babbitt has said, but in the seventeenth.) In this unpropitious atmosphere mysticism could not thrive; and, as Dom Chapman points out, there has been an almost complete dearth of Catholic mystics from the late sixteenth century down to the present day. Significant in this context is the remark made by Father Bede Frost, in his *Art of Mental Prayer*, to the effect that the great age of sacramentalism began in the nineteenth century. During the Middle Ages far less stress was laid on sacramental religion than is laid at the present time, far more on preaching and, above all, spiritual exercises and contemplation. An unsympathetic observer would be justified in pointing to the fact as a symptom of degeneration. A religion which once laid emphasis on the need to educate men's wills and train their souls for direct communion with ultimate reality, and which now attaches supreme importance to the celebration of sacraments (supposed in some way to cause the infusion of divine grace) * and to the performance of rituals calculated to induce in the participants a "subrational expansion of feelings," is certainly not progressing. It is becoming worse, not better.

Systematic training in recollection and meditation makes possible the mystical experience, which is a direct intuition of ultimate reality. At all times and in every part of the world, mystics of the first order have always agreed that this ultimate reality, apprehended in the

* The Council of Trent anathematized "si quis dixerit sacramenta novae legis non continere gratiam."

[340]

process of meditation, is essentially impersonal. This direct intuition of an impersonal spiritual reality, underlying all being, is in accord with the findings of the majority of the world's philosophers.

"There is," writes Professor Whitehead, in *Religion in the Making*, "a large concurrence in the negative doctrine that the religious experience does not include any direct intuition of a definite person, or individual. . . . The evidence for the assertion of a general, though not universal, concurrence in the doctrine of no direct vision of a personal God, can only be found by a consideration of the religious thought of the civilized world. . . . Throughout India and China, religious thought, so far as it has been interpreted in precise form, disclaims the intuition of ultimate personality substantial to the universe. This is true of Confucian philosophy, Buddhist philosophy and Hindu philosophy. There may be personal embodiments, but the substratum is impersonal. Christian theology has also, in the main, adopted the position that there is no direct intuition of such a personal substratum for the world. It maintains the doctrine of a personal God as a truth, but holds that our belief in it is based upon inference." There seems, however, to be no cogent reason why, from the existing evidence, we should draw such an inference. Moreover, as I have pointed out in the preceding chapter, the practical results of drawing such an inference are good only up to a point; beyond that point they are very often extremely bad.

We are now in a position to draw a few tentative and fragmentary conclusions about the nature of the world and our relation to it and to one another. To the casual observer, the world seems to be made up of great numbers of independent existents, some of which possess life and some consciousness. From very early times philosophers suspected that this common-sense view was in part at least, illusory. More recently investigators, trained in the discipline of mathematical physics and equipped with instruments of precision, have made observations from which it could be inferred that all the apparently independent existents in the world were built up of a limited number of patterns of identical units of energy. An ultimate physical identity underlies the apparent physical diversity of the world. Moreover, all apparently independent existents are in fact interdependent. Meanwhile the mystics had shown that investigators, trained in the discipline of recollection and meditation, could obtain direct experience of a spiritual unity underlying the apparent diversity of independent consciousness. They made it clear that what seemed to be the ultimate fact of personality was in reality not an ultimate fact and that it was possible for individuals to transcend the limitations of personality and to merge their private consciousness into a greater, impersonal consciousness underlying the personal mind.

Some have denied the very possibility of non-personal consciousness. McTaggart, for example, asserts that "there cannot be experience which is not experienced by a self, because it seems evident, not as part of the meaning of the terms, but as a synthetic truth about experience. This truth is ultimate. It cannot be defended against attacks, but it seems beyond doubt. The more clearly we realize the nature of experience, or of knowledge, volition and emotion, the more clearly, it is submitted, does it appear that any of them are impossible except as the experience of a self." This brings us back, once more, to the connexion between knowing and being. To those on the common levels of being, it does indeed "seem evident, as a synthetic truth about experience," that all experience must be experienced by a self. For such people "this truth is ultimate." But it is not ultimate to people who have chosen to undertake the mystic training in virtue and in recollection and in meditation. For these it is evident, "as a synthetic truth about experience," legitimately inferred from the empirical facts of their direct intuition, that there is an experience which is not the personal experience of a self. Such experience is not properly emotion, nor volition, nor even knowledge of the ordinary kind. Emotion, volition and knowledge are the forms of experience known to selves on the common levels of being. The experience known to selves who choose to fulfil the ethical and intellectual conditions upon which it is possible for an individual to pass to another level of being, is not their own emotion, their own volition, their own knowledge, but an unnamed and perhaps indescribable consciousness of a different kind, a consciousness in which the subject-object relation no longer exists and which no longer belongs to the experiencing self.

The physical world of our daily experience is a private universe quarried out of a total reality which the physicists infer to be far greater than it. This private universe is different, not only from the real world, whose existence we are able to infer, even though we cannot directly apprehend it, but also from the private universe inhabited by other animals—universes which we can never penetrate, but concerning whose nature we can, as Von Uexkull has done, make interesting speculative guesses. Each type of living creature inhabits a universe whose nature is determined and whose boundaries are imposed by the special inadequacies of its sense organs and its intelligence. In man, intelligence has been so far developed that he is able to infer the existence and even, to some extent, the nature of the real world outside his private universe. The nature of the sense organs and intelligence of living beings is imposed by biological necessity or convenience. The instruments of knowledge are good enough to enable their owners to survive. Less inadequate instruments of knowledge might not only lead to no biological advantage but might actually constitute a biological handicap. Individual human beings have been able to transcend the limitations of man's private universe only to the extent that they are relieved from biological pressure. An individual is relieved from biological pressure in two ways: from without, thanks to the efforts of others, and from within, thanks to his own efforts. If he is to transcend the limitations of man's private universe he must be a member of a community which gives him protection against the inclemencies of the environment and makes it easy for him to supply his physical wants. But this is not enough. He must also train himself in the art of being dispassionate and disinterested, must cultivate intellectual curiosity for its own sake and not for what he, as an animal, can get out of it.

The modern conception of man's intellectual relationship to the universe was anticipated by the Buddhist doctrine that desire is the source of illusion. To the extent that it has overcome desire, a mind is free from illusion. This is true not only of the man of science, but also of the artist and the philosopher. Only the disinterested mind can transcend commonsense and pass beyond the boundaries of animal or average-sensual human life. The mystic exhibits disinterestedness in the highest degree possible to human beings and is therefore able to transcend ordinary limitations more completely than the man of science, the artist or the philosopher. That which he discovers beyond the frontiers of the average sensual man's universe is a spiritual reality underlying and uniting all apparently separate existents—a reality with which he can merge himself and from which he can draw moral and even physical powers which, by ordinary standards, can only be described as super-normal.

The ultimate reality discoverable by those who choose to modify their being, so that they can have direct knowledge of it, is not, as we have seen, a personality. Since it is not personal, it is illegitimate to attribute to it ethical qualities. "God is not good," said Eckhart. "I am good." Goodness is the means by which men and women can overcome the illusion of being completely independent existents and can raise themselves to a level of being upon which it becomes possible, by recollection and meditation, to realize the fact of their oneness with ultimate reality, to know and in some measure actually associate themselves with it. The ultimate reality is "the peace of God which passeth all understanding"; goodness is the way by which it can be approached. "Finite beings," in the words of Royce, "are always such as they are in virtue of an *inattention* which at present blinds them to their actual relations to God and to one another." That inattention is the fruit, in Buddhist language, of desire. We fail to attend to our true relations with ultimate reality and, through ultimate reality, with our fellow beings, because we prefer to attend to our animal nature and to the business of getting on in the world. That we can never completely ignore the animal in us or its biological needs is obvious. Our separateness is not wholly an illusion. The element of specificity in things is a brute fact of experience. Diversity cannot be reduced to complete identity even in scientific and philosophical theory, still less in life which is lived with bodies, that is to say, with particular patternings of the ultimately identical units of energy. It is impossible in the nature of things, that no attention should be given to the animal in us; but in the circumstances of civilized life, it is certainly unnecessary to give all or most of our attention to it. Goodness is the method by which we divert our attention from this singularly wearisome topic of our animality and our individual separateness. Recollection and meditation assist goodness in two ways: by producing, in Babbitt's words, "a suprarational concentration of will," and by making it possible for the mind to realize, not only theoretically, but also by direct intuition, that the private universe of the average sensual man is not identical with the universe as a whole. Conversely, of course, goodness aids meditation by giving detachment from animality and so making it possible for the mind to pay attention to its actual relationship with ultimate reality and to other individuals. Goodness, meditation, the mystical experience and the ultimate impersonal reality discovered in mystical experience are organically related. This fact disposes of the fears expressed by Dr. Albert Schweitzer in his recent book on Indian thought. Mysticism, he contends, is the correct world view; but, though correct, it is unsatisfactory in ethical content. The ultimate reality of the world is not moral ("God is not good") and the mystic who unites himself with ultimate reality is uniting himself with a non-moral being, therefore is not himself moral. But this is more verbalism and ignores the actual facts of experience. It is impossible for the mystic to pay attention to his real relation to God and to his fellows, unless he has previously detached his attention from his animal nature and the business of being socially successful. But he cannot detach his attention from these things except by the consistent and conscious practice of the highest morality. God is not good; but if I want to have even the smallest knowledge of God, I must be good at least in some slight measure; and if I want as full a knowledge of God as it is possible for human beings to have, I must be as good as it is possible for human beings to be. Virtue is the essential preliminary to the mystical experience. And this is not all. There is not even any theoretical incompatibility between an ultimate reality, which is impersonal and therefore not moral, and the existence of a moral order on the human level. Scientific investigation has shown that the world is a diversity underlain by an identity of physical substance; the mystical experience testifies to the existence of a spiritual unity underlying the diversity of separate consciousnesses. Concerning the relation between the underlying physical unity and the underlying spiritual unity it is hard to express an opinion. Nor is it necessary, in the present context, that we should express one. For our present purposes the important fact is that it is possible to detect a physical and a spiritual unity underlying the independent existents (to some extent merely apparent, to some extent real, at any rate for beings on our plane of existence), of which our commonsense universe is composed. Now, it is a fact of experience that we can either emphasize our separateness from other beings and the ultimate reality of the world or emphasize our oneness with them and it. To some extent at least, our will is free in this matter. Human beings are creatures who, in so far as they are animals and persons tend to regard themselves as independent existents, connected at most by purely biological ties, but who, in so far as they rise above animality and personality, are able to perceive that they are interrelated parts of physical and spiritual wholes incomparably greater than themselves. For such beings the fundamental moral commandment is: You shall realize your unity with all being. But men cannot realize their unity with others and with ultimate reality unless they practise the virtue of love and understanding. Love, compassion and understanding or intelligence—these are the primary virtues in the ethical system, the virtues organically correlated with what may be called the scientific-mystical conception of the world. Ultimate reality is impersonal and non-ethical; but if we would realize our true relations with ultimate reality and our fellow beings, we must practise morality and (since no personality can learn to transcend itself unless it is reasonably free from external compulsion) respect the personality of others. Belief in a personal, moral God has led only too frequently to theoretical dogmatism and practical intolerance—to a consistent refusal to respect personality and to the commission in the name of the divinely moral person of every kind of iniquity.

"The fact of the instability of evil," in Professor Whitehead's words, "is the moral order of the world." Evil is that which makes for separateness; and that which makes for separateness is self-destructive. This self-destruction of evil may be sudden and violent, as when murderous hatred results in a conflict that leads to the death of the hater; it may be gradual, as when a degenerative process results in impotence or extinction; or it may be reformative, as when a long course of evil-doing results in all concerned becoming so sick of destruction and degeneration that they decide to change their ways, thus transforming evil into good.

The evolutionary history of life clearly illustrates the instability of evil in the sense in which it has been defined above. Biological specialization may be regarded as a tendency on the part of a species to insist on its separateness; and the result of specialization, as we have seen, is either negatively disastrous, in the sense that it precludes the possibility of further biological progress, or positively disastrous, in the sense that it leads to the extinction of the species. In the same way intra-specific competition may be regarded as the expression of a tendency on the part of related individuals to insist on their separateness and independence; the effects of intra-specific competition are, as we have seen, almost wholly bad. Conversely, the qualities which have led to biological progress are the qualities which make it possible for individual beings to escape from their separateness— intelligence and the tendency to co-operate. Love and understanding are valuable even on the biological level. Hatred, unawareness, stupidity and all that makes for increase of separateness are the qualities that, as a matter of historical fact, have led either to the extinction of a species, or to its becoming a living fossil, incapable of making further biological progress.

XV

Ethics

EVERY cosmology has its correlated ethic. The ethic that is correlated with the cosmology outlined in the preceding chapter has, as its fundamental principles, these propositions: Good is that which makes for unity; Evil is that which makes for separateness. Relating these terms to the phraseology employed in the first chapters we can say that separateness is attachment and that, without non-attachment, no individual can achieve unity either with God or, through God, with other individuals. In the paragraphs that follow I shall try to illustrate the application of our ethical principles in life.

Good and evil exist on the plane of the body and its sensations, on the plane of the emotions, and on the plane of the intellect. In practice these planes cannot be separated. Events occurring on one of the planes have their counterpart in events occurring upon the other planes of our being. It is always necessary to bear this fact in mind when we classify phenomena as physical, emotional or intellectual. But provided that we bear it in mind, there is no harm in our speaking in this way. This particular classification, like every other, fails to do full justice to the complexities of real life; but it has the compensating merit of being very convenient.

Let us begin by considering good and evil on the plane of the body. In general it may be said that any very intense physical sensation, whether pleasurable or painful, tends to cause the individual who feels it to identify himself with that sensation. He ceases even to be himself and becomes only a part of his body—the pain-giving or pleasure-giving organ. Self-transcendence thus becomes doubly difficult—though of course by no means impossible, as is proved by many examples of equanimity and non-attachment under suffering and under intense enjoyment. In general, however, excess of pain as of pleasure makes for separateness. All the oriental contemplatives are emphatic in their insistence on bodily health as a condition of spiritual union with ultimate reality. Among Christians there are two schools of thought—that which recommends mortification and that which stresses the importance of health. Pascal may be cited as a representative of the first school and the anonymous author of "The Cloud of Unknowing" as a representative of the second. For Pascal, sickness is the truly Christian condition; for, by mechanically freeing men from some, at least, of the passions, it delivers them from all manner of temptations and distractions and prepares them for living the kind of life which, according to Christian ethical theory, they ought to live. Pascal ignores the fact that sickness may create as many temptations and distractions as it removes—distractions in the form of discomfort and pain, temptations in the form of an almost irresistible impulse to think exclusively of oneself. There is, however, an element of truth in the Pascalian doctrine. When not excessive, sickness or physical defect may act as a reminder that "the things of this world" are not quite so important as the animal and the social climber in us imagine them to be. A mind which has made this discovery and which then succeeds, as a result of suitable training, in ignoring the distractions of pain and overcoming the temptation to think exclusively of its sick body, has gone far to achieve that "superrational concentration of the will" at which the religious self-education aims. In proclaiming the value of sickness, Pascal is advocating the physiological method of training through the mastery of pain. We have seen already that this method is a dangerous one. Only too frequently pain is not mastered, but achieves mastery— leads to attachment rather than non-attachment.

This being so, we can understand why the author of "The Cloud of Unknowing" should have taken the opposite view to Pascal's. For him, sickness is a serious obstacle in the way of true devotion to God and must be reckoned accordingly as a form of sin. The passage in which he comments on certain symptoms of what we should now call "neurosis" is of such interest that I make no excuse for quoting it in its entirety. "Some men," he writes, "are so cumbered in nice curious customs in bodily bearing that when they shall aught hear, they shall writhe their heads on one side quaintly, and up with the chin: they gape with their mouths as they should hear with their mouth and not with their ears. Some when they should speak point with their fingers, or on their own breasts, or on theirs that they speak to. Some can neither sit still, stand still, nor lie still, unless they be either wagging with their feet, or else somewhat doing with their hands. Some row with their arms in time of their speaking, as they needed to swim over a great water. Some be ever more smiling and laughing

at every other word that they speak, as they were gig-
gling girls and nice japing jugglers . . . I say not that
all these unseemly practices be great sins in themselves,
nor yet all these that do them be great sinners themselves. But I say if that these unseemly and unordained
practices be governors of that man that doth them,
insomuch that he may not leave them when he will,
then I say that they be tokens of pride and curiosity of
wit, and of unordained showing and covetyse of knowing. And specially they be very tokens of unstableness
of heart and unrestfulness of mind, and specially of the
lacking of the work of this book" (i.e., the work of
meditation as a training for the mystic experience).

This assimilation of physical deficiency to sin may
seem somewhat ruthless and unfeeling. But if sin is to
be judged by its results, then, of course, the author of
"The Cloud of Unknowing" is quite right in reckon-
ing among sins any bodily states and habits which cause
a man to concentrate on his own separateness, hinder
him from paying attention to his true relation with God
and his fellows and so make the conscious actualization
of union with them impossible. On the plane of the
body, sickness must generally be counted as a sin. For
by sickness and pain as well as by extreme pleasure, the
body insists on its separateness and all but compels the
mind to identify itself with it.

The saying that to him that has shall be given and
from him that has not shall be taken away even all that
he has, is a hard one; but it happens to be an extremely
succinct and accurate summary of the facts of moral life.
Those who sin physically by having some kind of bodily

defect may be made to pay for that defect in ways that are emotional and intellectual as well as physical. Some sick people are capable of making the almost superhuman effort that will transform the disaster of bodily defect into spiritual triumph. From the rest even that which they have, intellectually and emotionally, is taken away. Why? Because, on the plane of the body, they are among those who have not. "Men may be excusable," says Spinoza, "and nevertheless miss happiness, and be tormented in many ways. A horse is excusable for being a horse and not a man; nevertheless he must needs be a horse and not a man. He who cannot rule his passions, nor hold them in check out of respect for the law, while he may be excusable on the ground of weakness, is nevertheless incapable of enjoying conformity of spirit and knowledge and love of God; and he is lost inevitably." Weakness may be forgiven; but so long as it continues to be present, no amount of forgiveness can prevent it from having the ordinary results of weakness. These results are manifest in the present life and, if there should be some form of survival of bodily death, will doubtless be manifest in any subsequent existence.

Sex is a physical activity that is also and at the same time an emotional and an intellectual activity. If I choose to consider it here, it is not because I regard it as more physical than emotional or intellectual, but merely for the sake of convenience. It is an empirical fact of observation and experience that sexual activities sometimes make for a realization of the individual's unity with another individual and, through that other individual, with the reality of the world; sometimes, on the contrary, for an intensification of individual separateness. In other words, sex leads sometimes to non-attachment and sometimes to attachment, is sometimes good and sometimes evil.

On the plane of the body, sex is evil when it takes the form of a physical addiction. (All that can be said in this context about sex is true, *mutatis mutandis,* of the other forms of physical addiction—to alcohol, for example, to morphia and cocaine.) Like habit-forming drugs, habit-forming sex is evil because it compels the mind to identify itself with a physical sensation and prevents it from thinking of anything but its separate animal existence. Addiction cannot be destroyed by satiation, but tends, if indulged, to become more than a mere habit—a demonic possession. This is of course especially true in the case of civilized and highly conscious individuals—individuals who "know better," but who have nevertheless permitted themselves to become enslaved to their addiction. For uncivilized members of what J. D. Unwin has called "zoiṣtic" societies, or of the zoistic strata of civilized societies, sexual addiction is merely a pleasant habit that they indulge with a good conscience. It prevents them from putting forth that energy that will enable them to become conscious of themselves, to think about the strange world around them and to achieve civilization; but as they are unaware of the fact, they don't mind. Not so with civilized and self-conscious men and women. Of such people it cannot be said that "they know not what they do." They know only too well—know exactly what they are doing and exactly what they are losing in the process. For them the addiction is a real possession. The demon that inhabits them compels them to do what they know will harm them and what, with the best part of their being, they do not want to do. The nature of this demonic possession was described, with incomparable power, by Baudelaire in the *Fleurs du Mal*.

Une nuit que j'étais près d'une affreuse Juive,
Comme au long d'un cadavre un cadavre étendu . . .

Addiction persists—a true possession by a devil that malignantly wills the unhappiness of its victim—even when all physical pleasure has been lost, even in the teeth of disgust and loathing. Like virtue, it is its own reward; and the reward it brings is misery and the torment of body and mind.

Jamais vous ne pourrez assouvir votre rage,
Et votre châtiment naîtra de vos plaisirs.

Jamais un rayon frais n'éclaira vos cavernes;
Par les fentes des murs des miasmes fiévreux
Filent en s'enflammant ainsi que des lanternes
Et pénètrent vos corps de leurs parfums affreux.

L'âpre stérilité de votre jouissance
Altère votre soif et roidit votre peau,
Et le vent furibond de la concupiscence
Fait claquer votre chair ainsi qu'un vieux drapeau.

Loin des peuples vivants, errantes, condamnées,
A travers les déserts courez comme des loups;
Faites votre destin, âmes désordonnées,
Et fuyez l'infini que vous portez en vous.

The last line irresistibly recalls Royce's phrase to the effect that "finite beings are always such as they are by virtue of an *inattention* which at present blinds them to their actual relations to God and to one another." The addict is blinded by his addiction to "the infinite that he carries within him," to "his actual relations to God" and other beings. At the same time, he is generally aware, if only by a kind of nostalgia, by a hopeless longing for what he lacks, that "the infinite" exists within him and that his "actual relations to God" are those of a part to its proper whole. He is aware of the fact and he suffers from it; and at the same time the demon he has conjured up, that it may possess him, deliberately increases his suffering by forcing him "to fly from the infinite within him," to refuse, consciously and deliberately, to pay attention to "his actual relations with God."

It is not only when it takes the form of physical addiction that sex is evil. It is also evil when it manifests itself as a way of satisfying the lust for power or the climber's craving for position and social distinction. Love—and this is true not only of sexual, but also of maternal love—may be merely a device for imposing the lover's will upon the beloved. Between the Marquis de Sade, with his whips and pen-knives, and the doting but tyrannous mother, who slaves for her son in order that she may the more effectively dominate him, there are obvious differences in method and degree, but not a fundamental difference in kind. In such cases, the active party, by insisting on the right to bully, command and direct, thereby insists upon his or her separateness. At the same time, by refusing to respect the other's personality, the domineering lover makes it impossible for the beloved victim to pay attention to that *"infini que vous portez en vous."* Addiction degrades only the addict. The lust for power harms not only the person who lusts, but also the person or persons at whose expense the lust is satisfied. Non-attachment becomes impossible for both parties.

Sex as a means for satisfying social vanity is only less evil than sex as a means for satisfying the lust for power. There are people who marry not a person, but money, a title, social influence. Sex here is the instrument of avarice and ambition, passions that are in the highest degree separative and reality-obscuring. There are others who marry beauty or distinction for the sole purpose of flouting their exclusive possession of it before the eyes of an envying world. This is a special form of the lust for ownership, an avarice whose object is, not money, but a human being and that human being's socially valuable qualities. Such lust for ownership is as blinding and as separative as ordinary avarice and can do almost as much harm to the owned person as the maternally or sexually conditioned lust for power can do to its much loved and much tormented victim.

Sex is not always addiction, is not always used as an instrument of domination or as a means for expressing vanity and snobbishness. It is also and at least as frequently the method whereby unpossessive and unselfish individuals achieve union with one another and indirectly with the world about them. "All the world loves a lover"; and, conversely, a lover loves all the world.

"That violence whereby sometimes a man doteth upon one creature is but a little spark of that love, even towards all, which lurketh in his nature. When we dote upon the perfections and beauties of some one creature, we do not love that too much, but other things too little. Never was anything in this world loved too much, but many things have been loved in a false way, and all in too short a measure." Traherne might have added (what many poets and novelists have remarked) that, when "we dote upon the perfections and beauties of some one creature," we frequently find ourselves moved to love other creatures. Moreover, to be in love is, in many cases, to have achieved a state of being, in which it becomes possible to have direct intuition of the essentially lovely nature of ultimate reality. "What a world would this be, were everything beloved as it ought to be!" For many people, everything is beloved as it ought to be only when they are in love with "some one creature." The cynical wisdom of the folk affirms that love is blind. But in reality, perhaps, the blind are those who are not in love and who therefore fail to perceive how beautiful the world is and how adorable.

We must now consider very briefly the relation of sexual activity to mental activity in individuals and to the cultural condition of society. This subject was discussed by the late Dr. J. D. Unwin, whose monumental "Sex and Culture" is a work of the highest importance. Unwin's conclusions, which are based upon an enormous wealth of carefully sifted evidence, may be summed up as follows. All human societies are in one or another of four cultural conditions: zoistic, manistic,

deistic, rationalistic. Of these societies the zoistic display
the least amount of mental and social energy, the rationalistic the most. Investigation shows that the societies
exhibiting the least amount of energy are those where
pre-nuptial continence is not imposed and where the
opportunities for sexual indulgence after marriage are
greatest. The cultural condition of a society rises in
exact proportion as it imposes pre-nuptial and post-
nuptial restraints upon sexual opportunity.

"All the deistic societies insisted on pre-nuptial chastity; conversely all the societies which insisted on pre-
nuptial chastity were in the deistic condition.

"Is there any causal relationship between the compulsory continence and the thought, reflection and energy
which produced the change from one cultural condition
to another?

"One thing is certain: if a causal relation exists, the
continence must have caused the thought, not the
thought the continence."

Again, "the power of thought is inherent; similarly
the power to display social energy is inherent; but
neither mental nor social energy can be manifested except under certain conditions." These conditions arise
when sexual opportunity is reduced to a minimum.
Civilized societies may be divided into different strata,
representing every type of cultural condition from
zoistic to rationalistic. "The group within the society
which suffers the greatest continence displays the greatest energy and dominates the society." The dominating
group determines the behaviour of the society as a
whole. So long as at least one stratum of a society im-

poses pre-nuptial continence upon its members and limits post-nuptial sexual opportunity by means of strict monogamy, the society as a whole will behave as a civilized society.

The energy produced by sexual continence starts as "expansive energy" and results in the society becoming aggressive, conquering its less energetic neighbours, sending out colonies, developing its commerce and the like. But "when the rigorous tradition (of sexual restraint) is inherited by a number of generations, the energy becomes productive." Productive energy does not spend itself exclusively in expansion; it also goes into science, speculation, art, social reform. Where productive energy persists for some time, a factor, which Dr. Unwin calls "human entropy" comes into play. Human entropy is the inherent tendency, manifested as soon as the suitable social conditions are created, towards increased refinement and accuracy. "No society can display productive social energy unless a new generation inherits a social system under which sexual opportunity is reduced to a minimum. If such a system be preserved a richer and yet richer tradition will be created, refined by human entropy."

As a matter of brute historical fact, no civilized society has tolerated for very long the limitation to a minimum of its sexual opportunities. Within a few generations, the rules imposing absolute pre-nuptial continence upon females and absolute monogamous forms of marriage are relaxed. When this happens, the society or the class loses its energy and is replaced by another society, or another class, whose members have made themselves energetic by practising sexual continence. "Sometimes," writes Dr. Unwin, "a man has been heard to declare that he wishes both to enjoy the advantages of high culture and to abolish compulsory continence. The inherent nature of the human organism, however, seems to be such that these desires are incompatible, even contradictory. . . . Any human society is free to choose, either to display great energy or to enjoy sexual freedom; the evidence is that it cannot do both for more than one generation."

We have seen that, as a matter of historical fact, no society has consented to retain the tradition of pre-nuptial continence and absolute monogamy for very long. But it is also a matter of historical fact that these traditions have always hitherto been associated with the oppression of women and children. In deistic societies, wives have been regarded as slaves or mere chattels, having no legal entity. Custom and law have placed them at the mercy of their husbands. Discussing this fact, Dr. Unwin hazards the opinion "that it was the unequal fate of women, not the compulsory continence, that caused the downfall of absolute monogamy. No society has yet succeeded in regulating the relations between the sexes in such a way as to enable sexual opportunity to remain at a minimum for an extended period. The inference I draw from the historical evidence is that, if ever such a result should be desired, the sexes must first be placed on a footing of complete legal equality."

In this very brief summary I have certainly done much less than justice to Dr. Unwin's very remarkable book;

but though doing it less than justice, I do not think that I have misrepresented its main conclusions. The evidence for these conclusions is so full, that it is difficult to see how they can be rejected. They are conclusions which will certainly seem unpalatable to the middle-aged relics of a liberal generation. Such liberals are liberals, not only politically, but also in the sense in which Shakespeare's "liberal shepherds" (the ones who called wild arums by a grosser name than dead-men's fingers) were liberal. They have been "heard to declare," very frequently and loudly, that they "wish to enjoy the advantages of high culture and to abolish compulsory continence." Living as they do upon the capital of energy accumulated by a previous generation of monogamists, whose wives came to them as *virgines intactae*, they can make the best of both worlds during their own life-time. Dr. Unwin's researches have made it certain, however, that it will be impossible for their children to go on making the best of both worlds.

If Dr. Unwin's conclusions are well founded—and it is difficult to believe that they are not—how do they fit into our general ethical scheme? The first significant fact to be noticed is that "the continence caused the thought, not the thought the continence." Zoistic societies live in a condition of animal solidarity. In Dr. Unwin's words, "we begin with a society in which all the individuals are locked together by forces we do not understand; such a society displays no energy." Now, this animal solidarity has certain merits; it is preferable, for example, to the animal individualism of unrestricted intraspecific competition. But these merits are sub-ethical; in other words animal solidarity is below good and evil. People on the zoistic level are too much preoccupied with, and too completely de-energized by, unrestricted sexual indulgence to be able to pay attention to "their actual relations with God and with one another." Awareness is the condition of any moral behaviour superior to that of animals. The individual cannot transcend himself unless he first learns to be conscious of himself and of his relations with other selves and with the world. A measure of sexual continence is the precondition of awareness, and other forms of mental energy, conative and emotional as well as cognitive. But the pre-condition of moral behaviour need not itself be moral. As a matter of historical fact, the energy released by sexual continence has frequently been directed towards thoroughly immoral ends. Mental and social energy is comparable to the energy of falling water; it can be used for any purpose that men choose to put it to— for bullying the weak and exploiting the poor just as well as for exploring the secrets of nature and for creating masterpieces of art or for establishing union with ultimate reality.

Chastity is one of the major virtues inasmuch as, without chastity, societies lack energy and individuals are condemned to perpetual unawareness, attachment and animality. In another sense, however, chastity can rank only as a minor virtue; for, along with such other minor virtues as courage, prudence, temperance and the like, it can be used solely as a means for increasing the efficiency of evil-doing. Unless they are directed by the major virtues of love and intelligence, the minor virtues are not virtues at all, but aids to wickedness. Histori-cally, puritanism has been associated with militarism and capitalism, with war and persecution and economic exploitation, with every form of power-seeking and cruelty. Chastity is not necessarily correlated with char-ity; on the contrary, the human organism is so consti-tuted that there would seem to be a natural correlation between compulsory continence and energy that is malevolent at least as often as it is well-intentioned. (On the political results of this correlation Dr. Vergin's "Sub-conscious Europe" may be consulted; the book contains an over-emphatic and therefore somewhat dis-torted statement of a good case.) This natural and, I might almost say, physiological tendency for chastity to be associated with uncharitableness is manifested not only during the period when the energy created by sex-ual restraint is "expansive," but also, though perhaps with diminished intensity, when it is "productive."

Chastity, then, is the necessary pre-condition to any kind of moral life superior to that of the animal. At the same time, the energy created by chastity has a natural tendency to be, on the whole, more evil than good. By fulfilling the conditions upon which, and upon which alone, the higher moral life is possible, we transform our nature in such a way that it becomes easier for us to behave immorally than to behave morally. Our hu-man nature is such that, if we are to realize the highest ethical ideals, we must do something which automati-cally makes the realization of those ideals more difficult. Historically, progressiveness has always been associated with aggressiveness—the potentiality of greater good with the actuality of greater evil. This association "comes naturally" to beings constituted as we are, and can be broken only as the result of deliberate choice, directed by the highest ideals and the fullest knowledge of facts. As usual, the remedy is to be sought in awareness and good will. Only by consistently applying the major virtues of charity and intelligence can we prevent the minor, but indispensable, virtue of chastity from filling the world with actual evil as well as potential good. Dr. Unwin suggests that the modern world is confronted by only two alternatives: it may choose to be continent and energetic; or it may prefer sexual indulgence to mental and social energy. It would be truer to say that there are three choices. First of all, we can increase pre-nuptial and post-nuptial sexual opportunity, in which case our mental and social energy will decline. Alternatively, we can tighten up the system of sexual restraint, with a view to increasing the amount, without improving the ethical quality, of available social energy. This is the policy which is at present being pursued by the dictators of all the totalitarian states. Empirically and by a kind of rule of thumb, these men know very clearly that there is a correlation between puritanism and energy—just as they know (as was pointed out in the chapter on education) that there is a correlation between authoritarian discipline in youth and a militaristic psychology in later life. By combining a system of increased sexual restraint with a system of authoritarian education, the present rulers of totalitarian societies are providing themselves and their successors with a new generation of highly energetic militarists.

Significantly enough, in Germany and Italy the tightening up of sexual restraints has been accompanied by a lowering of the status of women. In the past, as Dr. Unwin has pointed out, absolute pre-nuptial chastity and absolute monogamy have always been associated with the subjection of women. Hitler and Mussolini are merely employing the old means to produce the old end—an increase of energy. This energy, as we have seen, has a natural tendency to take undesirable forms; but, not content with this spontaneous evil, the dictators are using all the means at their disposal to direct their subjects' energy along the channels of aggressive imperialism.

Finally, there is a third alternative—an alternative which has never been tried before. We can retain prenuptial chastity and absolute monogamy, at any rate for the ruling classes of our societies; but instead of associating these practices with the subjection of women, we can make women the legal equals of men. In this way, as Dr. Unwin suggests, and in this way only will it be possible to avoid that revolt against chastity which, in the past, has resulted in the decline of once energetic societies. By making compulsory chastity tolerable, such measures will prolong the period during which a society produces energy—will prolong it, perhaps, indefinitely. But they will do little or nothing to improve the ethical quality of the energy produced. Even the process which Dr. Unwin calls "human entropy" promises no ethical improvement—only increasing refinement and accuracy of thought and its expression. Hitherto, as history shows, sexual restraint has had the following results. The moral life has been made possible and some at least of this potential good has been actualized. Meanwhile, however, in the process of creating the potentiality for good, much evil has invariably been produced. Our problem is to discover a way to eliminate that evil, a way to direct all the energy produced by sexual restraint along desirable channels.

In the preceding chapters I have described the kind of political, economic, educational, religious and philosophical devices that must be used if we are ever to achieve the good ends that we all profess to desire. The energy created by sexual restraint is the motive power which makes it possible for us to conceive these desirable ends and to think out the means for realizing them. We see, then, that the particular problem of moralizing the energy produced by continence is the same as the general problem of realizing ideal ends. This being so, it is unnecessary for me to discuss it any further. The matter can be summed up in a couple of sentences. The third and only satisfactory solution of the problem of sex is that which combines the acceptance, at least by the ruling classes, of pre-nuptial chastity and absolute monogamy with complete legal equality between women and men and with the adoption of a political, economic, educational, religious, philosophical and ethical system of the kind described in this book.

I have discussed the problem of good and evil on the plane of the body and the problem of good and evil in relation to sex, as manifested on all the planes of being. We must now consider good and evil on the plane of the emotions. There is very little that need be said in this context. All the familiar deadly sins are the product of separative emotions. Anger, envy, fear—these insist on the various aspects of our animal separateness from one another. Sloth exists on all the planes, and can be physical, emotional or intellectual. In all its forms sloth is a kind of negative malignity—a refusal to do what ought to be done.

Some vices are animal, some are strictly human. The human vices, which are in general the most dangerous, the most fruitful in undesirable results, are the various lusts for power, social position and ownership. Pride, vanity, ambition and avarice are attachments to objects of desire which have existence only in human societies. Being completely dissociated from the body, such vices as lust for power and avarice are able to manifest themselves in a bewildering variety of forms and with an energy that is immune from the satiety which occasionally interrupts all physical addictions. The permutations and combinations of lust or of gluttony are strictly limited and their manifestations are as discontinuous as physical appetite. It is far otherwise with the lust for power or the lust for possessions. These cravings are spiritual, therefore are unremittingly separative and evil; have no dependence on the body, therefore can assume almost any form.

Under the existing dispensation, popular morality does not condemn the lust for power or the craving for social pre-eminence. European and American children are brought up to admire the social climber and worship his success, to envy the rich and eminent and at the same time to respect and obey them. In other words, the two correlated vices of ambition and sloth are held up as virtues. There can be no improvement in our world until people come to be convinced that the ambitious power-seeker is as disgusting as the glutton or the miser—that "the last infirmity of noble mind" is just as much of an infirmity as avarice or cruelty (with one or both of which, incidentally, it is very often associated), just as squalidly an addiction, on its human plane, as any physical addiction to drink or sexual perversion.

The human or spiritual vices are the most harmful in their results and the hardest to resist. (La Rochefoucauld remarks that men frequently desert love for ambition, but very rarely desert ambition for love.) Furthermore, their spiritual nature makes it hard for them to be distinguished, in certain of their manifestations, from virtues. This difficulty becomes particularly great when power, wealth and social position are represented as being means to desirable ends. (In the story of the temptation in the wilderness, Satan attempts to confuse the moral issue in precisely this way.) But good ends, that is to say a state of greatest possible unification, can be achieved only by the use of good, that is to say of intrinsically unifying means. Bad means—activities, in other words, that produce attachment and are intrinsically separative—cannot produce unification. The lust for power is essentially separative; therefore it is not by indulging this lust that men can achieve the good results at which they profess to aim. The political techniques by means of which ambition can be restrained have been discussed in the chapter on Inequality; the educational and religious techniques, in the two succeeding chapters. We cannot expect that any of these techniques will be very successful, so long as ambition continues to be popularly regarded, as it is at present, as a virtue that should be implanted in the growing child and carefully fostered by precept and example.

We have now to consider good and evil as manifested upon the intellectual plane. Intelligence, as we have seen, is one of the major virtues. Without intelligence, charity and the minor virtues can achieve very little.

Intelligence may be classified as belonging to two kinds, according to the nature of its objects. There is the intelligence which consists in awareness of, and ability to deal with, things and events in the external world; and there is the intelligence which consists in awareness of, and ability to deal with, the phenomena of the inner world. In other words, there is intelligence in relation to the not-self and there is intelligence in relation to the self. The completely intelligent person is intelligent both in regard to himself and to the outer world. But completely intelligent people are unhappily rare. Many men and women are capable of dealing very effectively with the external world in its practical, commonsense aspects and are at the same time incapable of understanding or dealing with abstract ideas, logical relations or their own emotional and moral problems. Others again may possess a specialized competence in science, art or philosophy and yet be barbarously ignorant of their own nature and motives and quite incompetent to control their impulses. In popular language, a "philosopher" is a man who behaves with

[372]

restraint and equanimity—one who loves wisdom so much that he actually lives like a wise man. In modern professional language a philosopher is one who discusses the problems of epistemology. It is not thought necessary that he should live like a wise man. The biographies of the great metaphysicians often make extremely depressing reading. Spite, envy and vanity are only too frequently manifested by these professed lovers of wisdom. Some are not even immune from the most childish animalism. Nietzsche's biographers record that, at the time when he was writing about the Superman, he was unable to control his appetite for jam and pastry; whenever, in his mountain retreat, a hamper of good things arrived for him from home, he would eat and eat until he had to go to bed with a bilious attack. Kant had a similar passion for crystallized fruit and along with it such an abhorrence for sickness and death that he refused to visit his friends when they were ill or ever to speak of them once they had died. In later life, moreover, he claimed a kind of infallibility, insisting that the boundaries of his system were the limits of philosophy itself and resenting all attempts by other thinkers to go further. The same childish self-esteem is observable in Hegel and many other thinkers of the greatest intellectual power. Such men are highly intelligent in certain directions, but profoundly stupid in others. This stupidity is, of course, a product of the will. Intelligent fools are people who have refused to apply their intelligence to the subject of themselves. There is also such a being as a wise fool. The wise fool is one who knows about himself and how to manage his pas-

sions and impulses, but who is incompetent to understand or deal with those wider, non-personal problems
which can be solved only by the logical intellect. The
wise fool does less harm than the intelligent fool and is
personally capable of enlightenment. The intelligent
fool, who has no knowledge of, or control over, himself,
cannot achieve enlightenment so long as he remains
what he is. However, if he so wishes, he can cease to be
an intelligent fool, and become an intelligent and wise
man. An intelligent wise man is capable not only of
achieving personal enlightenment, but also of helping
whole societies to deal with their major problems of
belief and practice. Under the present dispensation, the
educational system is designed to produce the greatest
possible number of intelligent fools. We inspire children with the wish to be intelligent about the phenomena of the external world and about abstract ideas
and logical relations; at the same time we teach them
the techniques by which this wish can be gratified.
Meanwhile, however, we make very little effort to inspire them with the wish to be intelligent about themselves and, on the rare occasions when we do make this
effort, we provide them with no devices for training the
inward-turning intelligence to perform its task efficiently.

One cannot deal intelligently with any matter about
which one is ignorant. If one is to deal intelligently
with oneself one must be aware of one's real motives,
of the secret sources of one's thoughts, feelings and actions, of the nature of one's sentiments, impulses and
sensations and of the circumstances in which one is

liable to behave well or badly. In general, it may be said that, on the intellectual plane, good is that which heightens awareness, especially awareness of oneself. No self can go beyond the limits of selfhood, either morally (by the practice of the virtues that break attachment) or mystically (by direct cognitive union with ultimate reality), unless it is fully aware of what it is, and why it is what it is. Self-transcendence is through self-consciousness. A human being who spends most of his waking life either day-dreaming, or in a state of mental dissipation, or else identifying himself with whatever he happens to be sensing, feeling, thinking or doing at the moment, cannot claim to be fully a person. McTaggart has objected that "to call a conscious being a self (or personality) only when it was self-conscious would involve that each of us would gain and lose the right to the name many times a day." Moreover, he adds, there is "a more serious difficulty. We are invited to define personality as being conscious of self. And consciousness of self is a complex characteristic which can be defined only when it is known what we mean by a self. Therefore, if self means the same on the two occasions when it enters into the statement, 'a self is that which is self-conscious,' we have a circular and unmeaning definition of selfness." It is quite true that such a definition is circular and unmeaning. But the facts of personality are not adequately accounted for in such a definition. Personality is not, as we have seen, an absolutely independent existent; persons are interdependent parts of a greater whole. In the commonsense universe, however, they possess a relative autonomy. There are degrees in this relative autonomy. Only when it has attained to the highest of these degrees does a personality become able, as all the mystics bear witness, to transcend itself and merge into the ultimate impersonal reality substantial to the world. To say that "a self is that which is self-conscious" is, of course, merely to make an unmeaning noise. But it is not absurd to say that, "there is an X (the totality of a human being's animal and conscious life) which emerges into selfness, or personality, when there is consciousne of X." That this definition involves each of us gaining and losing the right to the name of a person many times a day is no objection to the definition. Such happens to be the nature of things. The greater part of the life of the greater number of human beings is sub-personal. They spend most of their time identified with thoughts, feelings and sensations which are less than themselves and thus lack even that relative autonomy from the external world and their own psychological and physiological machinery, belonging to a genuine full-grown person. This sub-personal existence can be terminated at will. Anybody who so desires and knows how to set about the task can live his life entirely on the personal level and, from the personal level, can pass, again if he so desires and knows how, to a super-personal level. This super-personal level is reached only during the mystical experience. There is, however, a state of being, rarely attained, but described by the greatest mystical writers of East and West, in which it is possible for a man to have a kind of double consciousness—to be both a full-grown person, having a complete knowledge of, and control over, his sensations, emotions and thoughts, and also, and at the same time, a more than personal being, in continuous intuitive relation with the impersonal principle of reality. (St. Teresa tells us that, in "the seventh mansion," she could be conscious of the mystical Light while giving her full attention to worldly business. Indian writers say that the same is true of those who have attained the highest degree of what they call *samadhi.*)

It is clear, then, that if we would transcend personality, we must first take the trouble to become persons. But we cannot become persons unless we make ourselves self-conscious. In one of the discourses attributed to the Buddha, we read an interesting passage about the self-possessed person. "And how, brethren, is a brother self-possessed? . . . In looking forward and in looking back he acts composedly. (i.e. with consciousness of what is being done, of the self who is doing and of the reasons for which the self is performing the act.) In bending or stretching arm or body he acts composedly. In eating, drinking, chewing, swallowing, in relieving nature's needs, in going, standing, sitting, sleeping, waking, speaking, keeping silence, he acts composedly. That, brethren, is how a brother is self-possessed."

In the last paragraphs of the chapter on Education I have described a technique of physical training (that developed by F. M. Alexander), which is valuable, among other reasons, as a means for increasing conscious control of the body and, in this way, raising a human being from a condition of physical unawareness to a state of physical self-consciousness and self-control. Such physical self-awareness and self-control leads to, and to some extent is actually a form of, mental and moral self-awareness and self-control.

Of the purely psychological methods of heightening the awareness of self it is unnecessary to say very much. Self-analysis, periodical analysis at the hands of others, habitual self-recollectedness and unremitting efforts to resist the temptation to become completely identified with the thoughts, feelings, sensations or actions of the moment—these are the methods which must be employed. If they are not already known, they can easily be reinvented by all who choose to think about the problem. There is nothing abstruse about the theory of these methods of heightening self-consciousness. The principle is simple. What is difficult, as always, is its application in practice. To know is relatively easy; to will and consistently to do is always hard.

It is sufficiently obvious that the systematic cultivation of self-awareness may as easily produce undesirable as desirable results. The development of personality may be regarded as an end in itself or, alternatively, as a means towards an ulterior end—the transcendence of personality through immediate cognition of ultimate reality and through moral action towards fellow individuals, action that is inspired and directed by this immediate cognition. Where personality is developed for its own sake, and not in order that it may be transcended, there tends to be a raising of the barriers of separateness and an increase of egotism.

Under the Christian dispensation, personality has generally been developed in relation to the prevailing doctrines of sin, and of personal salvation at the hands of a personal deity. The results have been on the whole distinctly unsatisfactory. Thus, the obsessive preoccupation with sin and its consequences, so characteristic of Protestantism in the generations immediately following the Reformation, only too frequently produced an obsessive preoccupation with the separate self and its lusts for power and possessions. Modern capitalism and imperialism have a number of different causes; but among these causes must be numbered the Protestant and Jansenist habit of brooding on sin, damnation and an angry God, arbitrarily dispensing or withholding grace and forgiveness.

It is interesting, in this context, to compare the orthodox Calvinist attitude towards sin with that which was taken up by such mystics as Eckhart or the author of "The Cloud of Unknowing." These writers did not minimize the significance of sin; on the contrary, they regarded it as the chief obstacle in the way of the soul's union with God. But they saw that sin was the fruit of self-will and that self-will, in Bradley's words, "is opposition attempted by a finite subject against its proper whole." The important thing, they perceived, was to get rid of self-will and to cultivate, as quickly as possible, a state of being, propitious to knowledge of, and union with, ultimate reality. Such a state of being, they found empirically, could be reached by the practice of virtue and the raising of consciousness, first to the level of self-awareness, then, by means of meditation, to awareness of God. Obsessive preoccupation with past sins, they perceived, could result only in preoccupation with the self which they were so anxious to transcend. For this reason there is no insistence in the writings of Eckhart and the author of "The Cloud of Unknowing" upon their own or other people's sinfulness. They do not talk about themselves as miserable sinners; nor do they advise others to do so. They know, of course, that men are sinners and that sin is a barrier standing between souls and their God. Therefore, they say, men should make themselves aware of their sins and, having done so, proceed to stop sinning; after which they should concentrate all their attention on God and ignore the extremely uninteresting and unprofitable subject of their past, sinful selves. "It is a great grace of God," says St. Teresa, "to practise self-examination; but too much is as bad as too little, as they say; believe me, by God's help, we shall advance more by contemplating the Divinity than by keeping our eyes fixed on ourselves." Modern theologians, such as Otto, have blamed Eckhart for not being sufficiently conscious of his sinfulness, and have contrasted him unfavourably in this respect with Luther,* who spent his early manhood in the terrified conviction that he was "gallows-ripe." It is legitimate to inquire how far this conviction of his own ripeness for the gallows was the cause of that later conviction, expressed so forcibly a few years later, that the German peasants were ripe for the gallows and deserved extermination and enslavement at the hands of the ruling classes. There is a logical and a psychological connection between obsession with one's own sins and

* See "Mysticism East and West," by Rudolf Otto. (New York, 1932.) P. 129.

obsession with those of others, between haunting terror of an angry personal God and an active desire to persecute in the name of that God. At the risk of wearying my reader, I must repeat, for the thousandth time, that the tree is known by its fruits. The fruits of such doctrines as are taught by Eckhart, the author of "The Cloud" and the oriental mystics whom they so closely resemble, are peace, toleration and charity. The fruits of such doctrines as are taught by Luther and St. Augustine are war and the organized malice of religious persecution and the organized falsehood of dogmatism and censorship. On this point, it seems to me, the historical evidence is clear and explicit. Those who consider that the metaphysical theories of Luther and Augustine correspond more closely to the nature of ultimate reality than do the theories of Eckhart, Sankhara, or the Buddha must be ready to affirm the proposition that evil is the result of acting upon true beliefs about the universe and that good is the result of acting upon false beliefs. All the evidence, however, supports the opposite conclusion—that false beliefs result in evil and that true beliefs have fruits that are good. What we think determines what we are and do, and conversely, what we are and do determines what we think. False ideas result in wrong action; and the man who makes a habit of wrong action thereby limits his field of consciousness and makes it impossible for himself to think certain thoughts. In life, ethics and metaphysics are interdependent. But ethics include politics and economics; and whether ethical principles shall be applied well or badly or not at all depends on education and

[381]

on religion in so far as it is a system of self-education. We see then, that, through ethics, all the activities of individuals and societies are related to their fundamental beliefs about the nature of the world. In an age in which the fundamental beliefs of all or most members of a given society are the same, it is possible to discuss the problems of politics, or economics, or education, without making any explicit reference to these beliefs. It is possible, because it is assumed by the author that the cosmology of all his readers will be the same as his own. But at the present time there are no axioms, no universally accepted postulates. In these circumstances a discussion of political, economic or educational problems, containing no reference to fundamental beliefs, is incomplete and even misleading. Such a discussion is like Hamlet, if not without the Prince of Denmark, at least without the Ghost or any reference to the murder of the Prince's father.

In the present volume I have tried to relate the problems of domestic and international politics, of war and economics, of education, religion and ethics, to a theory of the ultimate nature of reality. The subject is vast and complex; this volume is short and the knowledge and abilities of the author narrowly limited. It goes without saying that the task has been inadequately performed. Nevertheless I make no apologies for attempting it. Even the fragmentary outline of a synthesis is better than no synthesis at all.

Index

INDEX

INDEX

Mitrany, D., 97
Montessori, M., 209, 213
Morgan, A. E., 234
Mussolini, 36
Mysticism, 335; direct mystical intuition of an impersonal God, 338; its relation to ethics, 347

Nationalism, 45; as a cause of war, 109; as an idolatrous religion, 311, 318
Nationalization of armaments no cure for war, 120
Naval Conference of 1927, 126
New Harmony, 148
Non-attachment, definition, 4; rarely described in imaginative literature, 240, 254
Non-violence, effectiveness of, 162ff.; in South Africa, 167; in Hungary, 168; in England, 169; seldom practised by governments, 170

Obedience, 63
Old Testament, 276, 328
Oneida Community, 148, 238
Otto, Rudolf, 380

Pain and Pleasure, their relation to ethics, 352
Pascal, 353
Peaceful change, the machinery of, 131
Persecution, historically related to belief in a personal God, 284
Personality, 277, 342, 375, 378
Philosophers, their theories contrasted with their practices, 373
Planning, its results, 43; may increase risks of war, 59
Police, increased efficiency of, 177
Population, decline of, 62
Power, lust for, 20
Preventive ethics, 17

Progress, definition of, 7; in Roman and British Empires, 30; biological, 303ff.
Propaganda, 180; new methods of, 244; need to build up resistance to, 245ff.
Pseudo-Dionysius, 336
Psychological types, 188ff.

Quakers, 152, 154

Reality, 345
Religious self-education, physiological methods, 268; emotional methods, 271ff.; method of meditation, 285ff.
Rhine, J. B., 300
"Righteous Indignation," 276
Rites, 261ff.
Roman Catholics, pacifism among, 125
Royce, J., 346, 358
Russell, B., 126, 208
Russia, education in, 213, 235

Sacramentalism, 340
Sade, Marquis de, 253, 312
Sanctions, military, 124, 127
Savages, non-violent treatment of, 164
Schweitzer, A., 347
Self-government, in industry, 81; most compatible with co-operative enterprise, 96; in schools, 233
Separateness, equated with evil, 349, 351
Sex, as physical addiction, 356; as lust for power, 358; as avarice, 359; as a force making for unity, 360; in relation to culture, 360ff.
Sin, results of preoccupation with, 380
Spanish civil war, 166
Spinoza, 355

INDEX

Spiritual Exercises, 154
Sport as a means of education,
215ff.
Suicide rate, decline of in war
time, 106
Synthesis, need of, 319

Tauler, John, 6
Telepathy, 300
Teresa, St., 377, 380
Theism, arguments in support of,
321ff.
Traherne, 360
Trappist rule, 148

"Unchronia," 166
Unity, underlies diversity, 348;
good is that which makes for
unity, 351
Universe of common sense, 295; its
illusory nature, 342, 346, 348
Unwin, J. D., 360ff.

Violence, effects of, 31, 127
Virtues, minor and major, 328; relation to mystical experience,
347, 349, 365

War, preparations for war incompatible with liberty, 71; incompatible with industrial self-
government, 95; nature of, 100;
Chinese attitude toward, 102;
Indian attitude toward, 104;
causes of, 106ff.; remedies, 139ff.;
conditions in which war may
lead to a lasting settlement, 159;
not remediable by economic reforms alone, 175; education for,
208, 217
Weakness, 355
Whitehead, A. N., 289, 340, 349
Wishes, sometimes a source of information, 329
Women, position of, 363

Zuni Indians, 22